An Author's Guide to Publishing

Fully revised and expanded edition

Michael Legat

ROBERT HALE · LONDON

© *Michael Legat 1982*
First published in Great Britain 1982
Reprinted 1982
Reprinted 1984
First paperback edition (with revisions) 1987
Reprinted 1990
Reprinted 1991
Fully revised and expanded edition 1991
Reprinted 1992 twice
Reprinted 1993
Reprinted 1994

ISBN 0 7090 4664 2

Robert Hale Limited
Clerkenwell House
Clerkenwell Green
London EC1R 0HT

Photoset in North Wales by
Derek Doyle & Associates, Mold, Clwyd.
Printed in Great Britain by
St Edmundsbury Press Limited, Bury St Edmunds, Suffolk.
Bound by Woolnough Bookbinders.

Contents

To the memory of C.J. and of Peter
and to all my friends in the writing business,
whether they are authors or agents or
publishers or booksellers or critics or
whatever, and of course to Rosetta

Foreword

This book is invaluable reading for all authors – and not simply beginners and those without agents. We can thoroughly recommend it as a balanced, helpful and informative guide to the profession of authorship.

Mark Le Fanu
The Society of Authors

Author's Note

I wish to make it clear that the ideas put forward in this book are not necessarily those of its publisher, nor of my other publishers, nor of my agent, nor of any publishing firm for which I have worked, nor of the Society of Authors nor of any other authors' organization. They are mine alone, so no blame will attach to the reader if he regards them with a certain suspicion. The views are, however, based on over forty-five years' experience of the book trade, and I hope therefore that the suspicion will not be justified too often.

I have used male pronouns throughout, and I apologize to feminists and to anyone else who finds this practice offensive. I have done so only to avoid the constant clumsiness of "he or she", "himself or herself", "his or her", and so on. Please read in the alternatives whenever appropriate. I do not wish in any way to suggest an inequality between the sexes in the world of books. Like many another dedicated reader, I do not choose my books according to the sex of the author, and I applaud the fact that few any longer sneer, as they may have done in past generations, at women writers, or expect them to be any less capable as authors than men; as for publishers, the editorial department is rapidly becoming the preserve of women, who are also well represented in every other area of publishing, from the office girl to the managing director. There have always been women in the ranks of agents, but again the balance seems to be changing so that the likelihood is that your agent, if you have one, will be a woman. Women publishers and agents are at least as perceptive and expert and effective as their male colleagues, if not more so – though they may also be rather more formidable and even terrifying, partly because, as one wit put it, "the trouble with business women is that they aren't always gentlemen".

Perhaps I should have used "she", rather than "he", throughout ... Ah, well, forgive me, please.

I should like to express my thanks to Mark Le Fanu, General Secretary of the Society of Authors, for his invaluable assistance and advice; to John McLaughlin and John Hale for their helpful comments and suggestions; to Philippa MacLiesh (formerly of the Society of Authors) and to Ian Rowland Hill (formerly of the Writers' Guild of Great Britain) for additional help.

I am also grateful to the following persons and organizations for permission to quote copyright material: Robin Denniston (an extract from his paper given to a meeting of the University, College and Research Section of the Library Association); the Hutchinson Publishing Group Ltd (a short extract from *Allen Lane: King Penguin* by Jack Morpurgo); Robert Hale Ltd (their formula for calculating the length of a typescript); the Society of Authors and the Writers' Guild of Great Britain (the Minimum Terms Agreement); the British Standards Institute (extracts from British Standard BS 5261: PART 2 1976 *Copy preparation and proof correction – Specification of typographic requirements, marks for copy preparation and proof correction, proofing procedure*); the Society of Authors (the Model Royalty Statement).

M.L.

1
The World of Books

Territories and Rights

Even those whose knowledge of geography is minimal are aware that the world is divided into the continents of Europe, Asia, North and South America, Africa and Australia, to which may be added the Arctic and Antarctic and a large number of islands scattered through the oceans and seas. The author writing in English has needed, for the last hundred and fifty years or so, to learn a different kind of geography, which is concerned with the division of territories by the various English language publishers who may bring out editions of his book. Until quite recently, there were likely to be two principal publishers only – the British and the American houses – and the world was divided into three: the exclusive British market, the exclusive American (i.e. United States) market, and the rest of the world, termed the Open market.

These divisions were easily defined: the British market consisted of the United Kingdom and the British Empire, including all its colonies and protectorates and a number of countries, such as Egypt and Iraq, where the British influence had been traditionally strong; the American market consisted of the United States of America and its colonies and protectorates; Canada was normally exclusive to the British publisher if the book were of British or British Empire origin, and exclusive to the American publisher if it were of United States origin; the rest of the world was non-exclusive territory. Even after the British Empire became the Commonwealth and certain countries such as South Africa and Malta became independent republics, the British publisher's traditional market remained a recognized entity.

In the 1970s, however, at the instigation of the United

11

States, it was agreed that the split of territories between the British and the American publisher should be re-defined in the case of each book, and the fact that a given country had been traditionally part of the exclusive market of one of the publishers should no longer mean that it was necessarily so for every book. Some territories which had always been regarded as belonging to the Open market could become part of the British or American publisher's exclusive area, and the growth of publishing industries in places like Australia, which previously relied almost entirely on Britain for its books, has further fragmented the old divisions. Canada, too, has a thriving publishing industry, and increasingly often, especially with agented books, the exclusive Canadian rights may be separately sold, and there is good reason to assume that other territories will be similarly treated in future. (This, incidentally, is going to pose a considerable problem for British publishers, who have always depended to a very large extent on their export sales – a problem which may be solved only when the trend to international publishing houses, with autonomous branches in a number of countries, has spread.) At the time of writing, however, for the majority of books which are published both in Britain and the United States, I think it can still be said that the world is divided into three, with some territories designated as exclusive to either the British or the American publisher, and the remaining countries being open to them both.

Within the British exclusive territory the British publishing house sells its edition of the book without competition from its American rival; equally, only the American publisher's edition sells in the American exclusive territory; in the Open market, however, both the British and the American publishers can sell their editions of the same book in direct competition with each other.

An additional problem has arisen recently as a result of Britain's membership of the EEC. Since trade barriers are prohibited within the Common Market, it is possible for a European wholesaler to purchase copies of a given book from the American publisher and then export them to Britain, thus infringing the British publisher's exclusivity in his home market, but relying on the provisions of the Treaty of Rome to be stronger than the agreement regarding territories between the British and American publishers.

The enterprise can be profitable to the wholesaler because of the fact that the British and American retail prices may differ considerably, and whereas in the past the British price was usually below that of the American edition, the reverse is often now the case. Fluctuations in exchange rates make this a volatile situation, and the problem will become more acute after 1992, when all trade barriers in the EEC are supposed to disappear.

Because of the dangers which the EEC regulations pose to their sales in Britain, which should really be the most inviolate of markets for them, some British publishers are attempting to add Europe, or at least the EEC, to their exclusive market, thus preventing the American publisher from selling the book in question in those territories, and obviating the threat of an invasion of the home territory. This move is clearly not popular with American publishers, some of whom have said that they will not sign up any books by British authors which do not allow them at least right of entry into the European territories. In some cases, in order to persuade agents and authors to grant these additional rights despite American disapproval, the British publishers have offered a full home royalty on sales within the EEC, instead of the normal export terms, which are considerably lower. The battle looks like continuing for many years to come.

It should be pointed out that the issue is one of potential market violation and not necessarily of infringement of the author's copyright. However, since in most cases it is the author who initially grants various exclusive and non-exclusive territories to the British and American publishers who may be in conflict in this matter, he may become involved in the dispute.

Of course there is less likely to be any problem if your book is bought by one of the Anglo-American conglomerates of which there are a number in the publishing business. Although the branches on either side of the Atlantic may operate independently, in many cases they will buy English language rights, and will control them throughout the world.

Foreign language publishers do not have the same problem of sharing out the world as English language publishers do. A German publisher, for instance, will usually have the whole world available to him for his

German language edition of a book, and most foreign language publishers similarly have exclusive rights throughout the world.

Incidentally, it should be made clear that sales of a British or American, or indeed Australian or Indian, English language publication in a foreign country have nothing to do with the Foreign Language rights, or Translation rights, as they are sometimes and perhaps less confusingly called, which are referred to in a British or American publisher's contract. These rights are concerned with the translation of the work from English into a foreign language. If the book is on sale in its English language editions in France, Germany, Japan, or any other foreign language country, such sales come under the British or American publisher's export sales, not under Foreign rights.

If you write in English and sell your book directly to a firm in Britain or the United States, the publisher will probably buy world rights, and will then attempt to sell either the American or the British rights in the book as appropriate; the details of which territories will be exclusive and non-exclusive to each publisher will be decided at the time of the sale. However, an agent, if you have one, will normally retain on your behalf the American rights (or in the case of an American author and agent, the British rights), and will then attempt to sell those rights. It is difficult to say which of the two methods is preferable, since it depends on the abilities of the agents and publishers concerned and on the varying percentages of the moneys earned which they may take. If the translantic rights are not sold, then in rare cases the British edition may be put on sale in the US (or vice versa), but the resulting sales are usually minimal.

Licence Periods

In most publishing contracts, the author gives the publisher the various rights defined in the agreement "for the period of copyright". This last phrase may be further defined by some such wording as "and all renewals and extensions thereof in each country". The effect, in most cases, is to give the publisher the rights in the book from the time of publication until fifty years after the author's death. If he goes on selling the book, he will of course go on paying the specified royalties to the author or, eventually, his heirs. If he does not keep the book in print, and/or under certain other circumstances which are usually clearly defined in the contract, the rights will revert to the author, though the publisher may be able to retain the rights if the book is still in print in an edition which has been sub-licensed to another firm or organization.

A granting by the author to the publisher of a licence for the entire period of copyright, as explained above, has been the tradition virtually ever since formal licensing agreements between authors and publishers (as opposed to the outright purchase of copyright) were first made. Such a tradition seemed to be immutable, but at the beginning of the 1980s campaigns led by the Society of Authors and the Writers' Guild began to bring about a change. Why should hardcover publishers not work on a limited licence of say, twenty years, or even ten years, with the right thereafter to negotiate a new contract for a further period if they wish to do so and if the author were willing for that publisher to continue to have the rights?

Although, not surprisingly, publishers in general were reluctant to abandon the traditional period-of-copyright licence, many contracts nowadays are based on a limited licence period. It seems to have done little harm. Authors feel that they have more control over their work, and that the arrangement should, at least in theory, make publishers more efficient, because if they fail to do a good job, they are likely to lose the author in question. Publishers, on the other hand, know very well that many books have a far shorter life than ten, let alone twenty years, so a licence covering that period will be adequate, while if a book continues to be active up to the time when the contract is due for renewal, the publisher can probably feel fairly certain of having done a good job, which will make the author think twice before taking the book away from him.

Packagers

Packagers are people who conceive and produce books for regular publishers to sell. Thus they do all the work of the ordinary publisher up to the marketing, publicizing, selling and distribution of the work. Very often the books are fully illustrated, with a considerable amount of colour work, and the packager's aim is to sell the book not just to a British publisher, but simultaneously to an American house and to foreign language publishers as well; if he sells foreign language editions, he will have to print the black plate which includes the text separately, but he will be able to print the colour for all the editions at one time, which will be much more economical than printing them separately, and since he can put several publishers' print quantities together, he can arrive at a total print run large enough to reduce all his origination costs to a very reasonable sum per copy. Having had an idea for a book, a packager usually commissions an author to write it, paying him a lump sum according to the number of copies printed, or in some cases making a handsome outright payment, or paying a substantial advance on account of a modest royalty on net receipts. The author might stand to gain more if he received normal royalties from all the publishers concerned, but any shortfall in this direction is made up for by the fact that he receives his money in advance, before the books have been sold into the shops, since the publisher will have paid the packager a sum inclusive of royalties to cover all the copies he has ordered. As a matter of principle any author who is asked by a packager to write a book should aim to get some kind of royalty rather than just an outright payment. After all, packaged books are often very successful. At the least a further sum should be payable if the book gets reprinted.

Sponsored Books

Sponsored books used to consist almost entirely of histories of large businesses, produced to celebrate some anniversary, paid for out of the firm's advertising budget, and distributed to the staff and customers. Such books were not usually on sale to the general public. Nowadays, however, many large organizations see the sponsoring of books, whether or not the subject is directly connected with the interest of the organization, as a useful kind of publicity. The books are usually published by a hardcover house in the normal way, the only real difference being that all or a proportion of the costs are paid by the sponsor, who often takes a share of the profits on the books, if any. Some sponsors have retailing facilities available or are prepared to spend considerable sums in publicizing the book, and this may result in an abnormally large print quantity being ordered. This is very pleasant for the author, although there are some cases where the sponsor will try to buy the author's copyright for an outright sum, and even if the amount is generous, the author may suffer from this arrangement. Or they may propose a low royalty, pleading the need to keep the retail price down and explaining that the author will still be well paid since the high sales envisaged should compensate him for earning less than the norm on each copy.

I was recently approached for advice by an author who was hoping to be commissioned by a company to write a history of the firm. They were insisting on owning the copyright so that they could exploit the history in any way they chose, and they made it clear that if the author did not agree to grant them the copyright there would be no commission for him. They suggested that he should become a temporary member of the company while he was writing the book; his salary (a generous one) would be payment for his work, while as an employee the copyright in that work would automatically be vested in the firm. As an alternative they were offering, rather reluctantly, an outright sum. Faced with a problem of this sort, it may be high-minded to insist on the principle that one should never surrender one's copyright. The author wanted to write the book, and needed the money. Seeing that my efforts to persuade him not to give up his copyright were fruitless, I suggested that he should opt for the outright payment, but try to push the sum up and also ask for an additional amount to be payable if the book were ever reprinted.

Vanity Publishing

Some authors who cannot secure commercial publication for their books pay to have their work published by vanity publishers. Vanity publishing is a technical term with a specific meaning. If you pay a printer to put your little volume of poems into print and you then sell the copies to your friends and anyone else who will buy them, it may be vain of you, but it is not vanity publishing; if the owner of a publishing house writes his memoirs and then publishes them under his own imprint, that may be vain of him, but it is not vanity publishing; if a regular publisher is persuaded to take your book on because you are prepared to subsidize it in some ways, perhaps by contributing to the costs or by promising to buy a large number of copies from him at trade prices, that is still not vanity publishing. In the first case, of that little volume of poems, you will be paying only for the cost of production and the printer's profit, and you will be able to retain all the moneys that you get from selling copies; in the case of the publisher who brings out his own memoirs, the book is unlikely to be taken on, even though he owns the firm, unless it is of publishable standard, and there will be a normal contract such as any other author would receive, allowing for the payment of an advance and royalties; similarly there will be a contract for the author who subsidizes his work and it will probably provide that the financial subsidy will be returned once the book has proved to be profitable and will certainly allow for the payment of royalties.

Vanity publishers, on the other hand, are the sharks who will express great enthusiasm for your work, however poor its quality, but will explain that publishing conditions are so difficult nowadays that they cannot go ahead unless you will make a "contribution" to the costs. You will get your money back, they say, because the royalties they will pay on sales (apart from the copies that you yourself purchase, which will be royalty free) will be exceptionally generous. In fact, you will be making more than a "contribution" – you will be paying for the entire costs of production and the publisher's profit too – and, strangely enough, the huge royalties never materialize. If you want to sign up with a vanity publisher, go ahead. It's your money, and you're entitled to do what you like with it. But whatever the vanity publisher may say about his large and extremely capable sales force, don't expect to see copies of your book in the bookshops – booksellers know the vanity publishers' imprints and refuse to stock their books. And don't expect to see any of your money back. You will get nicely produced copies of your book, but that's all, and you will have paid through the nose for them. Vanity publishers take your money and give your ego a boost that you could probably find much more cheaply in a bottle of liquor or a new dress or whatever turns you on.

How do you recognize a vanity publisher? By his contract (always an absolutely watertight document, so don't think you will get anywhere by suing him when he fails to meet your expectations), which will not bear any resemblance to the kind of contract discussed in Chapter 6 of this book, differing in such giveaway instances as not mentioning any advance payable by the publisher, specifying royalties of 33⅓ per cent (often not payable on the first 400 copies printed, and certainly not due on any copies purchased by the author), and of course the clause specifying the amount of subsidy that the author will pay. Before you have got to the stage of a contract, however, you can usually recognize a vanity publisher by the fact that they advertise, asking authors to submit their work – "Books wanted," they say, or "Authors wanted". Regular publishers have no need to advertise in that way – their problem is more likely to be how to cope with the vast numbers of typescripts submitted to them unsolicited and without any encouragement on their part.

Self Publishing

If you want to see your work in print and cannot find a regular publisher to take you on, then, rather than go to a vanity publisher, you might consider self publishing. Contact a reputable printer, who will produce the book for you. You may have to shop around a bit, but it is usually not too difficult to find a printer who is not only capable of doing a good job for you, but who will be willing to give you a great deal of advice on such matters as print sizes, paper quality, etc. Your biggest problem is likely to be distribution: how will you sell copies of your book without a sales force to persuade booksellers throughout the country – indeed, throughout the world – to put copies on sale? But even if all you can do is to sell copies to your friends and perhaps persuade your local bookseller to display the book (you will almost certainly have to supply him "on sale or return", so that he will only pay you for any copies that he has actually sold, and of course he will take a discount of at least a third on the sale) you are still likely to do considerably better than if you go to a vanity house. Two books which give helpful advice on self publishing are *Publishing Your Own Book* by Jon Wynne-Tyson (Centaur Press) and *How to Publish Yourself* by Peter Finch (Allison & Busby).

Desktop Publishing

The development of sophisticated word processors has made it possible for many authors to produce work in a finished state which can be described as "camera-ready". This term is usually used of a text which is heavily illustrated and for which the text has been set up in type and the pictures reduced or enlarged to the size in which they are to appear, and the whole has been pasted up into pages ready for the photographic process which will produce film from which the book will be printed. Authors who can produce work in this state are clearly in a favourable position for self publishing, but the term, "desktop publishing" is also used when they are simply supplying this material to a regular publisher. The publisher will normally pay the author an extra amount, or share with the author the savings on his production costs. The word processors which produce work of this quality and variety are priced beyond the means of many authors, but the costs are not in fact astronomic, and they tend to drop regularly (who would have believed in the early 1980s that a basic word processor would be available for hundreds, rather than thousands of pounds?). It can be confidently predicted that more and more authors, whose work is suitable, will become desktop publishers, and that self publishing will also increase.

The Net Book Agreement

Many years ago, after the introduction of the Restrictive Practices Act of 1956, which followed a Monopolies Commission investigation into restrictive practices, the British Publishers Association fought a long a battle in the Restrictive Practices Court over the question of whether it was in the public interest not to allow retail outlets to price books at their own discretion, but to maintain the arrangement of the Net Book Agreement, which had for many years ensured that the publisher fixed the retail price and the bookshops maintained it. The Act contained a number of tests designed to protect the public against restrictions on free competition. The Court had to consider the arguments in favour of competition and the arguments for allowing the market to fix its own prices, and was finally won over by the Publishers Association's arguments and the Net Book Agreement was allowed to remain in place. More recently, the Agreement was re-examined by the Monopolies Commission, but once again was approved, and is still with us. At the time of writing, one of our major bookselling chains is waging a campaign for the abolition of the Net Book Agreement, and threatens to continue a policy of putting certain titles on sale at discounted prices, despite the threat of legal action by publishers, most of whom strongly oppose any such move. A great deal of wind has been generated. If the Net Book Agreement does disappear, its supporters claim that the chief sufferers will be the small independent bookshops, which we cannot afford to lose; prices will rise; new authors will find it even more difficult to get into print. Those who would like to see it go believe that it can only increase sales, and even if the chief beneficiaries would be bestselling authors (whose books would be among the first to be discounted), attractive prices for their books would bring more people into the shops, and that in itself would be a Good Thing. In many parts of the world retail price maintenance has never existed – in the United States, for instance – or, as in Australia, has comparatively recently been abandoned. In the latter case it disappeared amid resounding cries of doom and gloom, and there would appear to be some evidence that its absence has harmed the development of the Australian book trade rather than made it more vigorous.

VAT

Another major concern within the book trade has been the possibility of the imposition of VAT on books. Purchase Tax, the forerunner of VAT, was first introduced in 1940 by the then Chancellor of the Exchequer, Kingsley Wood. He had every intention of imposing the new tax on books, but a strong campaign was mounted by authors and publishers, spearheaded by Stanley Unwin, who, in a celebrated letter to *The Times* argued that a tax on books was a tax on knowledge. His letter continued, "It would be humiliating if, in a war for freedom of thought," (the Second World War was, of course, raging at the time) "the sale of books in which man's highest thoughts are enshrined should be hampered by taxation." The Chancellor eventually gave in. Once Britain had joined the Common Market, it seemed likely that harmonization of taxes would mean that VAT would be levied on books, and in the late 1980s there was a strong expectation that the Chancellor of that period, Nigel Lawson, would indeed impose it. A campaign to keep books tax-free was launched, and was successful (the Chancellor claimed that he had never had any intention of putting VAT on books, so what was all the fuss about?), but few in the book trade doubt that eventually the tax will come. And what effect will it have? The price of books will be increased, sales will be affected (since the public at large foolishly already thinks of books as excessively expensive), new authors will find it more difficult to get into print, independent booksellers will go out of business, and so will small publishers. Perhaps. I certainly do not want to see a tax on books, and the next time the threat appears to be imminent, I shall join the campaign against it with enthusiastic vigour. Nevertheless, I have to say that I wonder whether the effect would be quite as disastrous as the prophets of doom predict.

Book Fairs

International Book Fairs are an important part of the publishing scene. They take place in almost all countries of the world. The best-known and largest Book Fair is the one that is held every autumn in Frankfurt. If a publisher says, "Are you going to Frankfurt?" or "See you in Frankfurt!" you can be sure that he is talking about the Fair. Other well-known Book Fairs include those held in London, Jerusalem, Moscow, and the ABA (American Booksellers Association) meetings which are held in a different US city every year. For publishers of children's books there is the annual Children's Books Fair in Bologna. Book Fairs provide opportunities for the sale and purchase of rights and also for foreign booksellers to order books, and the majority of publishers feel that it is essential to attend them (and often to spend a considerable amount of money on a stand to display their books and on hospitality for their customers). However, several other publishers stay away from them, save their money, and feel that they do not lose anything by not participating. Attendance by an author at any of the Book Fairs is far from obligatory, but probably worthwhile at least once. If you are a major "name" your publisher may want you to be there so that he can show you off – or indeed you may want to take the opportunity of meeting all your publishers over the world in one go, as it were. If you are not in that class but are the sort of author who likes to try to sell your work by personal approach, you will have the opportunity of speaking directly to dozens of editors and may persuade some of them to consider your book. If you are a quiet, retiring type, who has, perhaps, just had a first book accepted, you will probably be suitably humbled by the sight of the hundreds of thousands of books which, like yours, are going to be out there in the marketplace looking for people to buy them. The atmosphere at a Book Fair is always slightly unreal – it is hot, noisy, almost feverish, and the person you are talking to will probably be looking past you for most of the time, watching in case any of the passers-by is someone even more worth talking to than you.

Editorial Titles

Some editors are called simply "editors", while others have elaborate titles which may be very confusing. Such titles have proliferated in recent years, partly as a result of periods of wage restraint, when the only way to give someone a pay rise was to invent a new title for him as justification for a change of salary, and partly because of union insistence on job definition and differentiation. The titles used and the responsibilities of their bearers differ from company to company. There are two main editorial functions: one is the acquisition of new books, and the other the checking and preparation of authors' typescripts before they are sent to the printer. The functions may overlap, or both may be performed by the same person. In general, the former have titles such as "Acquiring Editor" or "Commissioning Editor" or "Sponsoring Editor", whereas the latter are more likely to be called "Copy Editor" or "House Editor". I have recently heard of a publishing house which refers to "Copy Editors", "Line Editors" and "Structural Editors"; apparently, the job of the first group is to correct punctuation and spelling, the second contingent check for consistency and accuracy, while the third section, who are usually also the acquiring editors, work with the author on major alterations to the book. Some acquiring editors may use a title referring to the section of the list which they handle, such as "Science Editor" or "Children's Books Editor". Many editorial titles are used only within the publishing house, and as far as the outside world and the author is concerned, the designation will often be restricted to "Editorial Director", "Senior Editor", "Managing Editor" (if used accurately, this title should suggest that its bearer is the person who allocates editorial work, whether acquisitional or copy-editing, among the personnel in the editorial department) or plain "Editor". If the title and the responsibilities of the person with whom you are dealing are not clear to you, then it is worth asking. It is always easier to work with someone if you know what he does and what he does not do. Moreover, your editor will probably enjoy explaining it all to you – most people respond readily when someone shows interest in the details of their work.

Translators

When a publisher buys the rights to a foreign language book, it is he who hires a translator to render it into his own language. Usually he will commission the translation on an outright basis, paying the translator an agreed flat sum per thousand words, but in some cases (and the Translators Association of the Society of Authors would advise this) it is possible for the translator to receive a royalty, particularly if the work concerned is out of copyright, so that the publisher has no royalties to pay to the author. English language publishers quite often receive requests for permission to translate books from the publishers' lists into foreign languages; the reply is always that that is the concern of a foreign publisher, that no such permission is likely to be given until a foreign language publisher has bought the rights for that particular language, and that he will then probably commission a translator who is already known to him to do the job.

2

Volume and Other Rights

The author who sells his book to an English language publisher normally retains the copyright in it (and indeed should always do so, unless there is very good reason for some other arrangement – see p. 205), but the right to sell the book in various forms is vested in the publisher. The latter, if buying direct from an author, will usually ask for control of all rights. This is to say that he not only has the right to produce various editions of the book, or to license others to do so, but also that he can sell serial rights, film, radio and television and a number of other subsidiary rights (which will be discussed in detail later in this chapter), in each case passing to the author an agreed share of the proceeds from such sales.

If, on the other hand, the publisher buys the book from an agent, it is likely that he will be restricted to Volume rights, which is to say the right to produce, or license others to produce, hardcover or paperback editions of the book, to sell bookclub rights, and usually second serial (i.e. serial rights sold after the first publication in book form) and anthology rights, the sale of all such rights often being subject to the agent's approval. All other rights are retained in the control of the agent, who will sell them, wherever possible, on the author's behalf. However, nowadays the hardcover publisher cannot even be certain of volume rights, for sometimes paperback rights are sold separately by the agent. Of course it is open to the author who deals directly with the publisher to follow the example of agents and to retain various rights, provided that the publisher is still willing to publish the book on those terms, but there is little point in doing so unless the author is equipped to sell the rights in question. Few publishers make no effort at all to sell the rights they are granted, for the very good reason that their share of any moneys resulting from such sales increases their profit or at worst diminishes their loss on the book in question.

It is very important, whatever arrangements have been made, to remember what rights you have granted to you publisher. If, for instance, you have given him the right to negotiate foreign language rights, and you then happen to meet a charming French publisher who expresses great interest in your book, you must not sell him your book, or even give him an option on it, and indeed it would be wise, I suggest, not even to give him a copy to read unless you make it perfectly clear that doing so does not commit your publisher in any way. Apart from the fact that you have handed control of foreign rights to your publisher and are therefore going against your contractual commitments, you may also cause quite a lot of embarrassment, especially, for instance, if your publisher is in the midst of delicate negotiations over the book with another French publisher. Instead, you should thank your French friend for his interest, tell him that you will let your publisher know of it, and do so. The same applies, of course, if it is your agent who has control of the rights. If the French publisher's interest is genuine (and do bear in mind that it could have been merely polite), and the book is not in the hands of another French publisher, your publisher or agent will probably be happy to submit it to your friend straight away, or to send it as soon as it is free of other commitments.

Hardcover Books

Books are sold in a variety of formats, and though there is some overlap in the markets for hardcover books, paperbacks, bookclub editions, condensed books and so on, it would appear that they are not totally competitive. Thus bookclubs, for instance, claim that their members are not on the whole regular buyers of hardcover books, and that they are therefore tapping a new, or at least different, market; equally there must be many thousands of homes where you will find large numbers of paperbacks but never a recent hardcover book in sight, apart perhaps from a mail order *Book of the Countryside* or something similar.

There are several hundred hardcover book publishers in

Britain, publishing an infinite variety of books. Some are specialist publishers, producing perhaps only medical or legal or school books, while others have a general list embracing fiction and non-fiction of all kinds, but also including sometimes books in a specialist field. Some are huge companies, bringing out hundreds of new books every year. In fact something like 90 per cent of the output of the British publishing trade is concentrated in the hands of just eight giant groups of companies. At the other end of the scale are the tiny concerns, sometimes run by one mad enthusiast who undertakes everything from the work of an office boy to that of the managing director, publishing perhaps only one or two books a year.

Two major developments of recent years have been the growth of the "fully integrated" publishing house and the proliferation of "conglomerates".

Many publishers have taken to issuing paperback editions of certain of their books, often producing both hardcover and paperback simultaneously, but sometimes publishing the book only in softcover form. Such paperbacks, usually known as "trade paperbacks", are in effect comparable to the cheap editions of the hardcover book which publishers used to produce; they are a somewhat different animal from the mass-market paperbacks published by such companies as Penguin, Pan, Corgi, etc, being printed in much smaller quantities and selling for a substantially higher price. The "fully integrated" publisher may produce a few such books, but usually earns its title because it owns a mass-market paperback division, and buys many of its books with the object of itself producing both the hardcover and the mass-market softcover editions.

In common with many other industries, publishing has become, in the last few decades, progressively more difficult a business to run economically. It has always been a gambling business, and its problems have been exacerbated because of the vast variety of books and the uncertainties of any business based on selling goods which are not essential in the way that food and clothing are, and which are no more than marginally profitable unless they achieve the rare status of bestsellerdom. In addition, publishing is a trade which demands substantial amounts of capital investment, and is therefore readily afflicted with cash-flow problems. One result of these difficulties in recent times has been the development of various forms of "conglomerate"; some publishing companies, including both large and small concerns, have been forced to seek the protection of giant, diversified groups which do not suffer from a shortage of cash, and who have been attracted to publishing partly because of its faintly glamorous and culturally commendable image, and partly because of a belief that the various businesses within the group will indulge, to the benefit of all, in a process known as cross-fertilization.

Another kind of conglomerate results from the banding together of two or three publishing houses, or even more, sometimes by voluntary amalgamation but often by purchase, when the wealthier concern swallows those in greater financial difficulty. In some cases the purchaser is an American publishing house (which may be itself already a conglomerate), and there has also been a considerable amount of traffic in the opposite direction with British firms buying into the American scene.

Conglomerates always say that their various editorial departments will maintain their individuality, and that what they are really doing is simply to amalgamate their service divisions (production, sales, warehousing) in the interests of economy and efficiency. Claims have also been made that, because of their greater resources, conglomerates can publish worthwhile books which might be uneconomic for small independent companies, and can afford to take on and nurture the talented author who needs time and experience to build up a reputation which will make him financially viable for the publisher.

The economic sense in all these changes is obvious, and the Americans who have bought British firms, or who have set up their own branches in this country, see great advantages in having both major English language markets under the control of one international company. However, the sense sometimes turns out to be somewhat superficial. The plans for editorial independence and for the economical management of every other area of publishing do not always work out; cross-fertilization does not take place; management by the yuppies who run the giant, diversified companies, who refer to books as "product" and who are motivated by a love of money, rather than a love of books, tends to stifle individuality and, what is worse, militates strongly against the discovery and nurturing of new talent.

For these reasons there is, at the time of writing, some feeling that decentralization may be the order of the day during the 1990s. It is also encouraging that several new publishing firms have been started up in the last decade and have managed, as a result of careful control, to thrive despite the difficulties of the economic climate.

Print quantities of hardcover books vary enormously, and so do the retail prices of the books, ranging from a few score copies of an extremely expensive limited edition, to fifty thousand or more copies of a major bestseller, which may be comparatively cheap. Nowadays very few books achieve a print quantity of anything like the copies just mentioned, and the majority of books on a general publisher's list are likely to have initial print runs of between fifteen hundred and ten thousand copies, with prices in a limited and familiar range.

Hardcover publishers sell their books primarily to bookshops and to libraries. In the first edition of this book, published in 1982, I wrote gloomily of the situation – the decline of bookshops, the squeeze on library spending, the shrinkage of the British publisher's traditional overseas markets, and his inability to maintain a backlist because of the cost of capital investment. As I prepare this revised edition, it seems to me that there are grounds for a little more optimism. Well-run small bookshops, even if still under threat, are mostly managing to survive, while the major chains are expanding and learning how to make their stores, in the current jargon, "user-friendly" – less intimidating for the casual customer who is not a regular book-buyer; libraries still feel the pinch, but nevertheless manage to buy sufficient books to keep their shelves up to date; and although publishers have not seen any substantial increase in their overseas markets, nor found any solution to the problem of reprinting slow-moving books, and although one hears regularly of firms which have found themselves in financial difficulty and are forced to go into liquidation or sell out to a larger company, the difficulties of the last decades have taught the survivors to cut their costs, to increase their efficiency and generally to be more ready than in the past to adapt to modern conditions.

The death of the hardcover book has been predicted for most of this century. Every new development in what might loosely be called the entertainment industry is seen as a mortal threat. So it was to die at the hands of the cinema, it was to wither because motoring would become the major leisure occupation, it was to receive a death-blow from the growth of paperbacks, it was to be killed off by television, and it is currently threatened by videos and talking books. Despite all this, it survives and, if you ask me, will go on for a long time yet.

Its survival could be guaranteed for a longer period, of course, if sales of the average hardcover book could be substantially increased. Despite the belief of some authors to the contrary, publishers do make efforts to sell their books – a book sitting on the warehouse shelf is of no use to anyone, and indeed it actually costs the publishers money to keep it there – and they try, by means of special book events and the willing support they give, for example, to television programmes about books, to promote sales. However, it has to be admitted that the public at large remains untouched. Since most people believe that hardcover books are expensive (forgetting to compare them with, for instance, the cost of a meal out, or the price of a theatre ticket), it will be difficult to convert them into hardcover book buyers.

If you listen to hardcover publishers talking together you will undoubtedly hear them saying that everything is more and more difficult and that they don't know how any of them will manage to survive more than a year or two more. I have heard that kind of talk for the past forty-five years. But there is one serious concern, which is that it is much more difficult nowadays for a publisher to foster a new talent by publishing that author's work, at a loss, until he has established a big enough reputation to make his books profitable. The economic pressures are such that the publisher can take on such an author with confidence only if he has the guarantee of being able to sell subsidiary rights, especially paperback rights; and where is there room for new unknown writers on the paperback racks which are dominated by the really big-name authors? Even this problem, however, may be a little exaggerated, for new authors continue to be published regularly.

The bulk of sales on a publisher's general list, and this applies particularly to fiction, will be sold on publication and in the first six months thereafter. Bestsellers may have a longer life (though even they can fade quite rapidly), and some books are fortunate enough to become backlist titles or standard works, and will go on selling steadily for a period of years. They are the exceptions, as are those very few books which suddenly come to vigorous life long after the initial impetus has disappeared (frequently because of a television series based on the book, or because it has become a "cult" book, or for some other equally unpredictable reason). Interest in an author's earlier books can sometimes be revived if he writes a particularly successful new book (this happens to most authors who win the Booker Prize), or if the author gradually achieves bestseller status. In some of the latter cases, the success may have come about because, over the years, the author's ability as a story-teller has vastly improved, and the republication of earlier, less well-written books may be somewhat embarrassing (though not so embarrassing as to prevent either publisher or author, or their bank managers, from enjoying the proceeds). In most cases, however, the author of a book will find that a very high proportion of the total sales will be shown on the first royalty statement received after publication, and indeed if the book came out at the beginning of the royalty period, the proportion may be as high as 80 or 90 per cent.

Many of those sales will have been to libraries. Demand has diminished substantially in recent years, not only because of cuts in local council spending but also because the libraries have improved their services to borrowers so that a single copy of a book can be more readily available in any branch of a group of libraries, whereas in the past that group would have purchased several copies and spread them around the branches. Nevertheless, British libraries have always been, and look like remaining, the best in the world. No other country has so extensive and well-stocked a system of public libraries, making books available at no cost (except indirectly to the ratepayer) to everyone. We may justly be proud of them as one of our greater national glories, but they are also a considerable millstone around the necks of publishers and authors, for they have turned us into a nation of book borrowers rather than book buyers. We have one of the smallest annual *per capita* hardcover book purchase figures among the affluent nations. How many authors have despaired at hearing their friends promise to get their books out of the library, as though this would be of great benefit to them? Admittedly, authors like to be read, but even though the Public Lending Right (which I shall come to shortly) has been a marvellous thing for many authors, bringing a welcome addition to their income, what they really want to hear is that their friends are going to *buy* copies of their books. This is not simply because the author gets a royalty on sales of the book, but because the more copies that are sold the more likely the publisher will be to accept the author's next book, the more likely the bookseller will be to stock all his works, the more likely he is to move towards bestsellerdom, or at least towards a greater success than he is presently enjoying.

Hardcover publishers sell their books to libraries either in bound form or in sheets which are then bound by library suppliers, though the latter method is far more rare nowadays than it used to be. When the library buys a book, the publisher makes a single sale only and the author receives a royalty only on that single sale, no matter how many times the book is borrowed and read. The unfairness has been ameliorated to a limited extent for the author by the introduction of Public Lending Right (see pp.225–7), but the publisher still receives nothing extra.

Paperbacks

There are far fewer mass-market paperback publishers than hardcover houses, with perhaps no more than a score of major imprints in this country. All of them are either owned by hardcover houses, or have close links with them, but they are usually separately managed, and do not only publish books which have first appeared on the lists of their parent companies. Some years ago it could be said that, on the whole, paperback publishers concentrated on very popular books, with fiction predominating, but although it is still in these areas that the major sales are achieved, virtually all the lists nowadays include an important section devoted to literary works, as well as children's books, non-fiction, illustrated books of various kinds – a very wide range indeed. There is also a considerable variety of format, and paperbacks appear in all sorts of shapes and sizes.

The variety of paperbacks available in the shops is increased by the fact that it is not only from the mass-market houses that paperbacks now appear. Almost all publishers now produce some of their books in softcover form, although, as I have already explained, these are really the equivalent of cheap editions rather than similar to the mass-market product.

Paperbacks are of course very much cheaper than hardcover books – not, as many people believe, because the thin board cover and the binding process (known as "perfect binding", the back edges of the signatures, or folded sheets, being guillotined off and the separate pages of the book then being glued together, whereas the hardcover book is still likely to have its signatures sewn together before the binding case is drawn on) are much cheaper than the boards and cloth and more complex binding of hardcover books, but because the paperback business is predicated on large quantities. The minimum print quantity for a mass-market paperback book is usually in the range of fifteen to twenty thousand (though it may drop as low as ten thousand), while bestsellers may be well be produced in quantities of a quarter of a million or more. Certainly the paper is of poorer quality and the binding is somewhat cheaper and the author's royalty rates are usually lower than for hardcover books, but it is the mass production of large quantities which keeps the retail price down. The publisher's profit is possibly limited to a very small percentage of the retail price – perhaps a few pence per copy only – but since he sells so many copies his sales income is sufficient to cover his overheads and give him a net profit and to provide for the large sums he often spends on the promotion of his bestsellers.

Paperbacks are of course very widely sold in regular bookshops, but they are also available in newsagents' and sweetshops, and increasingly in supermarkets, tobacconists, hairdressers, and other non-traditional outlets. Libraries too are beginning to take paperbacks in substantial numbers. Although paperback publishers do sell directly to some retailers, the bulk of their sales is made to wholesalers, who supply and service the thousands of small retail customers for the books, or to the central buying offices of the big chains.

The rights in the majority of paperback books are still bought from hardcover publishers, and though there are examples of both editions being published simultaneously, it is more usual for there to be a gap between the appearance of the hardcover book and that of the paperback of at least six months and more often a year or longer. This delay is imposed by hardcover publishers because, although it is true that paperback buyers are not in the main buyers of hardcovers, hardcover buyers can easily be seduced into the purchase of paperbacks, and hardcover publishers believe that publication of a paperback edition simultaneously with or very shortly after their own publication date does damage their sales. With major books, especially those of American origin, it is commonplace for the paperback edition to be published overseas in the Open market very much earlier than for the domestic market, and this is done in order to meet the competition of the American paperback edition of the same book, and indeed the British and American houses are often engaged in warfare over these lucrative export markets, each trying to produce his edition first so as to capture the bulk of the sales. It is as true of paperbacks as of hardcovers that, except with the most durable titles, the larger part of the sales will be achieved during the first six months after publication.

Although paperback publishers obtain most of their books from hardcover publishers, they publish an increasing number of "originals" (books published for the first time in paperback), and sometimes even commission them. Many originals are what are known as "category books" – westerns, romances, science fiction and non-fiction books on popular but specialist subjects such as gardening or home crafts. If you sell your book direct to a paperback house, you will receive a smaller royalty in most cases than you would from a hardcover publisher, but of course you will not have to split it as you would if the hardcover publisher had sold the book to the paperback house and then taken his share.

When a paperback publisher buys an original he will expect to control many of the subsidiary rights, just as a hardcover publisher would, and in recent years this side of the paperback business has expanded and become effective. Included among those rights would be that of licensing a hardcover edition, and this kind of reverse partnership between hard and soft cover has worked in a number of cases. If that kind of deal is made, the paperback publisher takes a share of the hardcover income, but it is usually a much smaller percentage than that of the paperback income taken by the hardcover house when the sale has been made in the more conventional way. Of course, the sums are usually very much smaller too.

There is, however, one very major problem facing the author who hopes to sell direct to a paperback publisher, and that is that the paperback houses (of which, remember, there are comparatively few) tend to be bestseller orientated. This means not only that they put almost all their efforts behind one or two "lead" titles every month, but also that if they have on their list a bestselling author who is also prolific, they are likely to keep a large number of his titles in print and this inevitably diminishes their appetite for less well-known authors. It also of course makes it much more difficult for the unknown book to find shelf space in the shops, and the display of a book and hence its immediate availability to the impulse buyer are essential in the paperback market; if a whole row of spaces in a rack of paperbacks is occupied by that bestselling author, it is very nice for him, but it doesn't leave much room for you. Paperback editors are well aware of this problem, and often try to encourage and introduce less well-known writers, but are sometimes hampered in this by their customers, the wholesalers, who will order the bestsellers in huge quantities, but may refuse to take even a token number of the book with a less familiar title and author's name. Even Penguin, the trendsetter, the company which brought about the "paperback revolution" which has so changed the face of publishing, having established itself in a position from which it was able to publish successfully books not aimed at the most popular end of the market, was eventually forced to take a number of steps to secure its continued existence. These included the addition to the list of popular bestsellers to compete with its more commercially orientated competitors, the introduction of pictorial covers, and the establishment of Penguin shops within bookshops, where the whole range of Penguin titles would be permanently available.

The major change of recent years in paperback publishing has been the increase in the number of "fully integrated" publishing houses. This term, as has already been explained, is applied to a hardcover house which also owns a mass-market paperback company, allowing the acquiring editors in the two concerns to work together in the purchase of books. Some people refer to the arrangement as "vertical" publishing. The joint deals of the two editors, buying both hardcover and paperback rights, can often involve huge sums of money, which become economically viable at least in part because they can think of the two editions of a potential bestseller as a single entity, co-ordinating the publicity, for instance, and generally working together to make sure of the book's success. (It is worth pointing out, too, that sometimes when publishers pay extravagant sums for certain popular authors, one of their objects in so doing is to attract other authors to their list – "if Messrs Rows & Crowne and their mass-market paperback house, King's Head Books, can pay a million pounds to get the hardcover and paperback rights in X's next three novels, they must be pretty good at selling books, for otherwise they're going to lose a lot of money, and if they can do that well for X, maybe they could do well for me, too.")

Bookclubs

Bookclubs sell by direct mail, offering hardcover books at less than the normal price, which they achieve by purchasing copies from the publisher at high discounts, reducing the author's royalty, and by binding their members to the purchase of a given number of books per year. This commitment, though the member's obligation is usually no more than the purchase of one book every quarter, gives the club a captive market. At regular intervals the club's latest "choice" is sent and billed automatically to the members, unless they return a form saying that they do not wish to receive it; undoubtedly many copies of the choice are sold by this method to members who do not really want the book, but are too lazy or forgetful to return the form rejecting it.

The quantities of books that bookclubs take vary from one or two hundred to tens of thousands. Booksellers abhor the clubs, especially when they offer new members the introductory opportunity of buying expensive books for a ridiculously low price, at the same time as the bookseller is trying to sell the same title at full price. Publishers, on the other hand, welcome a bookclub order, since it is usually given before the book is printed, and can thus increase the print order and spread the origination cost of the book. Sometimes bookclubs print their own editions of books, and this affects the author since he will probably receive a slightly higher royalty on these copies than he does when the publisher supplies the bookclub with copies from his own stock; the bookclub is unlikely to print its own edition unless it is expecting to dispose of very large quantities of the book, and it will usually cut costs by using the publisher's plant, so that it is in fact producing a reprint under its own name.

The support which the public gives to bookclubs seems to fluctuate; at the time of writing, they are thriving. In addition to those which take a very wide of range of books of general interest, there are many specialist bookclubs devoted to one particular subject, such as cookery, ancient history, religion, and so on. There are even bookclubs dealing only with paperbacks.

US Rights

If your book is sold to an American publisher, the contract will be basically similar to the agreement you sign with a British publisher, and will grant him much the same rights. It will almost certainly be a much longer document and may also be very much tougher on the author than most British publishing contracts. You should never, of course, sign any document without reading it carefully and understanding not only its benefits to you but your obligations under it and the restrictions it may place upon you, and care may be particularly necessary with American contracts. Royalties tend to be a little lower in the States than in Britain, but the quantities of books sold are often higher. If your book is lavishly illustrated, particularly if colour printing is involved, or if it is a somewhat elaborate production, it is quite likely that the British publisher will arrange to sell sheets of his edition to the American publisher who will buy them at a price only slightly above cost and inclusive of royalty. Your share will then be a percentage of the price received by the British publisher, and this is generally a ludicrously small amount in comparison with what you would receive if you were given a normal royalty on the American retail price of the book. It seems very unfair, but the economics of this kind of publishing rarely allow of a better deal for the author, and it is often a question of accepting this small reward or getting nothing at all. All moneys due from a US publisher (and the same applies to foreign language publishers) will be paid to your British publisher or to your agent, and of course their shares of the income will be deducted before it is passed on to you.

It may come about nowadays that you sign a contract with

the British branch of an American publishing house. Since such branches operate in many ways independently of their parent companies, the contract may not differ greatly from that which you would sign with any British house. On the other hand, you might be fortunate enough to find that both the British branch and the American owners want to publish your book, in which case you will be asked to grant world volume rights. This should of course be reflected in the size of the advance, and you should also aim at receiving full royalties on the American edition, rather than sharing them with the British branch.

If you sign a contract directly with an American publisher (or with a foreign language publisher) you will become liable for income tax in the United States (or in the foreign language country) unless you apply specially for exemption on the grounds that you pay your taxes in your country of residence. A large number of countries has reciprocal double tax exemption arrangements with Britain. The Society of Authors, the Writers' Guild, your agent or your bank manager or accountant would be able to advise you.

Foreign or Translation Rights

Translation rights can be very lucrative, despite the fact that the foreign publisher usually pays a lower rate of royalties (allowing him to include the cost of the translation in his budget without inflating the retail price). Let me repeat, sales of your original publisher's English language edition of your book in foreign countries do not come under Foreign rights, which are translation rights, sold to a foreign publisher who will bring out an edition of the book translated into his own language, whereas sales of the English language edition in foreign-speaking countries are export sales. It is customary for the foreign publisher to agree to publish a faithful translation of the book, and it should not be altered in any material way without your prior consent. You may well find, however, that minor changes have been made. In theory, the author should be consulted about all alterations, but in practice it is probably better to accept them with a good grace after the event, provided of course that they have not damaged your work, and enjoy the financial rewards. The foreign publisher will usually be granted volume rights in the book, and may therefore achieve for you a sale of the foreign language edition to paperback houses, bookclubs, magazines and so on in his country.

It is possible that with the lowering of barriers in Europe after 1992 we may see far more co-operation between British and European publishers, with further alliances, take-overs and conglomerations becoming frequent.

Subsidiary Rights

Serial

It is important to distinguish between first serial rights and second serial rights. First serial rights, which are not always granted to the publisher, but retained in the control of the author, refer to the appearance of the book, or extracts from it, in newspapers or magazines *prior to* its publication in volume form. Second serial rights, which are often controlled by the publisher, refer to the appearance of the book, or extracts from it, in newspapers or magazines *after* publication in volume form. However many times the book may appear in this way, after publication, the rights concerned are still second serial (not third, or fifth, or umpteenth), and to make it even clearer than mud, you might like to note that "serial" in this context is really another name for "magazine" or "newspaper" and does not mean a serial form of your book.

Anthology and Quotation

These cover the use of your work in anthologies of poetry or prose, and also cover the granting of rights to others to use extracts from your work in publications which cannot be described as anthologies. If you are quoting from another person's work, you must obtain permission to do so, and pay a fee for the privilege. Under rules known as "fair dealing" a limited amount from an author's work may be quoted without payment for purposes of criticism or review, but exactly how much may be used in this way is always a vexed question. Some time ago the Society of Authors and the Publishers Association set out the following standards for "fair dealing": a single extract of up to 400 words from a prose work; or a series of extracts, none of which is longer than 300 words, totalling not more than 800 words from a prose work; or extracts totalling not more than forty lines from a poem (but the extracts should not amount to more than a quarter of the complete poem). And your quotation must be used in the course of criticism or review or to illustrate a point that you are making, and not as part of an anthology.

Unless the material that you are quoting is very brief indeed, it is always as well to apply in writing for permission to use someone else's material, approaching the publisher of the work and giving details of the use you intend to make of the quotation. The publisher will tell you in what form the obligatory acknowledgement of the source should be made and what fee, varying from nothing to large sums for a lengthy quote from an author of note, will be payable. It may seem a chore to have to do this and you may resent having to make the payment, but the boot will be on the other foot when others want to quote from you. For poets and short story writers in particular Anthology Rights can often provide a substantial income.

Digest Book Condensation

Condensed books, mostly fiction, are sold by direct mail to subscribers. The shortening of the book may be a salutary experience for the author, demonstrating just how much of the original version was unnecessary verbiage; it may also cause him considerable pain at the disappearance of his fine writing and possibly the total elimination of scenes and characters which he considers essential to his story. The condensations are, however, done with considerable skill and as much sympathy as possible by the experienced editors employed by the condensed book publisher, and if the author is upset by what they do, his best course is to console himself with the cheque that he will receive for these rights.

Digest

This differs from "Digest book condensation rights" in that it refers to the right to publish a shortened version of a book in a newspaper or magazine, rather than in book form.

Strip Cartoon

To many people in this country, alas, a "book" is a magazine. To others, again alas, it may be a collection of strip cartoons, the contents of the original book having been abridged, the dialogue made brief and punchy, and excitement added with words like "POW" and "ZAP" and a proliferation of asterisks, exclamation marks and other typographical devices. It has happened to Shakespeare. It could happen to you. If it does, cry your way to the bank.

TV, Radio and Recorded Readings
TV and Radio Dramatization
Film and Dramatic
Sound and Video Recording

These rights are, I think, self-explanatory. It is perhaps worth noting that, if you are lucky enough and your book sells to a film producer or company, the moneys involved are sometimes supplemented by a share of profits on the film, which is fine if the term used is "gross profits", but rather less exciting if the share is of "net profits", since in the film industry net profits sometimes disappear altogether, even on the most successful films. Better deals are for a share of net or gross receipts. What happens most often with film rights is that an option is purchased for a comparatively small sum, and such options have a habit of lapsing without the film being made. There is nothing to be done about this except to be grateful that you received a sum of money for nothing.

Merchandizing

For most authors these rights remain unexploited, but if you should happen to be a Beatrix Potter or an Edwardian Lady just imagine how much you will rake in from the posters, notepads, money-boxes, coffee mugs and all the other products which will sell because of the use of your material.

One-shot Periodical

This term usually means the publication of the complete text of a book appearing in one issue only of a newspaper or magazine.

Hardcover Reprint and Large Print

Hardcover reprints are sometimes licensed to a firm which produces books in a special format, perhaps as a series ("Classic True Accounts of World War II", for example) or for promotional purposes. Large-print books, which are increasingly popular, are usually straightforward reprints of the original text, but set in a large size of type so that they can be read by the partially sighted. The specialist publishers of these books pay an advance and royalties in the normal way. If the US rights in the book have not been sold, the large-print publishers sometimes ask for the right to distribute their edition in the States. In contrast to large-print arrangements, it is customary when a request is received to translate a book into Braille to grant permission without fee for either author or publisher.

Electronic

Modern technology advances with extreme rapidity. We have become accustomed to the various storage methods used by word processors – floppy discs and hard discs and so on. CD Rom, a development of the compact disc, is capable of storing a huge amount of written material. Reproduction methods of this kind are covered by electronic rights, which, as we move towards and eventually into the twenty-first century, are likely to become of increasing importance.

Reprographic

Reprography (a term first used in the 1960s) is a portmanteau word, made up of "reproduction" and "photography", and its most common application is to the familiar photocopier. Reprographic rights are, in most cases, handled on the author's behalf by ALCS (the Authors' Licensing and Collecting Society) and on the publisher's behalf by PLS (the Publishers Licensing Society), these two societies controlling CLA (the Copyright Licensing Agency) which collects moneys due under the licences it issues (see p.228).

Public Lending

PLR (Public Lending Right), the payment made to authors when their books are borrowed from public libraries, is, by law, the author's money and no one else's. You should not therefore sign a contract in which a clause gives your publisher a share in your PLR. Even your agent, if you have one, takes no cut of it.

Other

There seems to be no end to the things that can happen to a book, and some contracts, after covering all the subsidiary rights that both parties to the agreement can think of, add a further clause which refers to other rights, and thus covers any rights that have been overlooked or any which do not exist at the time of the contract but which may come into being as a result of modern technology. Such a clause usually says that any other rights shall be reserved to the author, or that they shall be the subject of negotiation. If the former wording is used you have no problem, but if negotiation is called for, it will be worth taking advice as to what split of earnings should be regarded as acceptable.

3

Submitting Your Work
to a Publisher

Preparation of the Typescript

Handwriting was all very well for Jane Austen, but nowadays few publishers would be prepared to consider a manuscript (using that term in its true meaning of material written by hand). A typescript is required (even if it is often loosely and perversely referred to as a "manuscript"), and it should be in double spacing on one side of the paper only, with ample margins (say, a minimum of 2.5 cm) at top, bottom, right- and left-hand sides of the page. Why is this important? First of all, because your material will be easier to read. Double spacing will also allow room for corrections which do not warrant retyping. Margins at the sides will permit the compositor (the person who puts the book into type) to put each page into a kind of stand which has grips on either side to hold it in place while he copies it.

There are different rules for the layout of poetry and plays. Poems should be typed exactly as they are intended to appear in print, in single spacing with any indentations or other singularities just as you want them. Plays demand special and complex layouts, advice on which can be obtained from play publishers or from the BBC Radio Drama department, which has a useful leaflet on the subject.

The paper used should be A4 (210 x 297 mm), or what is known as American A4 (217 x 280 mm), which is the size of the "continuous" paper commonly supplied for word processor printers. I believe that most publishers would prefer you not to use the facility on your electronic typewriter or word processor which will "justify" the type on the right-hand side, spacing the words out so that the right-hand margin is a straight one. Do your best to keep to the same number and width of lines per page, and if you use more than one typewriter it is preferable that they should all have the same size of type – these considerations making it much easier to work out the length of the book, quite apart from the fact that the typescript will look neater.

Many authors tend to economize on typewriter ribbons. It doesn't help. Why put an obstacle in the way of your book by making it physically difficult for the publisher to read? Equally, masses of messy corrections are to be avoided. That doesn't mean that you can't make the occasional alteration, but the cleaner the typescript looks the better. If you do make a correction, make sure that the change is totally clear, and if it is of any length or complexity, retype the page.

You should make at least two carbon copies of your typescript. When submitting a book, always send the top copy to a publisher rather than a carbon. If he decides to take the book on, he will probably want a second copy, and your first carbon copy will be acceptable. The second carbon copy is for yourself, and you should retain it with the utmost care. You may want to refer to it in working with your publisher, and you will certainly need it if the other copies are lost or damaged. Typescripts sometimes go astray in the post or are mislaid in the most scrupulously monitored of publisher's offices (and not all are that!) or can be damaged by fire or flood, and if any such disaster should take place, it is much easier to have the book retyped or photocopied from your own carbon than to have to start writing it again from scratch. Photocopying is just as acceptable, if not more so, than carbon copying, if you can afford it. If you are using carbons, again don't indulge in false economy, but replace the carbons as soon as the copies begin to look grey.

Increasingly nowadays authors are working on word processors. A word processor is, in fact, a computer controlled by a program which allows the users to record whatever words they may wish to compose, the words then being stored on discs, from which they may be retrieved so that they may be read and, if necessary, altered, and from which copies may be produced on the attached printers. Word processors vary from the cheap and simple Amstrad PCW8256 (which at the time of writing is the cheapest machine on the market, and which many authors find entirely adequate for their purposes, although the quality of printing is less than perfect) to the expensive, luxury machines which allow of the production of graphics and other illustrations as well as of words, and which have a wide range of printing facilities, including the choice of many different type styles and sizes, colour work, and so on. If you are embarking on desktop publishing (see p.19) you will certainly need a fairly sophisticated word processor, even if not one at the very top of the range.

Among the many attractions of word processors are the ease with which corrections can be made, the speed with which the work can be printed, and the ability to produce as many additional copies as you like, without having to mess about with carbons. The use of continuous paper (217 x 280 mm, after the perforations at the sides have been torn off) makes the printing an even easier process.

However, the remarks above concerning typewriter ribbons apply equally to the ribbons used on word processors. Don't economize on them – make sure that your work is always easy to read. If you have the facility to produce work in either "draft" or "high quality" mode, use the former for your own copy of the typescript, but the latter, always, for work which you are going to submit to a publisher.

The pages of your typescript should be numbered consecutively from the first page to the last, not starting from "1" again at the beginning of each new chapter. If you have ever dropped a typescript of separate pages and tried to put it in order again, you will appreciate how much more difficult a task it would be if the chapters were each numbered separately. Put "The End" at the end, even if you don't want it to appear in the final printed version; endings are sometimes inconclusive, but if "The End" is there the publisher will know that that is where you intended to stop.

Publishers vary in their likes and dislikes about how a typescript should be fastened together. The universally unpopular method is that in which the pages are bound solidly together, which makes the book impossibly heavy and awkward to read. Looseleaf binders are often used; the ring variety is not too bad, but pages frequently slip out of the sort which relies on some kind of spring to keep them in place. Paperclips should be avoided, if only because other pieces of paper so easily get caught up in them. My own preference in my days as a publisher was for entirely loose leafs, the typescript either contained in the box the paper came in or in wallet-type folders or secured with rubber bands. However, stapling is acceptable, either in chapters or in batches of a regular number of pages, but only one staple, at the top left-hand corner, is needed.

How long should a book be? A glib, but nevertheless true answer is that it should be as long as it needs to be. If you set out to write, say, eighty thousand words, you may find that you have to pad your material or conversely to condense it. Let the book find its own length. There are no rules – very short and very long books do get published – but there are guidelines. In most cases, publishers do not want anything much under thirty-five thousand words (except for children's books) and tend to look apprehensively at anything which runs to more than a hundred thousand words. If you can keep to somewhere between fifty and eighty thousand words you will probably stand more chance. But, as I have already said, there are no hard and fast rules, unless you are writing for a series, when you may have to stick closely to a length decided in advance by the publisher. The best thing is to do your market research – find out the length of already published books which are similar in scope to yours, or write to a publisher and ask what length book of the type you have in mind he would be prepared to consider. But do make sure that a desired length does not become more important than the content – don't try to cram too much into a short space, when it will all seem under-written, or stretch your material out to fill up the pages, when it will seem thin and the padding will show.

How many chapters should your book have? Again, there are no rules. Some books have no chapters, and others are broken into hundreds of short sections. If you come to a "natural break" in your narrative, then you have probably come to the end of a chapter. But I doubt if any books have ever been turned down for having either too few or too many chapters.

It is not absolutely necessary to indicate on the front page of your typescript how many words it contains, since most publishers are practised at gauging the length of the books they receive, but it does no harm to show the extent, and indeed it may be a help. The publishers of this book, Robert Hale Limited, issue an excellent guide to the calculation of the length of a typescript and, with their permission, I shall now quote it:

> The purpose of calculating the wordage of any typescript is to determine the number of printed pages it will occupy. The precise word count is of no use, since it tells nothing about the matter of short lines resulting from paragraphing or dialogue (particularly important with fiction).
>
> Calculation is therefore based on the assumption that all printed pages have no paragraph beginnings or endings and the type area is completely filled with words.
>
> To assess the wordage proceed as follows:
>
> 1. Ensure the typewriting is the same throughout in terms of size, length of line etc. If not the procedure given below should be followed separately for each individual style of typing and the results added together.
> 2. Count 50 full-length lines and find the average number of words, e.g. 50 lines of 560 words gives an average of 11.2 words.
> 3. Average the number of lines over 10 characteristic pages, e.g. 245 lines on 10 pages gives an average of 24.5 lines.
> 4. Multiply the averages of 2. and 3. to get average per page, e.g. $11.2 \times 24.5 = 274$.
> 5. Ensure the page numbering is consecutive, then multiply the word average per page by the number of pages (count short pages at beginnings and ends of chapters as full pages.)
> 6. Draw attention to, but do not count, foreword, preface, introduction, bibliography, appendices, index, maps or other line figures.

Some authors are in the habit of putting "First British Serial Rights" on the front page of their typescripts, in the mistaken belief that this is what they are offering to the publisher. They should be offering volume rights, or at least British volume rights, or possibly all rights. First British Serial Rights are what you offer to a magazine or newspaper if you submit your book to them before or instead of showing it to a book publisher.

Do put your name and address on the title-page and last page of your typescript.

Words are the main tool of the author's trade, and they should be correctly used and spelt and punctuated. I have always considered that failure in these respects is the sign of an unprofessional approach. I do recognize that some writers have an impenetrable blindspot in certain of these matters, particularly spelling, and that even the most careful scrutiny of dictionaries and grammars cannot entirely solve their problems. In which case, I would suggest that before finally typing their books, or at least before submitting them if they are already typed, they should prevail upon a friend with the right capabilities to go through the books and make the necessary alterations. Such glamour attaches to authorship, that it should not be difficult to find a friend who will undertake this chore. Teachers are very suitable, though it is as well to choose one who has retired or is at least elderly – the younger ones may be as hopeless as you yourself. You may also find it worthwhile to get hold of a copy of my own book, *The Nuts and Bolts of Writing* (published by Hale), which was written with the specific aim of helping writers to improve the quality of their work in respect of such matters as spelling, punctuation and grammar. The book was, in fact, suggested to me by my publisher in a moment of anger and despair at the poor standard of punctuation, grammar and spelling in so many of the typescripts submitted to him.

Sending the Book Out

Having got your typescript ready, in the best possible condition that you can manage, where do you send it? In the *Writers' and Artists' Year Book* you will find a list of publishers and their addresses. Some indication of the kinds of books that each firm publishes is given, but the information is often too brief and general to be more than the roughest of guides. *The Writer's Handbook* gives rather more detail about publishers and their requirements, but even the additional help which it gives may not be entirely adequate. Rather than using a pin with either book to decide which publisher you will try, it is a good idea to visit your local bookshop and library and see which companies regularly produce books of the kind which you have written. It may be stating the obvious, but it is of little use to send, say, a romantic novel to a publisher who produces nothing but school text books, or an art book to a publisher who never ventures into that field. On the other hand, you should beware of working too closely on what you discover in the bookshop; if you have written, say, a new biography of Mary, Queen of Scots, it is probably a waste of time and money to send it to a publisher who has recently brought out a book on the very same subject, or who has a standard work on it on his backlist; try another house which has a list of biographies.

Should you choose a large publisher or a small one? You may prefer to be with a small publisher, on the grounds that it is better to be a big fish in a small pond than a small fish in a large pond. Of course, no matter what the size of the pond, if you're a bestseller you'll be a big fish, and if you're at the other end of the scale you'll be a small fish. Assuming, however, that you're just of medium size, you may feel that you will get more individual attention in the small firm, while you may benefit in the large one from its more efficient selling organization, but neither of these possibilities is necessarily so. It cannot even be said with any certainty that your work stands more chance of being accepted by a big publisher, despite the fact that he brings out a great many books every year – his standards are likely to be just as high as those of a small house. The best thing is to forget the size of the publisher and choose simply those which your market research tells you are the most likely to be interested in your book.

When you have selected your publisher you can simply send your typescript to him. In these days of very high postal costs for parcels it is, however, wiser to write first asking if you may submit the book. Tell the publisher, briefly, what it is about. If it is a novel, specify what genre it is ("straight", romantic, thriller, detective, western, etc), or if it is non-fiction, give a few details of your qualifications for writing it and possibly something about the market for which it is intended. You will have little chance of getting that biography of Mary, Queen of Scots published unless you are an accredited historian or have had access to new, unpublished material about her (though of course there are always exceptions to a statement of that sort – if you are a well-known writer, or have not found new material but a really new angle, or if you write so well that you have brought the lady to life as no one else ever has, for instance).

Do not tell the publisher that all your friends have enjoyed the book. He won't be impressed, partly because he does not know your friends and so has no idea whether or not he can respect their judgement, and partly because he will suspect that your friends will have told you that they enjoyed it even if in fact they loathed every word. On the other hand, if you happen to have had an endorsement from some eminent personage, especially if he is in the field in which you are writing, by all means say so. Equally, if you are writing, for instance, a book on safety in the home and have shown it to an organization such as RoSPA, who have given it their approval, say so. Or if the book is aimed at a specialist market, it will probably be worthwhile to give some details of the numbers of people likely to be keenly interested in the book.

Over the years I spent in publishing I received thousands of letters about books which the authors wished me to consider. Some were grovelling ("I would consider it an honour to be published by such a great firm as yours"), some were overbearing ("I have decided that you should publish this book. Kindly state your terms by return"), some were jokey ("My Mum thinks it's smashing, but I do recognize that she may be a teeny bit prejudiced in my favour"), some were apologetic and often tended to misquote ("A poor thing but my own"), some were so long that I felt I didn't need to read the book itself, and some were so illiterate that I knew I didn't have to.

Caroline Sheldon, the literary agent, lists three other letters that turn her off: those that begin "Don't miss this opportunity!", those that admit "the first three chapters aren't very good", and those that boast "this story won a prize in our village competition". The letters that she would like best, as I did, were those which are brief and to the point, businesslike, professional.

Send a stamped addressed envelope with your letter of enquiry. You may feel that the publisher should well be able to afford to pay for the postage on his letter back to you, but you should remember that you are in a buyer's market, and don't ask him to spend money on something which may not interest him.

It may be worth your while to find out the editor's name so that you can address your letter to him personally (not that, if it is a large editorial department, he will necessarily be the person to read it). If you do so, however, make sure that you get the name right. Some people are very sensitive about mispellings of their name (personally, I am inured to it after long experience) or to being addressed as "Ms" when in fact they are "Mr" or "Mrs" or even old-fashioned "Miss".

If the publisher says that he is willing to consider the book, then post it to him, or deliver it if you are near enough to his office. Enclose postage for its return. Don't, if you deliver it, expect to see anyone in the office – at that stage no one is interested in you. Your book is your ambassador. And if you feel that you have to see someone to explain about the book, then there is probably something wrong with it. Your book should speak for itself. After all, you aren't going to be able to stand in bookshops explaining it to potential customers, are you?

When you send your book to a publisher you should receive an acknowledgement of its arrival. If you do not receive such an acknowledgement it may mean that the parcel has been lost in the mail, or it may be simply that the publisher has decided to economize by not sending out those expensive (cost of stationery, secretary's time, postage) pieces of paper. Some authors enclose a stamped addressed postcard which the publisher can send off when the parcel arrives. It is all an additional expense for the author, but like paper, typewriter ribbons, carbons, and of course time and hard work, it is simply an investment that he has to make.

Synopses and Specimen Chapters

Instead of sending the complete book, you can send a specimen chapter or two and a synopsis. The practice of doing so has grown considerably in the past decade, partly, it would seem, because the present generation of editors is more willing than were their predecessors to consider submissions in this form, and partly because even untried authors are often unwilling to commit themselves to the work involved in writing a full-length book without some expression of interest from a publisher.

In the case of non-fiction books, the synopsis-and-specimen-chapters approach often works very well, provided that the publisher is given in addition sufficiently impressive information about the author's qualifications for writing the book (and perhaps also something about the potential market for it). Indeed, the non-fiction author can often begin simply by writing to a publisher about an idea for a book; if the publisher is interested, a detailed synopsis and a specimen chapter or two may be called for, meetings and discussions will follow, and the book may then be commissioned. Or, if you happen to be an expert in a particular field, the first approach may come from a publisher, inviting you to write a given book, in which case a synopsis and specimen chapters might be requested just to make sure that you really are capable of doing the work and that you and the publisher have the same concept of what the finished book is meant to be like.

For fiction, however, the situation is a little different, the problem being that in an imaginative work, which often depends heavily on the author's ability to create colour and excitement and to handle the crises in the story with a sense of drama, even the best of synopses and specimen chapters cannot give an entirely reliable picture of the book as a whole. When I was a publisher and was sent such a submission for a novel, only those which were quite hopeless got an outright rejection; if I found the material even slightly interesting, I responded by asking for the complete work to be sent to me in due course, and the same kind of letter went to those authors whose material seemed quite promising. In every case I was careful not to make any commitment. Had I really encouraged these authors? They may have felt so, but in effect I was simply saying that I was prepared to consider a full-length script only. Some publishers are perhaps more free with their encouragement than I was, but commissions to write a novel, based on showing no more than a small part of the material, are rarely given to untried authors.

(Incidentally, although the comment may brand me as an old reactionary, I must say that I have little sympathy with those would-be novelists who are unwilling to settle down to produce a book without first having a publisher's commitment to make it worth their while. New authors have to prove themselves. Few are so gifted that they can write an acceptable book without first learning their craft – and there is no better way to learn the craft than by actually doing it.)

If you are commissioned to write a book on the basis of a synopsis, you do not have to stick to it absolutely rigidly. Obviously, you must do your best to deliver the book that the publisher expects, but minor differences from the original synopsis will not worry your publisher too much. He is used to the fact that authors change their ideas sometimes in the course of writing, or find that something which sounds perfectly fine in brief will not work properly when it is expanded. If the changes are at all major, you should of course let your publisher know about them in advance, especially if they alter the scope of the book in some way.

Many established writers produce all of their books "on spec" – that is to say, without a contract until the book has been finished and accepted for publication. Others are fortunate enough to be commissisoned for each of their books, but in those cases, even though the author is very experienced and trustworthy, the publisher may ask him for a detailed synopsis. The main use of this will be for the editor to show to other people. For him, the title and your name may be sufficient. For others, both inside and outside his own publishing house, more details may well be useful.

Even less to be recommended than the synopsis and specimen chapter as a first approach is the submission which takes the form of two or three pages, taken apparently at random from a book. Intended to whet the publisher's appetite, such submissions are merely irritating and a complete waste of time and postage. It is in fact an unwritten law, known to all editors, that the authors who use this method of submission are generally entirely lacking in talent; one can always tell this, because if the pages sent represent the best of the writing in the book, then the rest of it must be abysmal indeed.

Multiple Submissions

Most tutors of Creative Writing and authors of books on the subject will tell you not to give up easily. They advise you not to be depressed if your typescript is regularly rejected, and they remind you of the number of rejections that John Braine received for *Room at the Top* before it was accepted and published with enormous success. But if each time you send out your work you have to wait for months before it comes back with a rejection slip, it may take you years before you too achieve your desired acceptance. Can you do anything about that?

Some years ago the majority of publishers would have held up their hands in horror at the thought of an author having the temerity to submit work simultaneously to more than one publisher. If they had discovered that such a crime had been committed the book would have been returned to the wicked author forthwith. However, manners and codes of behaviour change. Quite a long time ago now publishers began to accept the idea that agents would sometimes conduct an auction for a new book which was considered commercially important, sending copies to all the publishers who seemed to be possible contenders for it, and demanding that their best offers should be made by a due date. Having been forced to accept the principle of multiple simultaneous submissions in this particular way, the majority of publishers found it rather easier than they had imagined to respond to the increasing calls from non-agented authors to allow them to minimize the delays in awaiting verdicts by no longer objecting to looking at a typescript at the same time as other publishers were also considering it.

Multiple submissions are here to stay. However, there are still some dinosaur publishers who have not yet caught up with contemporary trends, and may therefore continue to object to the idea. It is probably sensible, when writing a letter of enquiry to a publisher about your work, to ask whether that house has any antipathy towards multiple submissions. If you prefer not to make that enquiry, but simply to assume that none of the publishers to whom you send your book will object to the fact that they do not have an exclusive offer, then at least I would suggest that you should inform them, as a matter of courtesy, that you have sent the work elsewhere at the same time.

Agents

You may decide instead of submitting your work directly to a publisher to send it first to an agent, and in many ways this can be a very wise move. The advantages of using an agent are many: he knows the state of the market much better than you are likely to, for he is in regular touch with all the principal publishers and is aware of the kinds of books they are looking for at any given juncture; he sends the book out at his own expense; he will negotiate the contract with the publisher, getting the best possible deal for his author, ensuring that the latter's rights are always preserved, and can often help to keep the publisher up to scratch, so that the book is handled well in every aspect; he collects any moneys due, and checks that they are correct; he will undertake the sale of many of the subsidiary rights; and, one of the agent's most important functions, he will stand between the author and the publisher in the case of any dispute, enabling the author to remain on friendly terms with his publisher despite the fact that, through the agent, they may be at loggerheads; he may also well be able to save you from having the dispute in the first place, for though he is your representative and therefore on your side, he does also have a wide experience of publishers and their problems (indeed, many agents have spent part of their careers as publishers) and may therefore be able to explain things that you don't understand, and tell you whether your complaint is justified or not; he will also probably be able to give you some advice about tax on your earnings as an author; and he will often give useful editorial advice on a typescript.

For all these services, the agent will normally charge the author 10 per cent of his earnings from the book, plus VAT, though he may take a higher percentage on foreign earnings. The higher rate on foreign earnings comes about because the British agent has made the foreign sale through a foreign agent who represents him in the country concerned. The foreign agent takes his cut on the moneys earned in that country, and transmits the balance to the British agent, who takes his percentage before passing it on to the author. Some authors resent having to pay a double commission in this way, and in certain circumstances their feelings may be justified. It is obviously a matter to be discussed directly with the agent.

The majority of agents do not charge for reading typescripts submitted to them by potential new clients, though the practice of asking for a fee has become more widespread recently, and will probably continue to grow. It is usually advisable to write to an agent first, asking if you may send your book for consideration (give a fair amount of information about it and about yourself, including any qualifications you have for writing the book, any details about its potential market, and something about your future writing plans).

Apart from the possible reading fee, no good agents, having taken you on to their list of clients, will take their percentage until they have sold your book and the money comes in. The agent's cut is usually (though not always) well earned, and any totally inexperienced author would be well advised to go to an agent. That is, if he can find one who is willing to act for him, which may not be easy. Agents are probably more difficult to find than publishers (there are, of course, fewer of them). They tend not to take on an author unless they are convinced that within a reasonable period they will be making enough money from him to cover their costs, their overheads and a profit. If an agent takes you on to his books he is undoubtedly hoping that within two or three years you will be earning upwards of £5,000 a year, and therefore contributing at least £500 a year towards his overheads and profit.

If you experience difficulty in finding an agent to take you on, and as already suggested it may be difficult at an early stage in your writing career, your best bet may be to try one of the newer, smaller agencies (look in the *Writers' and Artists' Yearbook* for the dates when they were founded.) You may not be getting the same expertise and experience, but the new agent's enthusiasm and need to establish himself may work to your benefit.

Do not despair if you simply cannot get an agent. It's an advantage to have one, but a huge number of highly successful authors have begun by submitting their work directly to publishers. There is a widespread belief that publishers do not like direct submissions from authors, preferring to receive all submissions through agents. There are certainly some publishers who discourage or even refuse direct submissions from authors, dealing only with agents, and there are others who go to the opposite extreme of regarding agents as enemies and refusing, as far as they dare, to work with them. But both these groups are minorities. Most publishers are quite happy to have a "slushpile". This is the name generally given to the pile on the editor's desk of unsolicited typescripts submitted directly by authors; it sounds a very derogatory term. The implicit contempt in it derives from the fact that well over 90 per cent of any publisher's slushpile consists of poor-quality material. Nevertheless, the majority of publishers devote considerable care and attention to the slushpile, searching for the very few publishable books that it may contain. Who knows? Nestling there may be a new Catherine Cookson, or the next Booker winner, or an even more successful diet book than those already on the market.

If a publishable book is found in the slushpile, it has some advantages for the publisher in not being agented, and these lie not so much in the fact that the terms in a direct contract may be slightly less favourable to the author than those in an agented contract – such differences are not likely to be really substantial – but in the opportunity a direct contract gives the publisher to control more subsidiary rights. For instance, most agented contracts with British publishers exclude US rights, which are then handled by the agent on the author's behalf; if the contract is a direct one, the publisher will probably handle US rights, and this can be of considerable advantage to him. It works like this: periodically British publishers go on business trips to the States with the hope of buying British rights in books controlled by American publishers, and selling American rights to American publishers in books which they, the British publishers, control, and American publishers come to Britain on similar buying/selling visits; it is obviously of advantage, when the publisher is setting out to buy, to have something to sell, and what the publisher has to sell, in this case, is not the agented book, in which he does not control the relevant rights, but something which has usually come from that apparently contemptuously described slushpile.

On the other hand, it must be remembered that a publisher who receives a book submitted by an agent knows before he has read a single word that it must have a modicum of merit, or the agent would not have agreed to handle it, and if the agent is one that he knows and trusts and the agent is very enthusiastic about the book, then he will undoubtedly give it special consideration. However, it is the book itself which will have to make the publisher enthusiastic, and that can happen whether it comes through an agent or directly from its author.

In the past, the idea that there should be a formal written agreement between a literary agent and his or her clients would have seemed very strange, and even the letters that may have been exchanged would often be very vague in many respects. The world changes, however, and nowadays it is becoming commonplace for an agent taking on a new client to present a formal agreement setting out the terms of the relationship. Such a contract is likely to be fairly simple, and especially if the agent belongs to the Association of Authors' Agents (members are marked with an asterisk in the *Writers' and Artists' Yearbook*) is probably not the kind of thing that you need to worry about before signing. Nevertheless, as with all contracts, you need to study such a document carefully before you do sign, and it will certainly be worth your while to seek advice on the matter if you have any doubts. The Society of Authors or the Writers' Guild, if you are a member of either, would be able to advise you.

Naturally, agents vary in their competence. You may find after a while that you are dissatisfied with yours. There is nothing to stop you changing to another agent if you can find one to take you on. However, you should give the first agent notice of your intention to change, and he is entitled to continue to act for you and to take his commission in respect of any books which he has handled for you, provided the original contract he negotiated has not been terminated. If you have a written agreement with your agent it will undoubtedly specify what is to happen regarding existing contracts with publishers in the event that you and the agent part company. If you do not have such an agreement, it is worth thrashing the matter out in some detail so neither party is in doubt about the situation.

Agents cannot of course perform miracles. If you get an agent to act for you, it does not necessarily mean that he will be able to sell all your ideas or completed books. Nor, though he may try to help his clients, is he usually in the business of teaching incompetent writers how to write. And though again, in very special circumstances, he may occasionally subsidize an author in a minor way, he is not, any more than your publisher is, in the banking business, and neither an agent nor a publisher should be expected to advance money to authors other than under the terms of a contract.

Waiting for the Result of a Submission

Having submitted your book to a publisher, how long can you expect to wait before receiving a verdict? Anything between two and eight weeks, and often – indeed, usually – longer. Some publishers are remarkably dilatory in this respect, and one frequently hears stories of books kept for a year or more before a decision is made. If the publisher has kept in touch with the author during that time to explain why it is taking so long to make a decision, the author may have less cause for complaint, but in most such cases, the author hears nothing. This seems to me to be quite outrageous.

Don't think, by the way, that this treatment is given only to new authors – it can happen equally to well-established writers, who have already had a number of books brought out successfully by the publisher in question.

As will be explained shortly, a decision as to whether or not to publish cannot always be arrived at swiftly, because there are a great many processes to be gone through. But some publishers contrive to make their minds up a lot more quickly than others – why can't they all? And if they positively cannot speed up their processes, why can't they have the courtesy to keep the author informed of what is happening?

Is there anything you can do about this situation if you encounter it? It is easy enough to say that you should withdraw your typescript from any publisher who delays decisions unreasonably, but we all know that authors, realizing that publishers are in a buyer's market, are reluctant to do anything which will possibly antagonize the very people they are hoping to impress and with whom they want to establish an amicable relationship.

Apart from withdrawing your typescript, there are not many options open to you. Of course, if you are an author of very high standing, even the most awful of publishers will be bowing and scraping and rushing round madly to convince you that you are dealing with a firm whose efficiency extends in every possible direction, including speed of decision-making. But for most of us the only answer is to suffer the delays. Do you suffer in silence? Yes, (unless you have been published previously by the firm in question, when you may be able to chivvy a little), for perhaps three months, after which it would be reasonable to write to the publisher and enquire politely what is happening. Some publishers will already have let you know by that time that they are tentatively interested in the book and will have explained that there will be a further delay while they prepare estimates, but in many cases there will simply be silence. If when you write after three months, you still get no satisfaction, then you have chosen an inefficient publisher (and there are many of them around). There is not a great deal that you can effectively do. At the end of six months without a decision, it is time to get stroppy, and demand the return of your typescript. That may mean the end of your chances with that particular publisher, but if he has already proved lackadaisical, you will be better off elsewhere. Nothing of course can compensate you for the lost time, and since there is little in the law books about the time that a publisher takes to make a decision, there is nothing to be gained from consulting your solicitor.

Reasons for Delay

So far we have been concerned largely with unreasonable delays in publishers' decision-making, but not all publishers are reprehensible in this respect. Nevertheless, there may be considerable variations in the time that an efficient publisher may take with different submissions.

Sometimes the work may be returned almost immediately upon receipt. This does not necessarily mean that your work has not been seriously considered, though it may be simply that you chose a publisher who was not interested at that juncture in the kind of book you had written. Often, however, a speedy return indicates no more than that you were lucky enough to send your book in when there was not a great pile of typescripts on the editor's desk waiting to be read, so that he was able to give you prompt attention. Now, he may not have read the book all the way through, and may in fact have read only a few sentences. Don't feel hard done by. Publishing may seem at times to be a particularly haphazard business, run largely by incompetent amateurs, but in fact the people who work in it are professionals, and that includes those who assess the typescripts which are submitted to the firm, such as your own. The easiest aspect of an editor's professionalism to learn is the ability to recognize those books which the firm will *not* want to publish. Mistakes can be made – most publishers, if pressed, will tell you of the great bestseller which they let slip through their fingers – but for the most part an editor really does know what he *isn't* looking for. And if he does stupidly turn down your masterpiece after the merest glance, and the next publisher it goes to pounces upon it with excited little cries and pays you an enormous advance for it, the first editor will shrug his shoulders and console himself with the thought that another interesting book will undoubtedly land on his desk before long.

If your book does not come back immediately, it may be that it has spent most of its time in the publisher's office working its way from the bottom of the pile to the top. It isn't always a steady progression. Sometimes a book will arrive at the publisher's office and usurp your position in the queue because it is by one of the publisher's established authors, or because an agent has sent it in suggesting that it is a potential bestseller and asking for a speedy decision. Most publishers receive a very large number of typescripts for their consideration, and delays are inevitable.

If your book does not come back from the publisher by return of post, you still may not have to wait long. It may be given a preliminary reading, perhaps by an outside reader, perhaps by a junior editor. If either of those persons feels that the book would not be of interest to his firm, then the typescript will come back to you soon thereafter. If, however, he finds it interesting, then a further reading will probably be arranged. Comparatively few books are taken by the publishers on the basis of one reading only, unless perhaps the book lands first of all on the desk of a director or a senior editor whose decision can be accepted without question. Even then, nowadays most publishers will prepare estimates in some detail before accepting a book, and this may take a considerable time, especially if the book is complicated (for instance, with diagrams to be inserted into the text, or numerous headings and subheadings and material to be set in different sizes of type, and so on).

Many books are rejected at the estimate stage. However enthusiastic the editor may have been, the publisher wants to see a profit on the book, and if the potential market for it is not large enough, then he will not be able to spread the costs of origination (that is to say, the setting of the book in print, the preparation of the jacket, and all the other costs which have to be borne before a single copy can be produced) so as to come to a retail price for the book which will not inhibit sales by being too high and which will still allow him to make his profit. A very few publishers are willing now and then to publish a book on which it is expected that they will make a loss – it might be a novel of exceptional literary merit, or perhaps poetry – but such instances are rare.

Perhaps this is an appropriate place to point out that when he commits himself to the publication of a book, the publisher is also, on average, committing himself to an expenditure in the region of £7,000, that being what it will cost him to pay the author his advance and produce an edition of a few thousand copies. The figure does not allow anything for his overheads, which will come out of the profits he makes if he sells sufficient quantities of the book to pass his break-even point. It is not surprising then that publishers check their figures with great care, and tend to take on only those books whose profitability they feel is certain.

Sometimes additional delay is caused, before a decision is made, because the hardcover publisher wishes to discover whether the book is likely to be taken for publication by a paperback publisher, bringing him a share of the advance and royalties paid. If he works in a fully integrated house, he will want to consult his colleagues on the paperback side to see the extent of their interest and support. If he is an independent, without an associated paperback company, he may submit a typescript which he is considering to one or more paperback houses to see if he has a good chance of selling the paperback rights. Some authors may query whether he is morally justified in doing so, arguing that the author has shown him the book in confidence, as it were, and that he has no right to let other parties see it unless the author has given him specific permission to do so. This procedure is, however, fairly common practice, and in many cases is an essential part of the process whereby a publisher decides whether or not to take on a particular book, since the addition of some kind of income from paperback or other subsidiary rights is often the only factor which makes it possible for the hardcover publisher to sign up a book which he does not expect to sell himself in large enough quantities to make his edition self-supporting. This, he would argue, is justification for trying to find the outside help he needs.

It is possible that the delay in reaching a decision is occasioned by the fact that the publisher has lost your typescript, an unfortunate occurrence which he is reluctant to confess. It does happen, even in the best-run offices. Most acknowledgement forms which publishers send out contain a statement to the effect that they accept no responsibility for the loss or damage of a typescript while it is in their possession, and you will not automatically get compensation for the loss, unless you have taken out your own insurance, which is a wise thing to do if you can afford it. That, however, really applies only if you have produced your typescript on a typewriter, and the only way that you can replace the lost material is by photocopying the carbon copy, assuming that it is of good enough quality, or by typing the whole thing again, which would probably take weeks. Now that word processors are so popular, the problem of a lost typescript has diminished in most cases to become a comparatively minor irritation, rather than the disaster it used to be. For the price of a few quires of paper and perhaps a new ribbon you will be able in the space of a few hours to make a new copy from your disc. And then you simply start the process of submission all over again.

The Rejected Typescript

If your book is rejected it will probably come back to you with nothing more than a formal statement that the publisher does not wish to take the book on to his list. There are a few publishers who take the trouble to explain briefly why they are turning a book down, but the majority do not, and I am not sure that you can expect it of them. It would of course be of immense value to you if the publisher told you what was wrong, but think of how many books he rejects every week – probably nine out of every ten scripts submitted to him – and then consider how much of that week he would spend, if he wrote in detail about the books he was rejecting, on books that he is not going to publish. If he does bother to write a letter explaining his decision, you may well take it as a hopeful sign – not that he is going to change his mind, but at least that he had found enough in your typescript to make him feel that it is worthwhile to take time to make the explanation. If, having received a formal rejection, you persist and write to ask why your book has been turned down, you may not even get a reply. This is not really as discourteous as it may sound. Many editors would like to correspond with the authors they reject, in an effort to help them, but they simply do not have the time. Looking after the books and their authors that they are going to publish leaves very few spare moments. Besides, they are paid to concern themselves with the interests of their employers, which do not include correspondence with rejected authors. Don't write even if you get a helpful rejection letter, apart perhaps from saying "thank you", unless the editor has plainly invited you to do so. Don't waste time on what will be a fruitless exercise. Simply send your book off to another publisher.

How often should you submit a book before giving up? The answer depends on your patience and how much you are prepared to spend on postage, and possibly on retyping the book, which is bound to get slightly tatty after several readings and which may require updating (though of course, if you use a word processor this will not prove a major difficulty). If you receive any kind of encouragement, despite the rejections, then it is certainly worth continuing to try. Publishers rarely hand out encouragement unless they really mean it, so you can take any such comments at face value. On the other hand, if you have received nothing but formal rejections, you should perhaps ask yourself, after the typescript has come back, say, six times, whether there is indeed something wrong with it. Of course you may find it quite impossible to see its failings, and friends are usually not much use in this respect, since they will rarely tell you the truth about the book if they don't think it's very good, for fear of hurting your feelings. If you put it away for a good long period – three months or more – you may find at the end of that time that you can judge it with better impartiality. On the other hand, you can just go on sending it out, hoping that one day it will find a home, and taking heart from the many stories of very successful authors who collected large numbers of rejection slips for their first book before finally placing it happily.

Your problem is to find someone in a publishing house somewhere who loves the book. Liking is not enough. You need an editor who is really enthusiastic, and who will if necessary fight his company to persuade them to take the book on. In some publishing houses this attitude is recognized to the extent of being known as "the love factor" and a book will not be taken on if it is missing.

Many would-be authors believe that you've got to "know someone" to stand any chance of acceptance. It isn't true. Of course there is no denying that it helps, but – cross my heart! – only to a very, very minor extent. Knowing someone in publishing will probably guarantee that your book will be read by someone fairly senior in the firm in question. But it will be a professional reading, and it will still be perfunctory if your book has no merit or is unsuitable for the list of that firm, despite the fact that you "know someone". What if the book is a bit better than that? Well, it will get a more careful reading – perhaps a number of readings – just as any other book of some merit would. But that doesn't mean that it's going to get published. Do you really suppose that publishers choose which books to publish on the basis of whether or not they know the author? No, my friend, I'm afraid that publishing is too tough a business to work on that sort of approach. The thing that gets you a contract is not who you know, but the quality of your work and its ability to bring out the love factor in an editor.

There is of course one sense in which "knowing someone" does work to an author's advantage. I know the publisher of this book, and he knows me, and he takes very seriously any suggestion that I make to him of a book that I could write for him (though he doesn't always agree to commission it), and he also sometimes suggests ideas for books to me (a development which, naturally, I welcome). But it's not really the fact that we know each other, or indeed that we can call ourselves friends, which makes this happen – it's because he knows *my work* (and, I hope, loves it).

If you don't succeed at first in finding an editor who loves your book, keep on trying. You can even try the same publisher more than once, after a decent interval, because publishing personnel change, and your book may land on the desk of a different editor from the one who saw it last time, and he may be the lover you're looking for. However, if you are going to send it to a publisher who has already rejected it once, you should not do so unless there was some kind of encouragement from him in the first rejection, and certainly not without indicating that it is a second submission.

4
What Are Publishers Looking For?

Primarily, these days, publishers are looking for books that will make money. In the good old days, when publishing was an occupation for gentlemen (nowadays, even if you feel that it is an occupation for incompetents, it is more accurately described as an occupation for business men), publishers were able to take an overall view, and if they had a bestseller on their list would be able to use some of the money that it made for them in publishing other books which were worthy but which would almost certainly make a loss. Provided that the year's results ended up in the black, it did not matter too much if you published, for instance, small volumes of poetry which might have been printed in red ink for all the contribution to the firm's profit that they would make. Admittedly, it was easier in those days; book prices were high in relation to the cost of production, overheads were low and so were taxes, and even a 25 per cent royalty, which was frequently paid on the higher sales of a bestseller, was not crippling to the publisher as it would be today. There were several other factors too which helped the pre-war publisher, such as his ability to bind only those copies of a book needed for fairly immediate sale, and the fact that he could dispose of his overstocks by reducing the retail price and still make a profit.

In recent years, accountants have increasingly dominated publishing. A few of them do understand what publishing is all about, including such concepts as undertaking the publication of unprofitable first novels in the belief that the author will ultimately become successful, but in many firms there is now an insistence that every single book must reach a fairly high level of profitability, and the editor's role has become subjugated to that of the money-man. It is a very unfortunate development – except, of course, if you think of Stanley Unwin's dictum, "The publisher's first duty to his authors is to remain solvent." The accountants would argue that without their control many publishing firms would simply go out of business.

Robin Denniston, formerly Academic Publisher of the Oxford University Press, in a paper given to a meeting of the University, College and Research Section of the Library Association, said,

> There are, it is true, areas of publishing (from which I exclude trade and consumer magazines) where market considerations are almost totally dominant – pre-eminently in mass-market paperbacks. Even there, however, I say "almost", because I have noticed throughout a longish association with such firms that the person who *makes the difference* in any list, however trashy it might appear, is the editor, whose own interests, subliminal drives, ambitions and egos (often huge) dictate ultimately what is acquired, for how much, and consequently the degree of emphasis placed on each new book. The shape and above all the flavour of the list is determined, here as elsewhere, by the editorial publisher.
>
> This may sound revisionist, but I believe it is such an important concept in the working life of a publisher that it cannot be repeated often enough – and the day when, in any firm, the accountant or even the marketing department finally takes over as publisher is a bad day in the life of that firm – bad not immediately and not purely in the quality of the list – bad, ultimately, for the profitability and well-being of that firm.

Although these comments were made several years ago, they are still applicable to today's publishing scene. It might be said that Mr Denniston was generalizing a little too freely – I am sure he would agree, as I have already said, that there are some accountants in the publishing trade whose attitude is liberal and enlightened – but his point is nevertheless valid. It is certainly largely because of the accountants' domination that it appears to be far more difficult nowadays for new novelists to find a publisher unless their books are immediately and obviously commercial. As I have already said in a previous chapter, since fiction sales are so often poor, publishers are very reluctant to take on new authors unless they can find a paperback publisher for the books in question (which will bring them a share of paperback royalties and so subsidize their own edition), and since there are comparatively few paperback houses and their lists are already at least half filled with bestselling authors, the outlook is not particularly rosy. This applies even to the fully integrated houses, the hardcover editor of which may not be able to persuade his paperback colleague that this or that book is saleable for them both.

For the book which deserves to be published but does not necessarily command a large enough mass-market appeal and for the author who needs time and encouragement while he is trying to perfect his craft and before his talent comes to full flower, some kind of sponsorship might seem to be the solution, whether it comes from the Arts Council or similar government-funded bodies or from commercial concerns in the public sector. However, there is a major problem – that there simply isn't enough money to go round. And how would it be possible to decide whether this author, rather than that one, had the appropriate degree of literary ability to justify a subsidy for his book? Of course, the Arts Council and the Regional Arts Associations do award bursaries to assist writers, and there are various other bodies which have funds available (see p.218), but in almost all cases such moneys are used to subsidize writers while they are working on their books, or because they have fallen on hard times, rather than to persuade a publisher to take on a book which seems to him worthy but likely to be unprofitable.

However, all is not woe. In some of the conglomerates and in some of the fully integrated houses a compromise has been reached which, while the accountants exercise enough control to fulfil the publisher's duty of remaining solvent, gives the editors sufficient freedom to encourage and nurture new talent. There are also new and comparatively small publishing houses which are successfully pursuing an enlightened policy, and there are a few survivors from an earlier era who have never allowed the powers of the editorial and accounts departments to get out of balance.

It is not just books which will make money that publishers want, but authors who will do so. Every publisher who takes an author on to his list hopes that he will produce more than one book, and indeed some titles are rejected on the grounds that the publishers believe that the author is a one-book writer. *The Egg and I*, a humorous book by Betty MacDonald, was a perfect example. Despite having had a considerable success in the States, it was rejected by many publishers at least partially on those grounds, and was finally taken on by the late Peter Guttmann of Hammond, Hammond (a publishing company which is, alas, no longer active), who himself doubted whether Betty Macdonald would write another book. In fact she wrote several more, and very successful they were, which was a bonus for Hammond, Hammond.

It is easy enough to say that publishers want books and authors which will make money for them – not necessarily a great deal of money, but sufficient to make a contribution towards overheads and a small profit in addition – and that the more commercial your book the easier it will be to find a publisher for it, but such comments, apart from stating the obvious, are not particularly helpful to the aspiring author.

Specific advice on what publishers want is hard to give, and few of them could tell you themselves. As Jill Black, a Director of The Bodley Head said, "The truth is that we don't know what we're looking for; but when we see it, it shines from the page." Nevertheless, there are some general points to be made.

In my days as an editor, I used to look for four A's:

A for Authorship
By this I did not mean just accurate spelling and punctuation, though, as I have said elsewhere, I believe that authors who do not take trouble over this side of writing are doing themselves a disservice. I was looking for a use of words which indicated mastery over them, and that included not only using them correctly, but also a sense of style, so that sentences were well phrased and the author knew when to begin new paragraphs and chapters, and had given his book a feeling of shape and construction. I was looking for an ability to communicate ideas with clarity, and an understanding of the effect the words chosen would have on the reader, getting to the point, avoiding waffle. And I was looking for the book to have something to say, by which I do not necessarily mean that it had to have some significant message, but that the author had an objective in writing his book, that he had indeed something to tell the reader,

whether it was how to decorate the bathroom or what James I was really like, or whether it was simply a good story.

A for Authenticity

I looked for credibility of characters and plot in a novel, for a true sense of period and place, and if a problem were presented, for a genuine solution to it rather than any *deus ex machina* contrivance. If I were asked to suspend disbelief, I was willing to do so just as long as the author remained faithful to the conventions he had originally established. I did not want anything to take me out of the story by forcing me to say, "I don't believe that". "A for Authenticity" belongs chiefly to fiction of all kinds, where realism or at least mock-realism is currently the fashion (and for the benefit of those long enough in the tooth and with sufficiently extensive memories, let me say that I believe this fashion was started in Britain by a serial about working policemen called *Z-Cars*, which was the first semi-documentary fiction that we saw on our television screens). It is not only this kind of realism that is required, but also a sense that the backgrounds and any research material have been adequately prepared – that the author knows what he is talking about. Although it is particularly a requirement for fiction, nevertheless, to some extent the same criterion can be applied to almost all books. You might sum it up by calling it "a sense of truth".

A for Action

In the detective novels which were popular between the two World Wars, it quite often happened that the first half dozen chapters were taken up with descriptions of the country house and the guests who were staying there, and it was only in Chapter Seven that a body appeared in the locked library. That approach is not much in favour nowadays, and readers want a body on page one, or very soon after, and the action must from that moment on be continuous and reasonably fast-paced. This criterion sounds again as though it applied only to fiction, and the special field of mysteries at that, but that is far from the case. I looked, whatever kind of book I was dealing with – the book on decorating the bathroom or the biography of James I are adequate examples – for my interest to be seized from the very beginning, and for the author never to relax the grip he had on me, a grip which is

achieved largely by a sense of immediacy. This is one reason
why first paragraphs are so important. So too is reader
identification, a term which is usually applied to fiction, but
which is relevant to any kind of book you can think of – the
reader has to feel involved and interested and, though he
may not recognize this consciously, that the book is written
for him.

A for Authority
This really applies only to non-fiction, and refers not only to
the fact that the author must have a full command of his
subject, so that he can write with authority about it, but also
that he should have acceptable qualifications for writing the
book. I have already, in the last chapter, touched on the
problem of the unknown, non-historian writer who produces
a new biography of Mary, Queen of Scots – unless he has
exceptional talents he will find it very difficult to force his
way into a sphere dominated by biographers who are either
accredited historians or well-known authors, and who
frequently can claim to be in both those categories. It applies
just as much to a book on gardening, or economics, or the
theatre, or whatever the subject may be. Of course, it is not
only a question of qualifications, but that the author's
authority also depends on his name being known at least to
some degree by those people who are likely to want to read
the book, a factor which makes it much easier to sell.

One other quality which publishers look for, needless to
say (or is it?) is originality, though it is true that there are
some houses which prefer to tread well-worn paths and
publish books almost indistinguishable from those that they
have brought out successfully in the past and which they
know exactly how to sell effectively. Even these conventional publishers, though looking for a book which is written
to a proven popular formula, will be drawn to the typescript
which is original in some aspect – the style, perhaps, or the
humour and wit, or the twist in the plot which gives a new
angle on a familiar theme. It is always difficult for authors to
be original without venturing into the experimental (which is
rarely likely to command a large enough market to interest
the average general publisher), but if you can bring a touch
of individuality to your book, it will stand a better chance of
success.

A highly controversial book is almost always of interest,

but not if it steps beyond the bounds of the publisher's taste, or if it is likely to run foul of the law (this kind of book is often libellous), or if it is too topical and its subject is likely to have faded from the news by the time the book could be published. Authors of controversial books do need too some authority, as defined above.

Naturally, there are exceptions to all these rules and guidelines – publishing is so individual and bizarre and multifaceted that every statement one makes about it needs qualification – and books which do not meet any of the requirements listed above, or which do so only partially, are frequently and often successfully published. It can be very confusing for authors, especially when they compare their own rejected work with books which have been published, perhaps by the very firm which rejected theirs, and decide, with as much dispassion as they can contrive, that the published books are inferior to their own work.

The first thing to remember is that you cannot compare like with unlike. If you are what is known as a serious novelist and you look at the romantic novels that are published and think how feeble and contrived and despicable they are in comparison with your own work, or if you are an academic who can see no justification for the success of certain pseudo-scientific books based on imagination rather than solid evidence, do remember that these books are not written for you, that they have their own market, their own techniques, and that the people who write them are mostly extremely capable craftsmen who know exactly what they are doing and do it with considerable flair.

"All right," you may say, "I will compare my work only with those who write in the same vein as I do. How is it that X and Y, who don't write as well as I do and whose subjects are more limited in interest than mine, get published when I can't? I can only think that they are friends of the publisher."

Well, they may be, but as I have said earlier in this book, publishers do not allow themselves to be influenced by a personal friendship with their authors and do not accept sub-standard books for such reasons. Even if they did, they would not continue to publish their friends' books unless the sales figures justified them in doing so. The reason why books which you consider to be of inferior quality are published may be simply a matter of taste – the publisher may disagree with your assessment of X and Y's work in comparison with your own, and has published them because in his opinion their books are better than yours. Books are accepted for publication not by some impartial and infinitely wise committee of assessors, but by individuals with their own likes and dislikes. Or it could be that X and Y are on that publisher's list because they submitted their books to him at a time when he was looking for just such work and theirs were the best that came along; now that he has them on the list, he has no room for your book, though he might even prefer it to one of the others. Or maybe X and Y are already established to some degree, and even though the publisher may not feel that their latest books are up to the standard he would like, he believes in them and wants to go on publishing them, hoping that their next books will be better. As I have already suggested, publishers are interested in authors rather than in books – by which I mean that they are looking for a writer who, with a number of books, will build up a reputation so that his books sell in increasing numbers as each new one comes out, or who, if his first book is an immediate success, will repeat that success with many more books.

Of course, the bigger name you are as an author, the more you have the publisher at your mercy, not only in securing better terms for yourself, but sometimes in persuading him to publish books that you have written at which he might otherwise have looked askance. If he refuses to take the book on, he knows that with your reputation you will find no difficulty in placing it with another house, which will be only too glad to publish it, however bad it may be, in order to get you on their list. I would suggest, however, that if you are just such a world-famous author and your publisher exhibits doubts about your latest offering, you should listen to him seriously before rushing into the arms of one of his competitors. Bad books can damage even the most brilliant of reputations.

The most important point to remember in what I have already said when, as a frustrated author once said to me, "you look at some of the rubbish that does get published", is that the publication of a book still depends, despite the influence of the accountants, on the personal tastes of an editor. Editors, believe it or not, are human, and the variety of their individual quirks and foibles is infinite. I could cite dozens of cases in which colleagues of mine in various editorial departments have been tremendously enthusiastic about books in which I could see no merit at all. Sometimes they proved me wrong, sometimes my doubts were justified. All editors make mistakes, all editors have successes which astonish their colleagues; all editors turn down books which subsequently become bestsellers, all editors champion books which do well against all the odds. *Jonathan Livingstone Seagull* is a fine case in point; the book landed on the desk of an editor called Eleanor Friede, who was enthusiastic about it and more or less forced through its publication; for some years the book seemed to justify the reservations of the Jeremiahs and was counted as a failure, but it then suddenly became a "cult" book and a world bestseller.

Some authors feel very aggrieved that certain books, often with little to distinguish them from the herd, and in some cases even of below average quality, get "hyped" into bestsellerdom. How does it happen? It usually begins with the enthusiasm of an agent, who begins to talk the book up and persuades a publisher to believe that the book is a potential bestseller, worth a lot of money. One such sale usually allows the bandwaggon to roll, and the book sells for extravagant sums all over the world. There is often an element of the Emperor's New Clothes about it. It certainly isn't fair, when much better books earn their authors little or no money, but then life isn't fair, and success in any field nearly always depends on a certain amount of luck as well as ability. You have to be in the right place at the right time; you, or your agent, must recognize that right time and right place and seize the opportunity when it comes – and there is a great element of luck in that too.

Do hyped books work? Well, sometimes, but often they fall flat. When they do succeed it is usually because the book which is chosen for such an exercise has the quality of being in tune with the reading public's mood. Of course, although publishers are generally agreed that advertising, other than to the trade, does not sell books, the hyped book is often very widely advertised, and that happens because, if the publisher is going to print, and presumably sell, a very large quantity of the book, he can afford to spend a large enough sum of money on advertising for it to have some effect on his sales.

(Incidentally, the advertising budget for a book really

does have to be pretty enormous to have any noticeable effect on sales. As well as large advertisements, often inserted several times, in newspapers and magazines throughout the country, the publisher will have to produce point-of-sale material such as posters, showcards, "dump bins" – special cardboard display stands – etc. Other options may include advertisements on buses, hoardings, in the London Underground. There will also probably be all the expenses of launch parties and a tour for the author. And then there is television, which is probably the most effective advertising medium available – provided that you produce a professional advertisement and screen it often enough for it to have an impact. In total, we are talking of many tens of thousands of pounds. And even then it may not work.)

Why, given two books of similar merits and accord with public taste, does one attract the hype approach while the other is neglected? Because of the irrationality of the human element, and because of the way the wheel of fortune turned. The hyped book just happened to appeal to a small handful of people who believed that it could be promoted into bestsellerdom and were prepared to spend money to push it in that direction; and it had the right kind of luck.

Since it is so difficult to be specific about what publishers want, it may be helpful to take the easier course of saying what they don't want.

Topical books
The normal publishing process takes about nine months from the acceptance of a finished typescript to publication – longer if the book is complicated in some way (e.g. any illustrated book with a complex layout). Books can be produced in a much shorter time, and sometimes are – almost instant publication has taken place in the past for such events as Winston Churchill's death, the raid on Entebbe (now virtually forgotten), and at least a couple of royal weddings, and no doubt instant books will appear in the future for equally newsworthy happenings. But these are exceptions, mostly appearing as paperbacks, and the event is of such wide interest that a really massive sale can be envisaged; thus justifying the enormous extra effort and expense that are necessary to whittle the normal nine months down to a few days. But a topical book without a

huge market will have little appeal to any publisher, especially as so often its topicality, which will have disappeared by the time the book comes out, is its only merit.

Categories of books not normally on his list
Publishers sell to booksellers, and booksellers tend to think of publishers as specialist in certain areas. Some houses, for instance, are known as publishers of art books. Now, if Rows & Crowne, a publisher who has not previously entered that field, brings out an art book, the bookseller's first reaction may often be, "If it were any good, one of the regular art book publishers would be bringing it out. Since Rows & Crowne are publishing it, it's probable that the specialist houses have turned it down. Therefore it can't be much good. QED. No, I won't order any copies, thank you." That is of course an over-simplification, and booksellers will deny that they can be so conservative and shortsighted as to turn down a saleable book simply because it bears an unexpected imprint, but it is certainly true that publishers often find it quite difficult to broaden the scope of their lists because of trade resistance. The moral from the author's point of view is that he must do his market research thoroughly, and if his book is a specialist one, not send it to a publisher who is unlikely to want to experiment with it in a field which is unfamiliar to him.

There is an additional reason for choosing a publisher who has some reputation for bringing out books in a particular category, and this is that some books of that kind have a market outside the normal bookshop – a book on gardening, for instance, may be on sale in gardening centres. The publisher who regularly brings out specialist books will know how to reach the specialist markets, and may also have a mailing list which will bring the books in question to the attention of those people who are most likely to buy it.

The jack of all trades
Publishers, booksellers and the public like to know where they are with an author. They like him to write the same sort of book each time, and it is certainly much easier to build a reputation as an author if you stick to one field, however loosely. But there is another reason why publishers tend to look a little doubtfully at an author who offers them a series

of widely differing books, and that is that the jack of all trades is so frequently master of none. If you can write a book on any subject under the sun, you may be quite brilliant, and therefore an exception – or possibly you deserve the rather uncomplimentary description of "a hack writer", with its implication that your work is of a low standard. The one thing that shrinking markets have done for books is to improve their overall quality. There is far less room for the hack than there used to be.

Autobiographies

Everyone, they say, has a book in him. True, but in most cases it should stay there, principally because so few people have the ability to get it out of themselves in a form that anyone else will want to read. But one of the other problems is that the book which most people have in them and want to write is their own life story. "I have had such an interesting life. I'm sure I could write a book about it," or, "After all your experiences, you should write a book – you really should." Unfortunately, thousands upon thousands of men and women lead lives which they and their friends find of riveting interest, but unless they are famous, or infamous, or can write superbly and perhaps evocatively of a bygone age, few readers outside their immediate circle will find it equally absorbing. And if you cannot claim fame or the pen of a Laurie Lee, who is going to buy the book? Your friends and relations will expect to be given copies, or will get the book out of the library; no one else will bother. Write the book, by all means, for your children and grandchildren to read, but don't expect to get it published commercially. This advice also applies to humorous accounts of your experiences – especially about moving house, a favourite subject for amateur authors. Almost everyone's experience of moving house is traumatic and, if you have that sort of sense of humour, funny, which means that in order to write about it successfully, your experiences or your humour (and preferably both) should be exceptional, so that the book is lifted beyond the commonplace.

Biographies of obscure historical personages

You may have discovered the truth about Sir Humphrey Drivell, the dull, stay-at-home eighteenth-century squire of the village of Upton Downbottom, but unless your account of his life, like *The History of Myddle*, for instance, also gives an unusual and detailed account of an eighteenth-century village community, few people are going to want to buy or borrow the book. No one has ever heard of Sir Humphrey Drivell, and that means that very few people will want to read about him. The same applies to a history of St Ethelwulf's Church, Upton Downbottom; you may be able to find a local printer who will produce a few copies for the benefit of the Upton Downbottom villagers and you and your relatives and friends, but the market for the book will be so small that no commercial publisher is likely to be interested. Again, I would not wish to discourage anyone from writing such a book, which might be fascinating and of immense value to its very limited audience. Just don't expect to get it published.

Short stories
I have never understood, nor, I think, have most publishers, why short stories are generally so unsuccessful. Everyone you talk to swears that he adores them, yet unless you are a very well-established writer, you are most unlikely to get a volume of short stories published, and even if you are at the top of the bestselling tree, your short stories will be given a much smaller print quantity than your new novel. Short stories do still get published occasionally in anthologies, and there is a limited market for them in collections of science fiction and horror.

Poetry
Despite the fact that public interest in poetry has grown very considerably in recent years, it is comparatively rare for a poet's work to be sold in quantities which make publication a profitable business, and such exceptions are almost always the result of the author having established his name as a poet over a long period of years, or perhaps being well-known in some other field. Therefore, and because the accountants nowadays wield such influence over the choice of books which a publisher brings out, unless you have an existing reputation, your poetry is likely to be turned down very quickly. Nevertheless, there are still a few houses with general lists who are prepared to publish volumes of poetry even though it may lose them money to do so, and if your work is of real merit, you will probably find recognition from one of these firms.

There is, however, some hope, even if you are not in the genius category, because there are hundreds of small concerns specializing in the publication of poetry in booklet form and in the so-called "little magazines" – sometimes in duplicated form. The financial rewards, if they materialize at all, are likely to be minuscule – in some instances you will get no payment other than a few free copies of the publication – but the appearance of your work in print may establish your reputation and lead you eventually to a slightly more lucrative offer from a regular publisher.

"Bandwaggon books"
As soon as a certain style of book becomes a bestseller – usually something which is sufficiently different from the normal range of publications to become almost a new genre – half the authors in the world seem ready to leap on to the bandwaggon, rushing to their word processors to produce imitations. Years after the James Bond books first appeared, would-be Ian Flemings are still slaving away at their pseudo 007s, and heaven knows how many world statesmen have come near to fictional assassination since *The Day of the Jackal* first appeared, while I have no doubt that there are many Hitch-hiker clones roaming around the galaxy, guidebook in hand. There are two reasons why they are not often successful: the first is that few of these imitators are talented enough to write books which are anywhere near as good as the originals; the second is that such fashions in writing can often change remarkably rapidly, and by the time you have written your imitation, and allowing for the normal delay in getting a publisher to accept it and then publish it, the fashion may have disappeared.

Obscene, scurrilous or politically extreme books
This is a question of doing your market research thoroughly. There are markets for books of this kind, but don't expect a publisher whose list is middle-of-the-road to take on an outrageously sexy book, or send your far-right orientated book to a left-wing publisher. As for the scurrilous books, beware of the laws of libel (see pp.207–10).

Children's books
The editors of children's books are usually people of enormous patience. Scores of mothers and grandmothers

make up stories for their little ones, decide when they are well received by their young audience that they could be published, and send them to a publisher, often accompanied by illustrations done by a friend whose lack of talent is equalled only by that of the story-teller. Writing for children is extremely difficult, and has not been made easier by the fact that nowadays it is essential to be non-sexist, non-racist, non-classist, and the length, complexity and especially the vocabulary of the story must be acceptable for the age range for which the book is intended. It is really a most difficult market to break into, and it becomes very little easier as you move up the age scale, coming eventually to teen-age novels. All writing for young people is difficult. If you can get it right, you will be welcomed, but be prepared for disappointment. And if you send in illustrations, do make sure that they are of professional standard.

Novels about failures
The plain fact is that failures are usually rather boring, simply because they are failures. You need exceptional skills to make them interesting.

Novels which have contrived plots
Do try to avoid stories which are based on, for instance, identical twins, or amnesia, or in which all the problems are solved through the generosity of a previously-unheard-of wealthy relative who arrives from Australia in the last chapter.

Expensive books
In general, publishers don't want books that are very expensive to produce because they are intended to be in odd shapes and sizes or because they involve the pasting in of pull-outs and pop-ups and other gimmicks, or which demand to be printed in seven colours throughout. Such books are published, of course – indeed, pop-ups have become very popular – but you probably stand a better chance by sticking to ordinary, common-or-garden books which can be produced in one of the standard formats such as Metric Demy 8vo, Metric Crown 4to or Metric Large Crown 8vo.

Libellous books
The threat of a libel action is enough to make the strongest

publisher go deathly pale. Quite apart from the fact that he may be involved in an extremely expensive court case and may have to pay very heavy damages, he will perhaps also have to withdraw and destroy all copies of the book that have been printed. And although in theory he can reclaim all his losses from the author (almost all publishing contracts carry a clause under which the author agrees to indemnify the publisher if his book contains defamatory material), in practice the author rarely has the resources with which to reimburse the publisher. See pp.207–10.

Let me repeat once more that there are always exceptions to prove the rule that publishers don't want the kinds of books listed above. Perhaps the chances for them are less, but you can never be quite certain because there are still a great many publishers about who are eccentric, unpredictable, erratic in their tastes as well as in the way they conduct their business. It is, after all, a fairly crazy business, in which every product is different, and each of them is, to a greater or lesser degree, a gamble. It is also a fascinating way of life (and "way of life" is the right phrase, for few people in publishing are involved in their work only during office hours), with constantly changing interest and problems, and those who work in the industry – even the maligned accountants – do so on the whole not just because of the financial rewards – there are comparatively few really rich publishers about, precisely because it is a gambling business and it is only too easy to lose on one book all the money you have made on another – but because they like books and, surprisingly, enough, authors.

It was Sir Frederick Macmillan, I believe, who first said, "Publishing would be fun if it weren't for authors." Undoubtedly he had his tongue in his cheek. Authors can be infuriating, childish, disloyal, temperamental, greedy, vain and any other pejorative adjectives that you can think of – just like other human beings. Publishers can be all those things too – just like other human beings. On the whole, publishers are eager to love and cherish their authors. They begin by loving a book, and with any luck, they will then transfer that love to its author.

That then is the message: publishers are not ogres, implacably hostile to all writers; on the contrary, they are always eager to find new books and authors on which they can lavish their affection. You don't believe it? Then send your work out and see what happens. But before you do, please remember that although the annual total of new books produced in Britain is still frighteningly high, and the figure rises every year, standards are rising too. Be as certain as you can that your book is equipped to fight its way into a crowded market. You need to be professional, just as you would if you were entering any other field, and that includes being sure that what you write will appeal to a wide enough public.

Despite all the difficulties, I have never believed and still do not believe that there are any mute, inglorious Miltons around, unless they wish to remain mute and inglorious. Talent, like murder, will out; it may be more difficult for it to out, but if you really have it, you will get published. Just keep on trying.

5

The Publishing Process

What happens between the time that you submit a book to a publisher and its publication? Why does it take so long? Processes vary from publisher to publisher, but in general it will go something like this:

Editorial

Your typescript will arrive on the desk of an editor, or possibly on that of a secretary whose job it is to log all incoming submissions in a ledger in which what happens to the material will also be recorded. When it reaches an editor, he will probably glance briefly at it. In some cases, he will make an immediate decision as to whether he should read it himself, or pass it to an outside reader, or give it to another editor in the house who specializes in that kind of book, or reject it immediately. However, in some publishing houses, such decisions will be taken at a weekly editorial meeting.

If the book is non-fiction, and especially if its subject is specific rather than general, it will almost certainly be sent to an outside reader who is an expert in that field, and very often to more than one such authority. Apart from these specialists, many publishers also employ general outside readers, and in some firms almost all books,including fiction, are given an outside reading, either before or after the book has been considered within the house. Who are these general readers, and what are their qualifications? They are often ex-publishers, sometimes themselves authors, sometimes merely friends or acquaintances of the publisher; they are expected to know something about the market for general books, and to be able to distinguish between good and bad writing; but their main qualification is quite simply that their tastes are known to the publisher, which allows him to evaluate their comments. In any case, their function is not entirely that of giving a verdict on the books they read; they also usually provide a detailed summary of the book's contents.

If you feel anxiety that your typescript may be delivered up to the mercies of a comparatively unqualified person, then be assured that most publishers use their general outside readers primarily as "weeders" or to confirm a judgement already made in the publisher's office. If the outside reader recommends rejection, he is usually right, provided that he is reasonably experienced (and if the publisher has any doubts of his expertise, then the book will almost certainly receive another reading before the final decision is made). Moreover, the report that he has written, and especially that part of it in which he gives his reasons for advising rejection, will be studied by a senior member of the editorial department, and if those reasons seem at all inadequate, again another reading will be called for. On the other hand, if the reader recommends publication, then the book will undoubtedly be read by other people too, to confirm that his enthusiasm is justified, before there is any question of acceptance. While the editor's decision may be final, therefore, that of the outside reader very rarely is, and few books, other than those by established writers will be accepted on the basis of one reading only.

As I mentioned earlier, some publishers use authors on their list to read books on similar subjects. If this happens to you, you can expect to be paid for the reading and report – not a great deal, of course, but a few pounds at least. If your publisher does not pay you, then you are being exploited, and you may well consider him something of a rogue.

Although the reports on a book may be generally favourable, the editor may not yet be ready to move to the next stage, the preparation of an estimate. The readers may indicate that the book is potentially publishable, but that additional work on it is needed before it can be accepted, and in this case, the editor will perhaps invite the author to come to his offices to discuss the matter with him. Some authors approach such meetings in an aggressively defensive mood, unwilling to concede that their work is less than perfect as it stands; it is their right to do so, but it is also the publisher's right in such circumstances to decline to go ahead. More sensible authors will listen to what is said, and accept the criticisms or at least discuss the proposed alterations in a reasonable way. Good editors can contribute materially to the improvement of a book, and indeed that is their object, or should be. Bad editors sometimes want to change the whole approach of a book, and in such cases the author is fully entitled to resist, though he must be prepared to accept the fact that such resistance may result in the publisher deciding not to publish the book.

Authors whose books are rejected speedily often believe that the books have not been read at all, and some even resort to various devices to prove this (such as putting one of the pages upside down, or carefully inserting a hair between two pages of the typescript). Apart from the fact that the publisher may spot these traps and leave them unaltered, just to annoy the author, you might as well face the fact that publishers do not read every word of every typescript submitted to them. Some are rejected at a glance because they deal with subjects that the publisher does not include on his list, or perhaps because they are not of book length (authors often submit short stories to book publishers in the apparent belief that they also publish magazines, while others seem to think that ten thousand words or less will make a full-length book), but most get more attention than that.

A few pages will be read – sufficient for the editor, who usually has a considerable amount of experience and who knows what kind of books he is looking for, to decide perhaps that the book is of no interest to his firm. Or perhaps he will read more, and get some way into the book before deciding that it is too dull, or too unauthoritative, or too controversial, or simply too badly written for him to bother with. Even if he is interested, he may skip a great deal, or use a technique which I call "skim-reading", whereby one turns the pages very rapidly, letting the eye travel swiftly over the page to get a general idea of the book without reading much of it word for word; it sounds a very cavalier way to treat a submission, but editors do become expert at coping with the vast numbers of typescripts that flow into their offices day by day, and rarely fail to recognize a book which needs more serious consideration. In many houses, even these rapid rejections will be discussed at an editorial meeting, and a book may get another reading from a different editor as a result.

Publishers do make mistakes and reject books which they should have taken, but you can be assured that any typescript with a certain amount of quality and which will fit the publisher's list will be considered carefully. It is for this reason that I dislike the term "slushpile", (used to describe all the unsolicited typescripts sent to publishers direct from the general public) because it suggests that publishers consider such material inevitably to be rubbish. As I have already said, earlier in this book, this is just not true. The majority of the books in the pile may indeed be worthless slush, but, apart from those few publishers who will consider only the books sent to them by agents, editors will always pay careful attention to *all* the books that come into their offices. There may be a nugget of gold there, and the publisher simply cannot afford to miss something worthwhile if he can possibly help it. Although he is in a buyer's market, the number of outstanding books that come his way is very limited, and he has no wish to let one get away. Adequate, publishable books are in better supply, but their numbers are vastly exceeded by the books which are of no interest to him, primarily because they are too badly written or do not fit his list.

Estimating

Assuming that the editorial reports are favourable and that any rewriting required is satisfactorily carried out, the book will probably be discussed again at an editorial meeting, and the go-ahead given for the preparation of an estimate. This involves consultation by the editor with the production department in order to assess the cost of manufacture, and with the sales department to gain their support for the project and to fix a tentative first print quantity and estimate of sales, so that the potential income can be calculated. Often the subsidiary rights department will also be consulted and asked to predict what subsidiary rights income may come in, and indeed in some cases the book will be shown to, for instance, paperback houses, in the hope of obtaining a firm offer for the paperback rights, the publisher's share of which will help to subsidize his hardcover edition. In the case of the fully integrated publisher, when a book is being considered for publication by the same organization in both hardcover and paperback, there may be a single estimate covering both editions.

Sometimes the estimate prepared will be unsatisfactory in that it does not show an adequate profit margin. In that case, the editor, or someone in one of the other departments, may suggest altering the specifications in some way – perhaps a smaller type face could be used, thus reducing the extent (i.e. the page length) of the book; perhaps a reduction in the number of illustrations could be considered; perhaps a cheaper printer could be used; perhaps the sales department could be persuaded to increase the print quantity or the retail price of the book, or both. Sometimes many estimates have to be prepared before the formula is right. When the estimate has been prepared it is then necessary in many firms to get approval from a number of department heads before the editor can finally write to the author to tell him that the firm wishes to publish his book. Often, after preparing several estimates, no satisfactory figures can be reached, and the editor then has reluctantly to reject the book.

The processes described are obviously time-consuming, which explains at least in part why authors so often have to wait so many weeks for a decision. During the waiting period it is often true that no news is good news, but equally a long delay, while it probably means that serious consideration is being given to the book, is no guarantee of ultimate acceptance.

Contract

If all has gone well, the publisher makes the author an offer to publish his book, usually specifying the advance that he is willing to pay and the basic royalties, but rarely going into other details, which await the preparation of a contract.

This will probably entail further discussions within the publishing house, so that whoever prepares the contract will get all the details right (though if the book is agented, the agent usually draws up the agreement on his own standard form). Authors should read each contract that they are sent with care. It is not a good idea, when you get your new contract from Messrs Rows & Crowne, to think that since you have already signed a number of agreements with them for previous books you can sign this one without reading it. They may have changed their basic contract form, or there may be a number of differences in the filling in of the blank spaces. If there is anything in the contract that you wish to query or change, write to the publisher about it – do not simply make alterations on the contract and return it to him, but settle any disputed points first. The Society of Authors and the Writers' Guild both offer their members detailed advice on contracts, so it will be worth your while to join, if you are not already a member. See also Chapter 6 for comments on what you should look for in an agreement.

Some publishers send the author two copies of the contract – one for him to sign and return and the other, already signed by the publisher, for him to keep. If there are any changes, mark them and initial them on both copies. Other publishers send one copy of the contract only, giving the author his counterpart only after he has signed and returned the first copy. In such cases it may be a sensible precaution to take a photostat of the copy sent to you to sign before you return it; otherwise you may not be absolutely certain that the counterpart you eventually receive is exactly the same – not that your publisher is likely to cheat in this way, for most of them are honourable, but it is a cheap and easy way of protecting yourself against the few unscrupulous publishers that do unfortunately exist.

When you return your signed contract, it will be filed by the publisher, and probably consulted thereafter quite frequently – whenever any subsidiary rights are sold, when it is time for royalty statements to be prepared, and so on. In some firms an extract of the contract is made, with all relevant details on it, so that the whole document does not have to be consulted every time.

In most cases, an advance or part thereof, is payable on signature of the contract by both parties, and a note will be passed to the accounts department so that an appropriate cheque can be drawn.

Copy Editing

Once you have accepted the initial offer, the book may be passed to a copy editor, though nowadays, in an effort to cut costs, some publishers are dispensing with this stage, relying on the author himself to have done a large part of the copy editor's work, and leaving the rest of it to the production department and/or the designer, or even to the printer. The increasing use of word processors is hastening the disappearance of the copy editor, because typescripts produced on a word processor tend to contain fewer typing mistakes – it is so much easier to correct your errors than it is on a typewriter, especially if your word processor has a spelling-check facility, which picks up literals as well as spelling mistakes. This is a pity – copy editors can contribute very considerably to good, efficient publishing. So what exactly does a copy editor do? His responsibilities go far beyond merely correcting the author's spelling and punctuation: he often checks the author's facts, he removes (or at least queries with the author) inconsistencies, he may rewrite phrases, sentences or even large parts of the book (there are many published books which should really bear the copy editor's name on the title-page as co-author), and he marks the typescript for the printer so that the latter has clear indications of, for example, italicization, indentation of paragraphs or of certain sections of the text, etc. Some authors resent the work of the copy editor, and with cause if they are unlucky enough to find one who interferes unwarrantably with the author's style or makes other totally unnecessary changes; but a first-class copy editor, who respects the author's intentions and knows his job, can make invaluable improvements. The good copy editor will in any case always consult the author concerning the changes he proposes, and a sensible author will listen co-operatively to what he has to say. Alterations should not in any case be made without the author's approval. But see also p.173.

Production

By this time, the author will probably have been asked to supply a second copy of the typescript, if he has not already done so, and this will have been sent to the Production Department, whose designer will decide the type in which the book is to be printed, the type area on the page, the way that chapters are to begin, and other such details. If the book is extensively illustrated, the designer has a much more exacting job, since he will need to work out the size and shapes of illustrations and their position, and the exact amount of text which is to appear on each page. Given the designer's instructions, the production department will send the typescript to one or more printers in order to get firm estimates for the manufacture. The production department will also decide on the method of printing the book and the binding process which is to be used, and will in due course order, or allocate from existing stocks, a suitable quantity of paper for the agreed print quantity for the text and the jacket, and cloth (usually imitation cloth nowadays) for the binding.

When the final copy-edited typescript is ready, the production department will send it to the printer for composition, together with the illustrations. With more and more authors using word processors it will increasingly often be discs, rather than a typescript, which the publisher sends to the printer; from the discs, with the addition of certain commands, the type for the book can be set without the text having to be re-keyed. The jacket design, together with the material which is to appear on the back and the flaps, will also be sent for preparation and proofing. The brasses with which the title, the author's name and the publisher's imprint are stamped on the binding will also be ordered.

In due course, proofs of the book will arrive from the printers. Two sets are usually sent to the author – one for him to correct and return, the other for him to keep. When correcting proofs it is advisable to use the proper markings and signs, and some of the most common of these are shown in Appendix I. Corrections are extremely expensive – out of all proportion to the initial setting charge – and should therefore be kept to a minimum. Mistakes made by the printer are his responsibility and are not charged for, and should be corrected in a different colour ink from that used for any alterations the author wants to make. The latter, if they exceed a certain percentage of the total setting costs, will almost certainly be charged by the publisher to the author, so the rule must be to get your typescript as perfect as possible before it is sent to the printer, and to make only those changes which are absolutely essential at proof stage. Also be sure to note all corrections in the set of proofs you keep.

Proofs sometimes come in galley form, that is to say on long sheets of paper, and not divided up into the pages which will finally appear in the book. This method of proofing is used if large numbers of alterations are expected (and have been allowed for in the costing of the book!) or if the layout of the book is particularly complex. Sometimes proofs come on what looks like a computer print-out. More often page proofs are supplied, which look very much as the final book will appear, except that they have a paper cover and are probably not printed on the same kind of paper as will be used for the finished version.

Normally the publisher allows the author two to three weeks for the correction and return of proofs. While he is reading them, they may also be read by someone in the publishing house – usually the copy editor, but sometimes someone in the production department. When the author's corrected proofs come in, his alterations and those of the publisher's proof reader will be incorporated in the marked set which will be returned to the printer.

When all proofs have been corrected and returned to the printer, and when a final decision on the print quantity has been taken, the production department will pass the relevant order to the printers and binders for the manufacture of the book, and will monitor its progress through all stages up to delivery to the warehouse.

Jackets

The jacket design is usually fairly widely discussed within the publishing house. Many publishers employ an art director, whose sole responsibility is jackets. He will probably discuss the design for each book on the list with the editor concerned and with the sales department. If it is decided to produce a jacket which is purely typographical or is based on a photograph or perhaps an existing painting (e.g. a contemporary portrait of the subject of a biography), he may design and produce the jacket within the house. In such cases, the art director may not see a word of the book itself, and it is not necessary for him to do so. If, on the other hand, the jacket is to carry a specially commissioned illustration, he is likely to read the book so that he can brief an outside artist, who will often be given a copy of the typescript or a proof so that he too can read it. The artist will then usually submit a "rough" – a sketch of what is proposed as the final art work. This will be considered and approved or rejected by the editorial and sales departments. Increasingly the author is consulted about jackets, and many publishers welcome comments, provided that the author does not make unreasonable demands. An author's complaint about the factual accuracy of the jacket design is entirely valid, but adverse comments on the overall effect or the basic design, though he should certainly make any such criticisms and the publisher should take note of them, are less likely to be matters on which he can put his foot down. In general, publishers take a great deal of care with jackets, knowing that they are a vital sales tool, and if the sales department in particular is satisfied with the general design, the author may have to bow to their belief that it is acceptable. Not unnaturally, publishers tend to believe in their own expertise, and may well tell you bluntly that your skill is in writing the book, and theirs in knowing how best to sell it.

The jacket of the hardcover book will also usually carry the blurb. The blurb is of course the description of the book normally to be found on the front flap of the jacket and very often on the first page of the book too. Your publisher may ask you to supply a blurb for your book, though he will usually discard your effort or rewrite it substantially, because most authors do not excel at describing their own books succinctly and appealingly, and however big their egos often shrink from using the adulatory adjectives beloved of professional blurb-writers. The back flap of the jacket may carry a continuation of the blurb or sometimes a brief biography and photograph of the author, while the back of the jacket, unless the illustration goes all the way round, will probably be used as an advertisement space for other books on the publisher's list – perhaps for books by the same author – or, if the book is reprinted, for favourable quotes about it from the reviews. The use that is made of the space available and the actual working of the material will probably be discussed and decided upon jointly by the editorial, publicity and sales departments. Again, it has become usual for the author to be consulted on the blurb and other material which appears on the jacket, but even the best publishing agreements, while giving the author the right of consultation, make it clear that the final decision on such matters rests with the publisher.

Subsidiary Rights

The work of the subsidiary rights department often begins at an early stage. Extra copies of the typescript may be made, but in other cases proofs will be supplied, so that the book can be submitted to paperback publishers, bookclubs, magazines and newspapers, and to foreign publishers. Some of these submissions may be delayed until finished copies of the book are available, but it is usually important to sell subsidiary rights, whenever possible, in advance of publication, especially where bookclubs are concerned, since the quantity taken by the bookclub may affect the publisher's print order.

The efforts of the subsidiary rights department are ongoing. Sometimes simultaneous submissions will be made (to all the leading paperback publishers, for example), but often it is a matter of trying one possible purchaser after another. Subsidiary rights managers are usually tenacious, and will often continue to try to sell their rights long after publication, and sometimes with considerable success. Of course, if your book is of a highly specialized nature, there may be a very limited number of potential outlets for it, and once they have all been tried, the subsidiary rights manager will understandably abandon the effort, to reactivate it only if some new buyer comes upon the scene.

The subsidiary rights department conducts the initial negotiations for the sale of rights, and in some firms is responsible for all details of the agreement, while in others the final arrangements will be made by the contracts department.

Sales

The sales department often plays a crucial part in the shaping of a publisher's list, not only in the decisions whether to accept this or that book, but also in reporting trends, sometimes suggesting specific titles or areas of publishing to the editors, and of course in the forecasting and budgeting processes which most businesses find essential.

In well-run publishing houses there is great rapport between the editorial and sales departments, each respecting the other. Unfortunately, all too often there is instead antagonism. "The sales department makes no effort with all the fine books I give them," says the editor; and the sales people reply, "If only the editors would find us some good books, we could improve our figures out all recognition." Authors may feel that there is more justice in the editor's complaint than that of the sales force; nevertheless, it is very rarely true that the sales department makes no effort. In most cases, the sales representatives, though they may have basic salaries, are also paid a commission on the sales they achieve, so they have a personal incentive in addition to the need to keep the firm in successful business and so retain their jobs.

The larger publishing houses have their own sales forces, a team which works exclusively for that house, but smaller publishers may group together to share a sales force, or use freelance representatives. Another possibility for small publishers is to arrange representation (and often warehousing, invoicing and despatch, too) by one of the large houses; for the very small new publishing house this is sometimes the only way that its books can be presented to the trade, but it is rarely satisfactory, because naturally the big publisher's representative will begin his spiel to the booksellers with the books on his own list and will come to the small publisher's titles only at the end of his time with that buyer, who may by then have spent all he intends to spend and is thinking anyway of his next appointment. It's pretty tough for new small publishers.

As soon as a new book is given a tentative publication date, or sometimes even when it is first signed up, the sales department informs the sales force, giving as many details about the book as possible at that stage, and selling then begins. However, the main vehicle of communication between the publishing house and its sales force in respect of new books is the Sales Conference, at which someone, often the editors concerned, will tell the salesmen about the books, endeavouring to enthuse them and trying to give them all the information which will help them to sell the books. Although many editors have never themselves been "on the road", especially nowadays when it is no longer the habit for new entrants to the publishing business to spend some time in every department, they all need to be salesmen too, for they have to "sell" their new books in the first place to the Sales Director before it is even signed up, and then to the representatives at the sales conference. If they fail to convince the salesmen of the value of the books, then, although they will still try hard, the reps will obviously not approach booksellers and other purchasers with the same confidence.

Sometimes authors are invited to attend the sales

conference. If this should happen to you, remember that you have two things to do: you have to convince the sales force of the quality and sales potential of your book, emphasizing any special markets which would be particularly interested in it; and you have to persuade them, if you can, that you are a likeable person, since it is after all a part of human nature to try a little harder for a friendly, pleasant author than for one who is perhaps too conceited or stand-offish or who talks down to the reps. If you are invited to speak at a sales conference and the whole idea terrifies you because, like many authors, you are extremely shy or because you know that you are an abysmal speaker, then it is probably best to decline and leave the job of presenting your book to the editor. Don't be surprised or hurt if you are not asked to attend a sales conference – it is a rare honour.

Of course it is not only to booksellers that the publisher sells his books. Wholesalers, library suppliers and, of particular importance to the British trade which depends so much on its ability to export, the overseas outlets all have to be canvassed. The publisher's bigger customers are called on at regular and fairly frequent intervals, but for some of the smaller shops the period between calls may be a long one, so it is important that the representatives should have all the necessary information about new books well in advance, so that they can be sure that everyone on whom they call will have heard of the book and had the opportunity to order – or rather, to be persuaded to do so. It is important to remember that there is no obligation on any bookseller to order any given book. He has to be persuaded by the publisher's rep that he should do so.

How the salesman does this is with personal enthusiasm, by using his knowledge of the customer (in some cases he may indeed "make no effort", knowing that the bookseller concerned has no market for that particular book), by trading on his own reputation (if he has guided the bookseller wisely in the past, his advice will be more readily taken) and that of his firm (which includes not only the quality of its list, but also its record in such matters as prompt delivery and its vigour in publicity and promotion). Of course, he uses jackets, catalogues and advance information sheets, which are the most common sales aids. Sometimes the bookseller will be given a proof copy of the book, so that he can form his own judgement. Very few of the sales that the rep makes nowadays are "firm" – almost all are "on sale or return", meaning that the bookseller has the facility of returning the books to the publisher for credit if, after a reasonable period, he has failed to sell any or all of them. Very often it is only by such methods that the rep can persuade the bookseller to order the book, and when you consider how many books are published every year, it is hardly surprising that he often fails.

Many of the chains of bookshops have central buying arrangements, and often it is the Sales Director himself who deals with these large accounts, and calls on them and sells the list.

The sales department is also primarily responsible for calling for reprints, which, incidentally, is always a matter for great care, for though all copies of the publisher's edition may have left his warehouse, the sales people have to be sure that they are also leaving the booksellers' shelves and that sufficient re-orders are likely to come to justify the reprint. The sales department also arranges special deals such as sponsored books (though the editors may take a major part in this), National Book Sales, and the kind of offer which involves saving the tops of cereal packets and sending them off in order to buy a book at a reduced price.

And then they sell "remainders". Remainders are those copies of a book which are left when sales have come down to an extremely low level or have ceased altogether. At that point, the sales department will probably decide that the book should be remaindered, and will approach a remainder merchant. The latter is a kind of specialist wholesaler, who purchases unwanted books from publishers at a very low figure indeed (usually less than the cost of manufacture), and then sells them, mostly through specialized outlets, to the public at knock-down prices. See also p.192.

Publicity and Promotion

Publicity and promotion are vital tools of the sales department, and in many firms the department is under the direct control of the Sales Director.

Since this is the area in which many authors feel that their publishers fail most dismally, I shall examine it in some detail.

When your book is accepted for publication, you will

probably be asked to fill in a form asking for such information as any bookshops where you are personally known, any papers or journals where your book has an especially good chance of being reviewed, any organizations which might be circulated with details of your book. Authors should fill these forms in with care, despite the fact that some publishers seem thereafter to file the forms away and to take no action on any of the author's suggestions. Good publishers do follow the information through, though sometimes they may neglect certain aspects, usually because of a lack of sufficient money in the publicity budget.

When hard times come (and they never appear to be totally absent as far as publishers are concerned), the publicity and promotion budget is almost always the first place where the publisher looks for economies, and the people who work in that department are used to doing so on a shoestring. The amount of money that they are allocated in any given year has to be spread among all the books that the firm is publishing in that period, and not surprisingly, when you stop to think about it, the books on which most money is spent are likely to be those which the publisher considers the major ones on his list, and this means that once they have been allocated their large share of the budget, the lesser books split the remainder between them, and end up with very little each. Hence, perhaps, your publisher's inability to produce the leaflet you envisaged, and hence almost certainly his reluctance to advertise your book in the National Press.

In fact, publishers believe, almost to a man, that National Press advertising is a waste of money. In the modern jargon, it is cosmetic, serving only to appease the author and satisfy his ego. "But if the book is not advertised," you may say, "how will the public know about it?" Well, there are other ways, which we will come to in a moment, but be honest – do you really buy books because you have seen them advertised in the National Press? All right, you do – but you are an exception. The vast majority of people buy books (or more often borrow them) because they have read a review, or because of recommendation by word-of-mouth or from a bookseller, or simply because they happen to see it (paperbacks in particular are known to be "impulse buys"). Publishers are slightly less grudging towards local newspapers, which charge much less for the insertion of advertisements and are possibly of some value if the author is known in the area where they circulate, but even then usually feel that their money can be better spent elsewhere. One of the truths of the advertising business is that a small amount of money is not nearly as cost-effective as a large amount, and alongside that principle it can also be said that something which is not already in demand can only be stimulated effectively by a blanket coverage. Indeed, two or three hundred pounds spent on advertising in the National Press is likely to achieve nothing, whereas several thousand may begin to bring results. If you don't believe me, ask any advertising agent.

Publishers prefer to concentrate on the trade, for it is to the trade that they sell their wares, not to the general public, and the battle for the success of a book is a long way towards being won if they can persuade the bookshops and the wholesalers to order good quantities.

The first thing that they do is to produce a catalogue of their new titles. Your book will appear in the catalogue, sometimes accompanied by an illustration – perhaps your photograph, or a reproduction of the jacket, or an illustration from the book – but almost invariably with the blurb. The catalogue information will also include a tentative publication date and price and various other details about the book, many of which pieces of information will turn out to be inaccurate, because catalogues are prepared a long time in advance of the publication of most of the books in them, and changes in plan frequently occur. Your position in the catalogue may give you cause for thought. How exciting to find your book occupying the leading position! How humiliating to find that your masterpiece is tucked away at the back and has been given no more than a quarter page! In the latter case, you may feel hard done by, but you just have to accept the fact that although most publishers believe all their geese to be swans until publication proves otherwise, they do recognize that some are swannier and some geesier than others. If your publisher sees your book as belonging in the geesier section of his catalogue, it's hard luck.

The catalogue is sent out to the trade (booksellers, purchasers of subsidiary and foreign rights, etc.) and some copies go to members of the public who have asked to be placed on the firm's mailing list. Sometimes the catalogue is used as an insert in the Export edition of *The Bookseller*, which is the major trade paper (well worth subscribing to) and which twice a year produces huge Export numbers in which almost all publishers present their lists of new books for the coming months. The Export number is a kind of gigantic multi-publisher catalogue. It also contains exclusive and informative editorial coverage of forthcoming books.

The publisher may also insert other advertisements for your book in *The Bookseller* and other trade papers. These will appear in advance of publication, but not usually as early as the Export numbers. He may also be willing to place advertisements in specialist journals catering for the section of the public for whom the book is intended.

Leaflets are sometimes prepared and sent out, but usually only for specialist books in which the recipients of the leaflet are likely to be keenly interested. The publisher needs to be sure of a good return from such publicity, for the cost of printing leaflets, plus envelopes and the labour of addressing them, and above all postage, is often prohibitive.

Sometimes a publisher will send proof copies of a book to well-known people, in the hope of getting pre-publication "puffs" from them, which might be quoted on the leaflet, if there is one, or on the jacket, or in advertisements. A proof copy may also go to those journalists who write about forthcoming books in the trade Press. Of course, they cannot mention every new book, so there is no guarantee that yours will be covered.

The publisher may also prepare showcards and other material for use in bookshops, including "dump bins", which are those cardboard stands which contain several copies of a book, with a sort of built-in showcard on the top. Paperback publishers also provide most of the solid racks and "gondolas" (the free-standing racks which you are likely see in the middle of a shop rather than against the walls) which hold their books. All this is known as "point of sale" material. Usually it is reserved for major titles, but if your local bookshop is willing to put on a display of your new book, your publishers may agree to supply a special showcard proclaiming the fact that you are a local author.

One of the most important weapons in the publicity department's armoury is the review copy. Most publishers send out large numbers of review copies of each book that they publish – sometimes as many as two hundred – to the literary editors of all major national and provincial newspapers and magazines, to specialist publications, to radio and television programmes, and indeed to any person or organization which might review the book. Many authors are bitterly disappointed by the lack of reviews for their books, and often blame the publisher. But it is not really his fault, and he is often as disappointed as you are. Reviews are important – even a bad one, unless it is totally destructive, is said to be better than none – and if you have any influence with a reviewer it is worth making sure that he gets a copy of your book. The publicity people will, of course, use any favourable quotes from reviews in advertisements, on the jacket of the book if it is reprinted, on the jacket of your next book, and in any other appropriate way. We have all heard stories of the misuse of quotes from reviews – for instance, the words "a magnificent ... play" being extracted from a review which actually said "a magnificent example of how not to write a play", but publishers are, as we all know, much too ethical to do anything like that.

A regular feature of publishing life is the parties that publishers throw to launch certain of their books. Some authors find it disheartening when their publishers tell them that they have no intention of celebrating publication in that way, and even decline an offer from the author to share the expense. Why should they refuse? Well, again it's a matter of cost-effectiveness. The guests at such a party are made up generally of the author and a few of his family and close friends, a fair sprinkling of the publisher's staff, a few journalists and literary editors, and a bookseller or two. Large amounts of liquor are consumed. The object of the exercise is to get publicity for the book and to persuade the booksellers to order it, but the amount of space that the Press gives on these occasions is usually very limited, and the booksellers present have already ordered the book if they are going to do so. So little is achieved. If your publisher does throw a party for you, you can consider yourself honoured indeed.

The publicity and promotion department also spends quite a lot of its time trying to get the firm's authors radio and television interviews, speaking engagements at literary luncheons, and the like. In the United States, where every city of any size has its own TV station, and television broadcasting is almost round-the-clock, a great deal of air time is taken up with "chat shows", which makes it comparatively easy to get authors the chance to talk about their books on TV. In this country, with our limited number of programmes, it is far more difficult, and the average author's chances of getting on a book programme or nationally-screened interview shows are very small. There are better prospects with radio, and while it still may not be easy to land an interview on one of the main radio channels, you may well have the chance of a broadcast on one of the local programmes, whether they are run by the BBC or are commercial stations – slots for phone-ins, for instance, are often available.

Luncheons and other impressive speaking engagements are fairly rare, and depend in any case partly on your ability to speak well. If you can work up a good talk it may prove worthwhile publicity for you and your book, and you may be asked to give it to Writers' Circles and local Literary Societies, and Women's Institutes and Townswomen's Guilds, and so on. You will also in most cases receive fees for your talks, or at least expenses, which are sometimes offered in an amount which will exceed your actual expenditure and therefore amount to expenses plus a small fee. It is impossible to give guidance on the fees that one might expect, which depend on the size both of the organization concerned and of the audience, not to mention your own fame. There is also the question of what is expected of you – a forty-minute talk, followed by questions, perhaps, or something more than that. All that can be said is that if your talk is sponsored by one of the Regional Arts Associations, you can expect at least £75, and possibly more, whereas the fees that Women's Institutes are prepared to pay are more likely to be in the £10–£15 range. Get as big a fee as you can, and if it is not very much, console yourself with the thought that the publicity is worth having. Incidentally, it *is* important to get as much as you can, not merely because it keeps the wolf away from your own door, but because it sets and maintains standards for other authors. Something else to bear in mind is that if you, a free-lance author, are being paid by a local authority, the officials there will often try to treat you as one of the authority's employees and will deduct tax from your fee; the best way of avoiding this is to get the authority to agree in advance that you are providing a one-off service which does not constitute employment and that therefore they are not entitled to deduct tax; you will undoubtedly have something of a battle before they give in (it can help to give details of the tax office which deals with your affairs), but it is worth persisting.

The publicity and promotion department will also be involved, along with the sales department, in film tie-ins and other similar marketing opportunities, and arranges tours for some authors, though again these are usually reserved for the more famous. Tours are exhausting – a series of frantic train and car journeys, interspersed with drink parties and a great deal of hand-shaking with local booksellers, journalists and other worthies. They also usually involve signing sessions. Most publishers, and most booksellers hate signing sessions. They are surprisingly costly to arrange, so that only the most successful of them are profitable. And how many are really successful? Very, very few – usually only when the author is a nationally known "personality". Far more often it is an extremely depressing occasion, with the bookshop manager, the publisher's publicity manager and his local representative making embarrassed conversation while the author sits miserably behind a pile of his books, waiting for the customers who don't come. And if one does come, it is quite likely to be the representative's wife, summoned by a desperate phone-call. Pretending to be an ordinary member of the book-buying public, carefully not looking at her husband, she will purchase a copy of the book, be grateful for the author's signature on it, and later will hand it back to her husband, who will either put it back in the bookshop, getting a refund from the bookseller, or, more likely, tell his wife to keep it, and that he will put it on his expenses, disguised as "entertainment". Do everyone a favour, including yourself, and don't ask your publisher to arrange a signing session for you.

In some ways you yourself can do as much for the book as anyone else, and you should not be shy about blowing your own trumpet. Unless your book is too technical for them, your relations and friends will read it. Don't hesitate to ask them to recommend it in turn to their friends and to give copies of it for Christmas and birthday presents. Most non-writers find authors curiously glamorous, and you should not hesitate to capitalize on this. Tell a stranger that you are an author, and he will almost always show immediate interest and ask what sort of books you write. Don't be modest, but do your best to make him resolve to go and buy a copy. If your book is going to be paperbacked, keep quiet about it for as long as you can, so that people buy the hardcover edition instead of waiting for the cheaper version. Use every trick you can think of to increase your sales.

By the way, that includes not being too generous with your complimentary copies. You will probably be forced to give free copies to your nearest and dearest, but make the others buy their own. You can promise that when they've done so you will sign the copy for them.

Final Print Quantity, Price and Publication Date

After the proofs have been returned, a final decision about the print quantity will be taken. This may vary from the figure originally discussed for the purposes of the estimate when the book was first under consideration. Very often, alas, the print quantity is lowered. Why? Because publishers, who are among the world's optimists, become less so as the time approaches for them to commit themselves to spending large sums of money on the gamble of manufacturing a book. Additionally, it is often difficult to maintain the initial enthusiasm – new books have come along to engage the editor's attention, and he may be far more interested in the one that he is about to sign up than in the one on which, although it is not yet published, his work was completed months ago. That does not mean that he has lost his enthusiasm totally – it is a matter of degree. Sales departments like to be cautious, and the editor may not fight them as vigorously now as he would have done earlier to keep the print quantity up or even increase it. Other circumstances may affect the decision too. For instance, the failure to sell subsidiary rights may have lessened confidence in the book or the market may have changed in some respect, or the book have been pre-empted by another publisher's book on the same subject, or advance orders may, for these reasons or for no discernible cause, have been disappointing. Equally of course there may have been reasons why the print quantity should be increased – bolstered by success in the subsidiary rights market and initial reactions from booksellers, excitement about the book may have mounted. Or it may be that the publisher is going to stick with the number he first thought of. Whatever print quantity is decided upon, new sets of figures will probably be prepared, now that the costs of the book are more accurately known, and again approval for the estimate will have to be obtained from various departments within the publishing house.

The book's price will also be fixed. This is not an easy matter. The public at large believes that books are expensive, though in fact they are remarkably cheap when you compare them with the ephemeral delights of eating out, or going to the cinema or theatre, or indeed if you compare them with almost any other consumer item. Be that as it may, the publisher needs to price his books so that the return to him covers his manufacturing costs, the author's royalty, his overheads, and gives him a profit, since he is in business, after all, to make money. If he prices the book too cheaply, he will lose on it; if it is too expensive, he may find it unsaleable. The more copies he prints, the easier the decision is, for the fixed costs on the book (i.e. the composition or setting of the book in type, the preparation of the illustrations, the setting up of the printing and binding machines, the costs of originating the jacket, including the artist's fee, and other similar items) are spread over the entire printing, which means that the total costs per copy diminish the more copies are printed. With a small print quantity, however, he often finds himself in great difficulty, especially if the book is fiction, for there is a convention within the trade and among the public that a novel should cost less than a non-fiction book of similar length and size. A biography, for instance, is liked to be priced at a minimum of £2 more than a novel of comparable length, and if it is heavily illustrated may easily cost £7 or £8 more.

The cost of a book in relation to its retail price varies from publisher to publisher and from book to book, but very roughly it could be said that the average discount to wholesalers and retailers is about 40% (this allows for the higher discounts given to overseas customers), manufacturing costs work out at about 20% and the author's royalty at 10%, leaving 30% to cover the publisher's overheads (including wages, telephone and mailing costs, rent, rates, interest on capital, advertising and promotion, distribution, heating and lighting, depreciation, and the cost of the books that he does not sell, either because they are given away for promotional purposes or because he has printed too many

copies) and profit, not to mention tax. The formula works
out slightly differently for paperbacks, the average discount
being 48%, manufacture 17.5% and the author's royalty
7.5%, leaving 27% for the publisher's other expenses and
his profit, the net amount of which may not exceed 3%. It is
not a formula for instant wealth for publishers, any more
than it is for authors, and indeed it is worth remembering
that publishing is in fact a small and not over-lucrative
business. The turnover of the entire British publishing
industry does not approach that of a single firm such as ICI,
and even at the highest level those who work in the business
rarely earn high salaries and certainly do not have the same
sort of regular inflow of wealth that some of their bestselling
authors enjoy. Bear in mind also that the publisher's profit is
more often than not ploughed back into the firm for use on
future projects, many of which will not come to fruition for
many years, and the next time your affluent publisher takes
you to an expensive lunch, just think how many books have
to be sold to pay for it.

At the same time as the print quantity and price are
decided, the publication date will probably be firmly fixed.
Publishers tend to bring out their books on dates which are
regular to the firm concerned – the last Thursday in the
month, for instance, or the first and third Tuesdays – and
usually publish more than one book on those days, so that
the titles can be invoiced and despatched at the same time.
The decision about which month in which to bring out a
particular book depends on a number of issues. First of all,
there is the question of when the manufacturing processes
will have been completed and stocks delivered to the
publisher's warehouse, and this in turn depends on
everything going through as planned, without an unexpected
delay at proof stage, for instance, or a sudden essential
change of jacket design, and with the manufacturers keeping
to the scheduled dates and producing work of acceptable
quality; secondly, it will depend on the balance of the
publisher's list – he will not want to publish all his major
titles in the same month, nor, if he is a general publisher, to
have nothing but fiction one month and nothing but
non-fiction the next; thirdly, he will be concerned about the
time of year and sometimes with specific dates – it is no use
hoping to catch the important Christmas market by
publishing in November or December, by which time the

booksellers will have ordered all that they want for the gift season, nor is there much to be gained by publishing a book about Wimbledon, as an example, in August when the Tennis Championships are over. Incidentally, it is worth pointing out that the Christmas market is important for a limited number of books only. Some books for children, including annuals, certain practical books, annuals for adults, and those books which would in any case be bestsellers may have substantial Christmas sales, but the vast majority of books sell no better then than at any other time, and often less well.

Sometimes authors feel that their books have been hampered by being published at the wrong time of year. There is little that can be done about this, since it is entirely the publisher's province to decide when a book will appear. Nevertheless, most publishers, being business men, try as often as circumstances will allow to publish at the most suitable time for each book on their lists, because it is in their own interest, as well as the author's, to do so. At the same time, you have to understand that not every book can be published in September or October (which many consider to be the best possible months), since the list has to be spread throughout the year. If you ask your publisher, he will probably be able to tell you good reasons in favour of every month of the year – e.g. "January is a splendid time to be published – far fewer books come out then, so you stand a better chance, to say nothing of all those people wanting to spend their book tokens – besides which, the shops have been cleared of Christmas cards and all the other space-consuming seasonal material." Equally, when he decides to delay the book until February, he will be able to tell you that "January is a rotten month anyway – all the booksellers are stocktaking, and don't want to order any new books, especially if they've got Christmas overstocks to get rid of – whereas by February they're looking for important new books like yours to give their New Year sales an impetus."

Invoicing, Warehousing and Despatch

Once the salesmen start selling the book, orders begin to flow into the publisher's office, where they are stored until the time comes for the preparation of invoices. Almost certainly other books will be published on the same day as yours, and the orders will be collated so that the books due for publication can all be invoiced, packed and despatched together. Books ordered before publication are "subscribed" and the total of such orders is "the subscription".

The preparation of invoices used always to be done by hand, but in almost all firms nowadays a computer is used. The computer is also programmed to recognize "stopped accounts" (those which the publisher will no longer supply – perhaps because they do not pay their bills) and other outlets with which, for one good reason or another, the publisher does not wish to do business, and it will also know the discounts applicable to each outlet.

Meanwhile, the books have been delivered to the warehouse from the printer and/or binder, on a date previously arranged with the warehouse manager, who must make sure that he has space to keep them near the packing benches. Later, the books will be stored on racks, ready for repeat orders. Bulk supplies of slow-moving titles will probably be kept on the top racks, from which a fork-lift truck will be needed to remove them. They may well stay there until the book is remaindered.

The books are "looked out" – that is to say, the requisite copies of each title on the invoice are brought together from the stocks – and packed, and then distributed so that, whether they go by post, rail or road, they will arrive in the bookshops in time for publication, but not too much before, since the booksellers do not want to have their stockrooms full of books which they cannot put on sale. It is important, of course, that the book should not be on sale earlier in one outlet than another, especially if the shops are rivals in the same town, so publishers try hard not only to see that booksellers stick to the publication date, but that they themselves give the shops no excuse for not doing so. It is a tricky and complex job to get all the books out for the right date, especially as the warehouse will simultaneously be packing and despatching other, non-publication, orders, dealing with returns, answering queries, and keeping in regular touch with head office (most publishers' warehouses nowadays are separate from the administrative offices).

Publication Day

It is perhaps not surprising, with all these processes to go through, that the publication of a book is a lengthy process, usually taking at least nine months, and often longer. Bear in mind too that the various departments of your publishing house are dealing not just with your book but, at their various stages, with all the other books that they will be publishing during the next nine months, and often far ahead of that. And they will have their other problems too, of general administration, staff changes, office accommodation and the like.

When publication day comes at last, you might expect, as I did when I first entered publishing as a boy of eighteen, that the place would be humming. I envisaged presses thumping away in the basement, green-eye-shielded editors frantically answering three telephones at once and passing scribbled messages to a stream of messengers scurrying in and out. The images came, I suppose, from newspaper offices as depicted by Hollywood. In fact, publication day in a publisher's offices is like any other day – if anything, quieter. All the work on the books coming out that day has been done, and the books themselves are in the shops waiting for customers. Occasionally, with a roaring bestseller, the publisher's phone may start to ring with repeat orders, but even that is more likely to occur several days after publication, when the bookseller is certain that his stocks are reducing rapidly and that there is sufficient continuing demand to justify the re-order. If you are lucky, your editor may remember to write to you to congratulate you on publication, or may even take you out for a celebratory lunch, but don't expect it as a matter of course. If he is taking anyone out to lunch to celebrate it is likely to be the author of the most important book to be published that day, but in any case he may have forgotten, in the pressure of work on books still far away from publication, that it is indeed publication day.

After Publication

What happens to your book after publication? Probably very little, unless it has a considerable success and reprints are required. The representatives will continue to try to sell your book, but it will now be part of the backlist, and though for the first few weeks after publication they will be asking their customers for repeat orders, unless these come in regularly, the book will receive a diminishing amount of attention. This is sad, but inevitable – they have to devote the bulk of their energies to the new books which are coming out.

For a while at least, the publicity and promotion people will continue to be active, but unless something happens to revive public interest in you or the subject of your book, they will ultimately give up – there is nothing more moribund, if not dead, than the majority of last year's books, unless of course you are in the happy position of having written a bestseller or a standard work, or of being a very well-known author.

(It is interesting, by the way, to compare these three categories. The bestseller will continue to be active for quite a long time, but even in this case – unless it is one of those extraordinary books like Stephen Hawking's *A Brief History of Time* which go on and on selling in the original hardcover edition – the activity is more likely to be in the area of subsidiary rights, such as bookclub and paperback editions, foreign sales and so on. The standard work is an interesting phenomenon, and one which can be immensely pleasing to the author, for though its sales may not be large, they continue with a remarkable steadiness, until the happy day when the publisher tells the author that it is time for the book to be revised and updated, after which it can look forward to a new lease of life. The book by the very well-known author may, of course, be a bestseller or a standard work or both, but it is the author's persona – perhaps as a politician or a pop-star – which keeps the book active rather than the book itself.)

The subsidiary rights department will go on beavering away for a long time, and is often surprisingly successful with books that have otherwise been forgotten by everyone except the author.

If you are fortunate, your editor or someone else in the publishing house may give you some information from time to time about how your book is going, but in many cases authors have to wait until the royalty statement appears to know the best or the worst. You are not being kept in the dark deliberately, though it may seem so; it is largely a question of out of sight, out of mind – your editor finds it takes all his time to deal with the new books going through, and tends to forget all about you, or to think to himself, "I really must write to So-and-so," but never actually does so. It may also be, especially in some of the larger houses, that he really has little idea of how sales are going, since, absurd though it may sound, some sales departments tend to keep their information to themselves, only passing it on to the editorial department if it is either unusually good or completely disastrous. It is very frustrating for the author not to know how his book is doing, but if you ring up daily or even weekly after publication, you will probably be regarded as a considerable nuisance; on the other hand, if the publisher volunteers no information, you can reasonably ask occasionally and be justified in expecting a rather more detailed reply than, "Oh, it's doing quite well – I think."

The royalty statement, when it does arrive, may be rather less comprehensive than you might hope. The royalty arrangements on nearly every book are different, and many publishers use a kind of shorthand on their statements which makes them hard to understand. However, in recent years considerable improvements to the form of royalty statement have been made in many publishing houses, and it is to be hoped that all publishers will follow suit. The Model Royalty Statement drawn up by the Society of Authors and appoved by the Publishers Association is shown as Appendix II.

Although some publishers attempt to supply annual royalty statements only (and, alas, succeed in so doing), the tradition in the trade is for six-monthly statements, which appear three months after the royalty period has ended. Thus the statement for the period January 1st to June 30th in any year is due on the following September 30th, and that for July 1st to December 31st in any year on the following March 31st. The three-month gap was a necessity in the days when all statements were prepared by hand, partly because of the complications and the variety of the information included on royalty statements (the terms for so many books, even by the same author, often differing from contract to contract), and partly because of the need to have all the statements ready at the same time (a reasonably large publishing house might have to prepare many hundreds of statements for every royalty period). It is many, many years now since publishers first began to use computers in their accounts departments, but until comparatively recent times they have nearly all claimed that it was impossible to write a programme which would cope adequately with something as complex as royalties. That is no longer true, and more and more publishers are computerizing their royalty calculations. In doing so, their last justification for the three-month delay has vanished. Since earlier payment of royalties may exacerbate their cash-flow problems, publishers will almost certainly be reluctant to abandon the old practices, but authors will probably feel little sympathy for them and will hope that one day, in the not too distant future, quarterly and even monthly royalty statements will be sent out.

In the meantime, at least in the less progressive publishing houses, the three months after the end of the royalty period are a time of hectic work for the royalty department. After the statements have been sent out, the department is naturally less busy, and then is a good time, if you find the statement baffling, or if you think the figures are wrong (and it pays to check them carefully, because mistakes do occur), to go to see the Royalties Manager and ask for his help. He will probably be pleased to see you, since he comparatively rarely meets the authors whose names and sales are so familiar to him, and the poor chap often thinks of authors as glamorous persons (which you and I know not to be true!).

By this time, you will perhaps be well on the way with your next book, and the whole process will begin again. If you are a beginner, this second venture should be in some respects easier, since you know what to expect – but be prepared for variations on the theme. One of the great pleasures of a publisher's life is that his work is rarely of a totally routine nature, but changes with almost every book. The differences between one book and another can mean pleasure or disappointment for the author, so be prepared.

6

Contracts

"Barabbas was a publisher," said the poet Thomas Campbell, who was also the perpetrator of a toast to Napoleon, which horrified his fellow guests at a dinner for authors until he went on to explain, "I agree with you that Napoleon is a tyrant, a monster, the sworn foe of our nation. But, gentlemen, he once shot a publisher!" Many, many authors would agree with Campbell that publishers are thieves, or if not thieves, at least totally unscrupulous in the way that they exploit authors. Publishers naturally reply that any such statement is grossly libellous of a profession which has high risks and low profit margins, and whose honest businessmen would not retain authors on their lists if they were as wicked as that. They would admit that there are some rogues among their ranks, just as there are in any profession in the world, but they would claim that such publishers tend not to survive for long, since authors, and particularly agents, soon find them out. As for exploiting authors, they might point out that it is always easy to level that accusation at those who are in a buyer's market. There may be comparatively few wildly successful books to be found, but there is never any shortage of works which some publisher somewhere will consider publishable; if you, as the seller, do not like the terms which they, as the buyer, propose, they will probably be able to find another author of a similar book who will happily sign on the dotted line and not feel that he is being exploited – on the contrary, considering the publisher's terms generous.

One of the difficulties facing authors is that publishers' contracts vary from firm to firm, and from book to book within each firm. This is neither surprising nor evidence of sharp practice – one of the truisms of the book world is that every book is different. Equally, every publisher is different, and there are good ones and bad ones and vast numbers of them who are just average. Thank God it is so. Publishers will only be alike when they are all State-owned and State-run, which Heaven forfend, when they will probably all be equally bad. You should not expect all publishers to behave the same way and to offer the same terms, any more than you should expect a first novelist to receive the same treatment as one with a worldwide bestselling reputation. Nevertheless, it is all rather confusing.

Moreover, precisely because publishers are perpetually in a buyer's market they have been able, if not to exploit authors outrageously, at least often to be niggardly towards them, and this has perhaps been particularly true in their refusal to share more generously with the author in the rewards of a successful book. They have also been assiduous in maintaining that they alone should control every aspect of the publication of a book, many of them refusing to consult the author on any matter concerning his book and neglecting to tell him what was happening to it. An author was someone who wrote a book, amended it in accordance with a publisher's wishes, accepted gratefully whatever terms were offered for its publication, and then disappeared smartly into limbo (in which state his publisher had no wish to disturb him) while he got on with writing the next book.

Unless he is consistently in the bestseller class, in which case he or his agent will probably be able easily to obtain a favourable contract, the individual author has little chance of fighting successfully for improved terms, especially since he may not fully understand the wording of the agreement, not to mention the ease with which the publisher can say, "This is our standard contract," with the implication that all his other authors accept it without demur, or even more tellingly, "This is standard practice throughout the trade," a statement which the author will be in no position to contradict. Such a fight can only be won if all authors band together, or if sufficiently influential bodies fight on their behalf.

It is for this reason that the Society of Authors and the Writers' Guild produced in 1980 a form of contract, known thenceforth as the Minimum Terms Agreement. In this document they set out not only to lay down standards on financial matters, such as the royalty rates and the various splits of subsidiary earnings which they considered acceptable, but also to allow authors the right to be kept informed of publishing plans for their books and to be consulted on such subjects as jackets, blurbs and publicity. The Society and the Guild jointly tried to persuade the Publishers Association to adopt the MTA on behalf of all its members. The PA predictably argued that it could not bind its individual members in any way, but drew up a "Code of Practice", to which it hoped they would adhere. The Code was both bland and unenforceable. The Society and the Guild then set about persuading individual publishing firms to sign the MTA (or a form of it, for it was soon realized that each firm was likely to want to negotiate certain changes to the basic formula). Progress, despite vigorous efforts, has been lamentably slow. By 1990, ten years on, the list of firms which had signed was a short one, consisting of BBC Books, Bloomsbury, Century Hutchinson (including Jonathan Cape and the Bodley Head), Chapmans, Faber & Faber, Headline, Hodder & Stoughton, Methuen London, Penguin (including Michael Joseph, Hamish Hamilton and Viking) and Sinclair-Stevenson. It is interesting that the list should include four houses of some size (Bloomsbury, Chapmans, Headline and Sinclair-Stevenson) which have been set up since the MTA was first launched.

It is to be hoped that more publishers will adopt a form of the MTA in the near future. Meanwhile, however, although the signatories are few, the existence of the MTA has undoubtedly influenced a large number of other publishers so that they have improved many aspects of their dealings with authors. They will not all concede your *right* to consultation on the jacket design, for instance, but at least none will now look at you with horrified incomprehension if you ask for it, and many will in fact show you the design in advance and allow you to comment on it (whether they listen to your comments and act on them is naturally a different matter). The point is that some kind of progress is being made in getting publishers to look upon their relationships with authors as a *partnership*, and for that we must all be grateful to the Society and the Guild and those of their staff and members who have spent so much time in fighting for the MTA.

A typical MTA is reproduced in the next pages, followed by comments on various matters which perhaps deserve special attention.

AN AGREEMENT

AN   AGREEMENT   made   this   day
of   199 between the Society of Authors and
the Writers' Guild of Great Britain of the one part
and   (hereinafter called "the Publisher")
of the other part WHEREBY IT IS AGREED AS FOLLOWS:

A Scope of the Agreement
This Agreement confirms the minimum terms and conditions
to be observed in all contracts signed on or
after   199 ("the contract") between the
Publisher and authors who are members of the Society of
Authors or of the Writers' Guild of Great Britain (any such
member being called "the Author") in respect of any original
literary work first published in the UK in volume form but
excluding the following:

1 Illustrated works being either:
  a) books in which the proportion of space taken up with
  illustrations is 40% or more; or
  b) specialist works on the visual arts in which the
  proportion of space taken up with illustrations is 25% or
  more.
2 Books involving three or more participants in royalties.
3 Technical books, manuals and reference works.

B Nature of Agreement
1 The terms and conditions of the contract shall be no less
  favourable to the Author nor in any way detract from or
  qualify the terms and conditions specified in Section C
  hereof, except in so far as may be requested or may in
  exceptional circumstances be agreed by the Author or
  his/her agent.
2 This Agreement may be terminated on either party giving
  to the other three months' written notice expiring at any
  time after the fifth anniversary hereof. For the avoidance
  of doubt either party may wish to ask for specified terms
  within Clauses 10 to 12 of this Agreement to be reviewed
  on three months' written notice if unforeseen changes in
  the trade seem to make this imperative (but this provision

shall not be invoked more than once in any 12 month period).

3 The contract shall contain the words "drafted in accordance with an Agreement with the Society of Authors and the Writers' Guild of Great Britain".

C Terms of the Contract between the Author and the Publisher

1 *The Typescript and its Delivery*

(a) The contract shall specify full details of the work including its title, length, number and type of illustrations, index etc, and may refer expressly to a synopsis, specified correspondence between the Publisher and the Author and any other relevant material submitted by the Author. There shall also be stated (without being binding on the Publisher) the number of copies the Publisher plans to print initially, the proposed format (i.e. hardback and/or paperback) and the anticipated retail price(s). In the case of commissioned works, the planned print run and anticipated retail price(s) may alternatively be disclosed on delivery of the typescript. The Author shall deliver by the date specified in the contract two legible copies of the typescript of the work, which shall be professionally competent and ready for press.

(b) Within 30 days of delivery the Publisher shall notify the Author if any changes to the script are required (or if the script is to be rejected). Within a further 30 days (or such reasonable necessary longer period as may be notified to the Author) the Publisher shall specify the changes required (or provide detailed reasons in writing for rejecting the script).

If the typescript is rejected because of the Author's failure to comply with Clause 1(a) he/she shall be liable to repay, if so requested, the part of the advance already received.

(c) Should the Author fail to meet the agreed delivery date, the Publisher may agree with the Author a later date or give the Author reasonable notice in writing to deliver the work and should he/she fail to do so the Publisher shall be entitled to terminate the contract in which event the part of the advance received shall be returnable and all rights shall revert to the Author.

2 *Warranty and Indemnity*

The Author shall warrant:

(i) that the work is original, that he/she is the owner

thereof and free to contract, and that the work has not previously been published in volume form elsewhere; and

(ii) that the work will not contain anything that infringes copyright or is libellous or obscene or otherwise unlawful; nor will it infringe third parties' rights; and

(iii) that all statements purporting to be facts are true and that any recipe, information, formula or instructions contained therein will not, if the reader were reasonably to act thereupon, cause injury, illness or any damage to the user or third parties.

The Author shall indemnify the Publisher against costs, expenses, loss and damage resulting from any breach of the foregoing warranties or any claim alleging breach thereof (excluding any claims which are reasonably deemed by the Publisher to be groundless, vexatious or purely malicious). The indemnity shall survive termination of the contract.

The Publisher reserves the right to request the Author to alter or amend the text of the work in such a way as may appear to the Publisher appropriate for the purpose of removing any passage which on the advice of the Publisher's legal advisers (in association with the Author's legal advisers, if he/she so wishes) may be considered objectionable or likely to be actionable at law, but any such alteration or removal shall be without prejudice to and shall not affect the Author's liability under the warranties and indemnity on his/her part. If the Author declines in such circumstances to alter or amend the text, the Publisher reserves the right to terminate the contract and seek reimbursement of the advance.

3 *Copyright Fees and Index*

(a) The Publisher shall pay any copyright fees for agreed illustrations, unless otherwise agreed (in which event the Publisher will contribute at least £250). The responsibility for clearing and paying for quotations shall be a matter for individual negotiation.

(b) If in the opinion of the Author and the Publisher an index is required, but the Author does not wish to undertake the task, the Publisher shall engage a competent indexer to do so and the costs shall be shared equally between the Author and the Publisher, the Author's share being deducted from money due to the Author.

4 *Licence and Review*

(a) The copyright in the work shall remain the property of the Author who shall grant to the Publisher the sole and exclusive right for a period of 20 years from the date of first publication ("the initial term") to print, publish and sell the work in volume form in the English language (or in any language as the case may be) in the territories specified in the contract and to sub-license such rights specified in Clauses 15, 16, 17 and 18 hereof as may be agreed in the contract. The Publisher will inform the Author of all sub-licences granted (excluding anthology and quotation rights) and supply copies thereof on request. In particular the Author will be fully consulted and have an adequate opportunity to discuss and comment (without undue delay) on all proposed major sub-licences (including but not limited to serial, paperback, American, film, television and merchandising deals).

(b) On every tenth anniversary of the publication date (or within a reasonable time thereafter) either party may give written notice to the other that it wishes specified terms in the contract to be reviewed, in which case those terms shall be considered in the light of comparable terms then prevailing in the trade and shall be altered (with effect from the date of the notice) to the extent that may be just and equitable. Failing agreement on what may be just and equitable the matter shall be referred to arbitration under Clause 28.

(c) If the work is in print (as defined herein) at the end of 17 years from the first publication, the Publisher may inform the Author in writing of the date that the contract is due to expire and invite the Author (or his/her executors, as the case may be) to negotiate in good faith with the intention of reaching agreement on revised terms for a further period. The Author, if so requested by the Publisher, shall inform the Publisher of the terms offered (if any) by other publishers and the Publisher shall be given an opportunity to match such terms but the final decision shall rest with the Author.

(d) If, with the Author's consent (such consent not to be unreasonably withheld), a licence is granted by the Publisher extending beyond the initial term, the reversion of rights to the Author (if applicable) shall be without prejudice to the continuation of that licence and the Publisher's entitlement to the

Publisher's share of the proceeds therefrom. But the Publisher shall not be entitled to extend or renew, without the Author's consent, any licence granted which is due to terminate after the initial term (unless and until a further agreement is reached under (c) above).

5 *The Publisher's Undertaking to Publish*
The Publisher shall publish the work at the Publisher's own expense and risk within 12 months (unless there are particular reasons for later publication or unless the Publisher is prevented from so publishing by circumstances beyond its control) of delivery of the typescript and any other material specifed in the contract. Should the Publisher decline to publish the work for any reason other than the Author's failure to meet the specifications in Clause 1(a), the advance stipulated in Clause 9 (including any balance unpaid) shall be paid to the Author without prejudice to any additional compensation to which he/she may be entitled for breach of contract.

6 *Production*
   (a) All details as to the manner of production and publication and the number and destination of free copies shall be under the control of the Publisher who undertakes to produce the book to a high standard.
   (b) The Publisher shall consult the Author and obtain his/her approval on copy editing and the final number and type of illustrations (unless, because of the topicality of the book, time does not permit), such approval not to be unreasonably withheld or delayed. The Publisher shall consult the Author about publication date. The Author shall be shown artists' roughs (or, if that is impracticable, proofs) of the jacket and shall be fully consulted thereon and on the blurb in good time before publication, but the final decisions shall be the Publisher's.
   (c) No changes in the title or text (other than changes made to conform to the Publisher's house style) shall be made by the Publisher without the Author's consent, such consent not to be unreasonably withheld.
   (d) In ample time before publication the Author shall be sent a questionnaire inviting him/her to supply personal information relevant to publicity and marketing, to suggest who should receive review/

free copies and to say whether he/she wishes the typescript to be returned.

(e) The Publisher will disclose to the Author, on request, the size of the first and subsequent print runs.

(f) Within 30 days of publication the Publisher shall return to the Author the typescript of the work, if so requested.

(g) The Publisher shall ensure that the provisions contained in (c) above are included in any contract for sub-licensed editions of the work.

7 *Approval of Final Edited Script and Correction of Proofs*

(a) Unless the Author has already seen a copy of the edited typescript or does not wish to see it, he/she shall be sent a copy for approval – normally at least 10 working days before it goes to the printers – and he/she shall respond as soon as possible.

(b) The Author shall be sent two complete sets of proofs of the work. The Author shall correct and return one set of proofs to the Publisher within 15 working days (or such other period as may be agreed). The Author shall bear the cost of proof corrections (other than printers' or publisher's errors) in excess of 15% of the cost of composition, such cost to be deducted from the advance or royalties.

8 *Copyright Notice and Credit to the Author*

A copyright notice in the form © followed by the Author's name and the year of first publication shall be printed on all copies of the work and the Author's name shall appear prominently on the jacket, binding and title page of the work and in all publicity material. The Publisher shall ensure that an identical copyright notice appears in all sub-licensed editions of the work.

9 *Advance*

(a) Unless the Author requests a lower figure, the Publisher shall pay the Author an advance against royalties and earnings of not less than the following percentage of the Author's estimated receipts from the sale of the projected first printing:

(i) 65% if the work is to be published by the Publisher only in hardback or only in paperback

(ii) 55% if the work is to be published by the Publisher in both hardback and paperback.

(b) In the case of a non-commissioned work half the

advance shall be paid on signature of the contract and half within one year of signature or on publication, whichever is the sooner (or as may be otherwise agreed at the Author's request).

(c)   In the case of a commissioned work the advance shall be paid one-third on signature of the contract, one-third on delivery of the final and revised typescript and one-third within one year of delivery of the typescript or on publication whichever is the sooner (or as may otherwise be agreed at the Author's request).

(d)   The provisions of (b) and (c) may be varied by agreement when the work is to be published first in hardback and then in paperback under the Publisher's own imprint.

10 *Hardback Royalties*

(a)   *On home market sales in the UK and Irish Republic*
10% of the British published price on the first 2,500 copies, 12½% on the next 2,500 copies, and 15% thereafter except on works for children when the royalty will be 7½% rising to 10% after 3,000 copies. [In exceptional circumstances involving long works of fiction being published in short print runs for libraries or works of drama or poetry being published in short print runs, the Publisher may wish to ask the Author to consider accepting a lower starting royalty for specified reasons.]

(b)   *On overseas sales*
10% of the price received on the first 2,500 copies. 12½% on the next 2,500 copies and 15% thereafter, except on works for children when the royalty will be 7½% rising to 10% after 3,000 copies. If the work is published abroad in a separate local edition, royalties will be paid at a rate to be mutually agreed on the local published price.

(c)   On reprints of 1,500 copies or less the royalties shall revert to the starting royalties, except that the Publisher may not invoke this provision more than once in 12 months without prior agreement of the Author.

(d)   *Cheap and other hardback editions*
The Publisher shall pay to the Author a royalty to be agreed on any hardback edition published at less than two-thirds of the original published price, on any "special" hardback edition under the Publisher's imprint (e.g. an educational or large-print edition), and on any other edition not covered by (a) or (b) above.

11 *Paperbacks*
  (a) Should the Publisher publish a paperback edition
      under one of the Publisher's own imprints the
      Publisher shall pay to the Author on home sales
      7½% of the British published price on the first
      50,000 copies and 10% thereafter. On works for
      children, the Publisher shall pay 5% to 10,000
      copies and 7½% thereafter. The royalty on copies
      sold for export shall be 6% of the British published
      price (4% in the case of works for children). If the
      work is published abroad in a separate local edition,
      royalties will be at a rate to be agreed based on the
      local published price.
  (b) Should the Publisher sub-license paperback rights
      to an independent paperback publisher, all moneys
      accruing under such sub-licences shall be divided in
      the proportion 60% to the Author 40% to the
      Publisher up to a point to be negotiated and then
      70%: 30% thereafter.

12 *Returns*
  The Publisher shall have the right to set aside as a
  reserve against returns 10% (h/b)/20% (p/b) of the
  royalties earned on the first royalty statement (after first
  publication or reissue) and to withhold this sum up to and
  including the second (h/b)/third (p/b) royalty statement,
  following which all moneys shall be paid in full and the
  Publisher shall accept responsibility for any over-
  payments resulting from subsequent returns.

13 *Remainders and Surplus Stock*
  If the Publisher wishes
  (a) To sell copies at a reduced price or as a remainder,
      the Author will be given the option to purchase
      copies at the remainder price and will be paid 5% of
      the net receipts of other sales;
  (b) To destroy surplus bound copies, the Publisher will
      notify him/her accordingly and the Author shall have
      the right to obtain free copies within 20 working days
      of the notification.
  There shall be no disposals under this clause within one
  year of first publication.

14 *Royalty Free Copies*
  No royalties shall be paid on copies given away free to
  the Author or others, review or returned copies, or those
  destroyed by fire, water, in transit or otherwise.

15 *Bookclub Rights*
Should the Publisher sub-license simultaneous or reprint bookclub rights the Publisher shall pay the Author as follows:
(a) On bound copies or sheets sold to the bookclub: 10% of the Publisher's receipts.
(b) On copies manufactured by the bookclub: 60% of the Publisher's receipts.

16 *United States Rights*
If the Author grants to the Publisher US rights in the work, the Publisher shall make every effort:
either to arrange the publication of an American edition of the work on a royalty basis, in which case the Publisher shall retain not more than 15% of the proceeds inclusive of any sub-agent's commission;
or to sell bound copies, in which case the Publisher will endeavour whenever reasonably possible to see that the Author is paid royalties (the percentage(s) to be agreed) related to the US published price. If the Publisher is unable or does not consider it reasonably possible to secure a royalty, the Publisher shall offer copies or sheets for sale inclusive of royalty, in which case the Author will be paid 15% of the Publisher's receipts, unless the discount is 60% or more in which case the Author will be paid 10% of the Publisher's receipts.

17 *Translation Rights*
If the Author grants to the Publisher translation rights in the work, the Publisher shall retain not more than 20% of the proceeds from any foreign language edition inclusive of any sub-agent's commission.

18 *Subsidiary Rights*
(a) The Publisher shall pay to the Author the following percentages of the proceeds (after the deduction of any sub-agent's commission in the case of merchandising) from the licensing of the following rights:

(i)	Second (i.e. post volume publication) serial rights	75%
(ii)	Anthology & quotation rights	50%
(iii)	Condensation rights – magazines	75%
	Condensation rights – books	50%
(iv)	Strip cartoon rights	75%*

(v)	TV, radio and recorded readings	75%*
(vi)	Merchandising	80%*
(vii)	One shot periodical	75%
(viii)	Hardcover reprint, loose leaf, and large print	50%

* These rights may or may not be granted to the Publisher according to the terms of the contract. If necessary, the Author will, at the Publisher's request, join in the granting of any such rights.

(b) If the Publisher wishes to act as agent for the sale of any of the following rights (for which there is no collective licensing scheme) and the Author so agrees, the Publisher shall pay 90% of the net proceeds to the Author:

First serial rights, TV and radio dramatization, film and dramatic rights and electronic publishing rights. Any legal fees or professional charges incurred directly in connection with the sale of film or video rights will be charged against the gross income.

(c) Reprographic rights shall be granted by the Author and the Publisher to the ALCS and PLS respectively. Any other income from reprography not covered by collective licensing schemes shall be handled by the Publisher and the income divided 50:50. In relation to editions of the work published by the Publisher, these provisions shall survive the termination of the contract.

(d) Public Lending Right and all other rights not specified above shall be reserved by the Author.

19 *Author's Copies*

The Author shall receive on publication 12 free copies of the work and shall have the right to purchase further copies for personal use at 50% discount if payment accompanies the order or 35% discount if credit is to be extended to the Author or if the amount is to be charged to the Author's royalty account. Should a paperback edition be issued under Clause 11(a), the Author shall be entitled to 20 free copies. If the work has more than one author, the free copies shall be divided accordingly.

20 *Accounts*

(a) The Publisher shall make up accounts at six-monthly intervals and shall render such accounts and pay all moneys due to the Author within three months thereof.

(b) Any sum of £100 or more due to the Author in respect

of sub-licensed rights shall be paid to the Author within one month of receipt provided the advance has been earned.

(c) Each statement of account shall contain at least as much information as is given in the Model Royalty Statement agreed between the Publishers Association and the Society of Authors. In particular print runs and opening and closing stock figures will be stated. The Publisher shall supply copies of statements received from sub-licensees, unless such statements contain information about other authors in which case information will be provided on request.

(d) The Author or his/her authorised representative shall have the right upon written request to examine the Publisher's books of account (during normal working hours) in so far as they relate to the work, which examination shall be at the cost of the Author unless errors exceeding £50 shall be found to his/her disadvantage in which case the costs shall be paid by the Publisher.

21 *Actions for Infringement*

(a) It is agreed that if the Publisher considers that the copyright or any one or more of the Publisher's exclusive licences in the work has been infringed and the Author after receiving written notice of such infringement from the Publisher refuses or neglects to take adequate proceedings in respect of the infringement, the Publisher shall be at liberty to take such steps as the Publisher considers necessary for dealing with the matter and if the Publisher desires to take proceedings shall be entitled to do so in the joint names of the Publisher and the Author upon giving the Author a sufficient and reasonable security to indemnify the Author against any liability for costs and in this event any sum received by way of damages shall belong to the Publisher. If the Author is willing to take proceedings and the Publisher desires to be joined with him/her as a party thereto and agrees to share the costs then if any sum is recovered by way of damages and costs such sum shall be applied in payment of the costs incurred and the balance shall be divided between the Author and the Publisher in proportion to the Author's and the Publisher's shares of the costs.

(b) The provisions of this clause are intended only to apply in the case of an infringement of the copyright in the work affecting the interest in the same granted to the Publisher under the contract.

22 *Revised Editions*
If the Publisher and the Author agree that the work should be revised in order to bring it up to date, the Author, subject if reasonable to the payment of an agreed advance, will undertake such revision. In the event of the Author being unable by reason of death or otherwise to edit or revise the work, the Publisher may procure some other person to edit or revise the work and, subject to the approval of the Author or his/her executors, such approval not to be unreasonably withheld, may deduct the expense thereof from all moneys payable to the Author under the contract.

23 *Assignment*
The Publisher shall not assign the rights granted to the Publisher in the contract or the benefit thereof without the Author's written consent (such consent not to be unreasonably withheld).

24 *Termination*
(a) If the Publisher fails to fulfil or comply with any of the provisions of the contract within one month after notification from the Author of such failure or if the Publisher goes into liquidation (except a voluntary liquidation for the purpose of reconstruction) or has a Receiver appointed, the contract shall automatically terminate and all rights shall revert to the Author.
(b) When all editions of the work published by the Publisher are out of print the Author may give notice in writing inviting the Publisher to decide whether or not to reprint or reissue the work. Within 6 weeks the Publisher shall notify the Author in writing:
(i) that the Publisher does not intend to reprint or reissue the work, in which case the contract shall terminate automatically and all rights granted shall revert to the Author when stocks are exhausted or within 6 months whichever shall be the sooner; or
(ii) that the Publisher will reprint or reissue the work, in which case the Publisher shall do so within 8 months of receiving the notice from the Author; or
(iii) that the Publisher wishes to issue a revised edition, in which case the provision of Clause 22 will apply.
The work shall be considered out of print if fewer than

50 copies of the hardback and 150 copies of the paperback remain in stock (as to which the Publisher will inform the Author). The rights shall not revert until any money owed by the Author to the Publisher has been paid.

(c) Termination under (a) or (b) shall be without prejudice to:

    (i)   any sub-licences properly granted by the Publisher during the currency of the contract, and

    (ii)   any income due to the Publisher if termination is under (b) above, and

    (iii)   any claims which the Author may have for moneys due at the time of such termination, and

    (iv)   any claims which the Author may have against the Publisher in respect of breaches by the Publisher of the terms of the contract.

25 *Advertisements*

The Publisher shall not insert within the work or on its cover or dust jacket any advertisement other than for its own works without the Author's consent and shall use its best endeavours to see that a similar condition is contained in all sub-licences.

26 *First Refusal*

The Publisher may ask the Author for first refusal on his/her next work, in which case the Publisher will make any offer for the next work within 3 weeks of receipt of a synopsis or within 6 weeks of receipt of a complete typescript as the case may be.

27 *Moral Rights*

The Publisher shall observe the moral rights conferred on the Author under the Copyright, Designs and Patents Act 1988. The Author's right of paternity shall be "asserted" in the manner recommended by the Society of Authors and the Writers' Guild.

28 *Disputes*

Any dispute arising in connection with the contract, which shall be interpreted in accordance with the law of England, shall be referred to a single agreed referee on terms to be agreed between the parties informally. Failing agreement about the appointment of a suitable referee the matter shall become subject to arbitration in accordance with the Arbitration Act 1950 or any amending or substituted statute for the time being in force.

COMMENTS ON THE MINIMUM TERMS AGREEMENT

A Scope of the Agreement

Note that only those authors who are members of the Society of Authors or the Writers' Guild are entitled to the full benefits of the MTA from the present list of publisher-signatories (another good reason for joining).

Note also that the terms of the MTA do not apply to highly illustrated books, to books involving three or more participants in the royalties, or to technical books, manuals and works of reference. It is unfortunately impossible here to advise the authors of such excluded books on the terms which they should try to obtain, but of course the main principles of the MTA should still apply. If in doubt about what is or is not an acceptable contract for such works and if you do not have an agent, you can if you are a member seek advice from the Society of Authors or from the Writers' Guild.

C Terms of the Contract between the Author and the Publisher

Clause 1 The Typescript and its Delivery
Sub-clause (a). Note the requirement that the typescript "shall be professionally competent". Legally it might be extremely difficult to define exactly what "professionally competent" means, but the spirit of the words is crystal clear, and if all authors abided by them, there would be far fewer publishers wanting to include a provision for "acceptance" of the typescript in their contracts. In its *Quick Guide to Publishing Contracts*, the Society of Authors points out that if a clause is included which makes the publisher's obligation to publish subject to his acceptance of the book (and this is sometimes merely implied in that part of the advance is "payable on delivery and acceptance"), then the agreement has been turned into nothing more than a promise to consider the book for publication, and it strongly advises all authors not to accept an "acceptance" clause. It argues that publishers have the means, by insisting on receiving detailed synopses and specimen chapters before commissioning a book, of satisfying themselves that the author is competent to write it. However, believe it or not,

not all the rogues are on the publishing side of the book business, and every publisher can cite cases in which, despite the most careful precautions and sometimes involving well-established authors, books turned out to be unpublishable when delivered. Publishers really do feel that they need some protection against the incompetent or unscrupulous author.

As a matter of fact, the majority of books which have an acceptance clause do eventually get published by the house whose contract it is. And publishers who use the acceptance loophole to protect themselves from the obligation to publish a poor book may argue that if the acceptance clause is to go they will have to take fewer risks in commissioning books, and that will mean fewer commissions. However, even if that is the end result, authors should do their utmost to resist the inclusion of an acceptance clause.

It may also be worth clarifying with the publisher the meaning of the words "ready for press". I know of a publisher who has argued that a book is not ready for press, and therefore the part of the advance due on delivery is not payable, until his copy editor has completed work on the typescript.

Sub-clause (b). If a publisher does ask for alterations, authors should listen carefully. Publishers don't usually suggest changes for changes' sake, but in the hope of improving the book and its sales. Accept the criticisms if you can, but, as I have said elsewhere, fight for your work if you really believe that you are right. Most good editors recognize that there is a point beyond which the competent author should not be pushed – it is his book, not the editor's, and he should be allowed the final say.

Incidentally, if you happen to be a bestselling author, do try not to get so grand that your publishers don't dare to make editorial comments in case you take umbrage and take yourself off to another publisher. However good you may be, an informed comment from an experienced editor is always worth having, and you should let your publisher know that you welcome constructive criticism and will not be upset by it.

Clause 2 Warranty and Indemnity
Publishers' contracts vary widely in the scope of their warranty and indemnity clauses, which are often a cause of

strife. When signing an agreement, beware especially of any mention of the author's responsibility to indemnify the publisher against expenses resulting from any *threat* of action, even if it is not pursued. There is really no reason why the innocent author should be expected to bear such costs, which should surely be part of the publisher's normal expenses.

Do take the warranty clause seriously. If you have the slightest fear that your book might infringe another author's copyright or might be libellous or might contain some other unlawful material, tell your publisher about it. He may refuse to publish such material, which will be a blow for you but less of a blow than a subsequent expensive legal action against you; he may set your fears at rest, or help you to clear any obstacles in the way of publication; he may be willing to assume any risks himself, in which case make sure that you obtain from him a statement to the effect that he accepts full responsibility for the publication of the material about which you have warned him.

Sub-clause (i). The warranty "that the work has not previously been published in volume form elsewhere" would clearly not apply in some cases (if your book had appeared first in the United States, for instance), but this would be a simple matter to clarify with the publisher.

Clause 3 Copyright Fees and Index
This clause is one of the minor triumphs of the MTA. Many publishers in the past and still today would baulk at paying all the author's expenses in respect of copyright fees, except perhaps by increasing the amount of the advance, which, unless part of it remained unearned, meant that the author was still paying the whole sum. Others would not go beyond sharing the costs. Different authors and different books will have different needs, and obviously there is room for negotiation. It is very important that a firm agreement should be reached between the author and his publisher on this subject, and it is advisable to have a separate document (a letter is adequate) setting out the arrangement in full and unambiguous detail, so that neither party is in doubt of where they stand.

Clause 4 Licence and Review
This is undoubtedly the most controversial clause in the MTA, and not all those who have signed an agreement with

the Society of Authors and the Writers' Guild have accepted its inclusion in full. Hardcover publishers have been in the habit of buying rights for the full term of copyright. No one ever thought of working in any other way until the Society and the Guild began to argue that this is a restriction of an author's freedom, pointing to the fact that hardcover publishers normally grant sub-licences for a limited period only, and what is sauce for the goose should be sauce for the gander too. Why do publishers restrict the licence period when they sell subsidiary rights? So that at the end of the period they can either get the rights back, and perhaps sell them elsewhere, or renew the licence, if the sub-licensee has been doing an effective job, in either case possibly obtaining better or more appropriate terms. Circumstances change, and the terms of an agreement which were fair and reasonable when it was signed ten or twenty years ago may now seem very unfavourable. Authors should be able to renegotiate their agreements with publishers after a reasonable period. Publishers of course fear that if the licence period is limited (and a ten-year period would be even more desirable from the author's point of view than the twenty years specified in this clause, and may yet become the norm for licence periods), not only might an ungrateful author at the end of that time take himself elsewhere while his book was still selling well, but an unscrupulous rival publisher might tempt the author away with outrageously better terms. Both things could happen, but the more enlightened publishers have realized that they have little to fear if they treat their authors well (i.e. as partners) and do a good job with their books.

Clause 5   The Publisher's Undertaking to Publish
The commitment from the publisher to publish the book within a reasonable time after delivery of the typescript is an essential part of an agreement. It is of course subject to negotiation if there are legitimate factors which will delay the book's appearance, but in the event of late publication, or indeed non-publication, due solely to the publisher's dilatory attitude, the penalty of having to pay the balance of the advance should concentrate his mind wonderfully, not to mention the fact that the author may be able, if the firm publication date in the contract is not adhered to, to cancel the agreement if he so wishes.

Clause 6 Production

The whole of this clause marks a great step forward in author/publisher relationships. Not so many years ago it was unheard of for an author to be consulted over catalogue copy, jacket design and the like, publishers kept the size of their print runs as the darkest of secrets, and quite ruthless copy editing could be carried out without the author's consent. It was little wonder that many authors felt that they were being treated by publishers as second-class citizens. Fortunately, and largely as a result of the MTA and the efforts of the Society and the Guild, attitudes are improving. However, there are still some unenlightened publishers around, so if you are offered a contract which does not include provisions similar to those in this clause, fight for them.

Clause 7 Approval of Final Edited Script and Correction of Proofs

Sub-clause (b). The more usual percentage of the composition cost above which the author pays for proof corrections is 10%. Prudent authors avoid any likelihood of a charge by making sure that the final typescript is as perfect as possible. In the case of topical books, where changes may have to be made at the last minute, special arrangements regarding alterations in proof should be made with the publisher.

Clause 9 Advance

Sub-clause (a). Publishers who do not subscribe to the MTA appear to pluck a figure out of the air when deciding what advance to offer. In fact, the figure is usually based on an expectation of earnings from the first printing, but the amount offered may be a small proportion of that sum. Setting out a firm percentage would seem to be a fairer method of calculation. However, while some authors may feel that it is important to obtain as large an advance as possible (in order to ensure that the publisher puts in the maximum effort), others may believe that it is more important to fight for respectable royalties than to worry about the advance – and I think that in most cases they are right.

Clause 10 Hardback Royalties
Sub-clause (a). Royalties offered to authors in the past have varied enormously, some not rising from a basic rate at all, others jumping at widely differing points. Some publishers may argue that to increase royalties after 2,500 copies and again after 5,000 copies will mean that the retail price of books will have to be increased, with a possible reduction in sales. Not true. If the home sales have reached, 2,500 copies, let alone 5,000, the publisher should be making enough money to afford the extra royalty percentage on additional sales without having to increase the retail price. On the other hand, publishers do have increasing difficulty in publishing books economically if the initial print run is likely to be small, and it seems reasonable that they should have the freedom to negotiate less favourable terms in such cases.

Suggestions are made from time to time that royalties on home sales should be based on publishers' receipts, as with export sales, rather than on the published price of the book. There are considerable advantages to the publisher in this method, since it simplifies his royalty accounting and allows him freedom to change the discounts at which he sells to certain of his customers in the hope of achieving larger sales (his argument here being that royalties based on the published price sometimes prevent him from selling books at high discounts – and he goes on to point out that although the author might earn less per copy from books sold at a high discount, at least the books would be sold, which otherwise they might not have been). Authors are right to be wary of such proposals, since even if extra sales do result they are likely to be much worse off. The only way that the system would not damage your earnings is if the percentage of the net receipts payable to the author is substantially higher than normal royalty rates. If the publisher's average discount is 45% (and it may well be higher than that), then an 18.2% royalty on net receipts would be necessary to be the equivalent of a 10% royalty on the published price. Incidentally, if the enemies of the Net Book Agreement succeed in getting it abolished, publishers could well argue that a royalty based on net receipts would be much fairer than one based on a recommended retail price which no one was observing. They would still have to offer a high percentage for it to be acceptable.

Sub-clause (c). You may wonder why a lower royalty should be payable on a reprint when the origination costs of the book should have been absorbed by the first printing. The simple fact is that the start-up costs of a reprint are so high that unless the print quantity can be raised above 1,500 copies the whole thing may not be economically viable, especially if burdened with a 12½% or 15% royalty.

Clause 11 Paperbacks
Sub-clause (b). For many years it was standard practice for the publisher of the hardcover edition to retain 50% of all royalties received on a sub-licensed paperback edition, and his arguments for doing so were that if he had not published the book in the first place, the paperback edition would not have appeared; that he had invested money in building up the author's reputation, publicizing his book, securing reviews for it, and so on, and that if he had not done so the paperback publisher would not have been interested in it; that the growth of paperback sales had eradicated his ability to sell cheap editions of the hardcover book, making his initial risk that much greater; and that without a substantial share of the paperback income, he would be unable to publish many new books, and especially new fiction. However, thanks largely to the concerted efforts of authors' agents, the concept of the invariable 50:50 split has virtually disappeared. Hardcover publishers have survived, and new books have continued to be published – even fiction – although it is certainly true that new novelists find it difficult to get into print unless their books have a potential paperback sale. A 60:40 split, rising to 70:30 should be regarded as standard.

Clause 12 Returns
The Society of Authors, the Writers' Guild and agents used to be implacably opposed to the idea of royalties being withheld against returns. However, the realities of life have to be faced, one of them being that the practice of sending out books on a "sale or return" basis has become the norm. Books sent out on sale or return are entered in the publisher's ledgers as sales, but may be nothing of the sort, since the booksellers and wholesalers have the right to return for credit any copies that they have not sold after a given period. Suppose a publisher has sent out 1,000 copies

of a book on sale or return; they are counted as full sales and royalties on them paid to the author at the end of the accounting period; but in the subsequent royalty period, 250 of those books are returned for credit, which means that the author has been paid royalties on books which have not been sold. This will not matter if a further 250 firm sales are made, because the returns can be offset against them, but often no more sales are made. Equally, it would not matter if authors were prepared to refund any royalties paid on books which turned out not to have been sold, but in practice, although the advance is supposed to be the only non-returnable payment made to an author, publishers have long come to accept that any moneys paid to authors are lost to them for ever. The problem of returns has been even more acute with paperbacks – not surprisingly, perhaps, since they are so dependent on exposure for their sales. So the principle of a reserve against returns has become generally accepted. You may well find that your own publisher will ask for more than the 10% reserve for hardcover editions and the 20% for paperbacks specified in this version of the MTA.

Clause 13 Remainders and Surplus Stock
Sub-clause (a). Another minor triumph of those in the Society and the Guild who have negotiated the MTA is to have persuaded its signatories to pay a royalty on remainders. Publishers have resisted doing so for years, arguing that they should not have to add to their losses (remainders are usually sold to remainder merchants at less than the cost of manufacture). Since the books eventually reach the public at prices considerably above the cost of manufacture, it seems only fair that the authors should get something out of the deals, however little.

Sub-clause (c). Many agreements in the past contained clauses which did not allow publishers to remainder or pulp books until two years after publication. Publishers argued that a large number of the books concerned can be seen to be unmitigated disasters within six months of publication, and that they should be free to dispose of them then. Twelve months seems a reasonable compromise.

Clause 15 Bookclub Rights
Sub-clause (a). 10% of the publisher's receipts is a much fairer share than a small royalty (usually 3¾%) on the

bookclub's price to its members, which is often specified in publishers' agreements.

Clauses 16, 17 and 18   United States Rights, Translation Rights, Subsidiary Rights
The author's shares in these three clauses are at least equal to and in many cases higher than it has been the normal practice of hardcover publishers to pay. It is perhaps worth pointing out that many of the rights covered by the clauses may or may not be granted to the publisher. Agents will normally retain US and Translation rights, together with those rights in Clause 18(a) which have been asterisked, and all the rights listed in Clause 18(b). However, if the author has no agent, he may well be advised to allow the publisher to handle such rights for him, since the publisher will probably be better equipped than he is himself to deal with them. Reprographic rights should always be granted as specified in Clause 18(c), and Public Lending Right should always be retained by the author.

Clause 19   Author's Copies
Standard practice has been for the author to receive six copies only of a hardcover book. The provision of six extra free copies is one of the least costly things a publisher can do to keep his author happy. It is good too to see that the discounts at which the author may buy additional copies have been specified, which is preferable to covering the matter with such phrases as "at best trade terms" or "at the lowest trade price". Although the clause refers to the purchase of copies "for personal use", and does not include the wording "not for resale", it is always advisable if you want to sell copies of your book to obtain the publisher's permission to do so.

Clause 20   Accounts
Sub-clause (a). It is to be hoped that at some future date the computerization of royalty accounts will allow authors to receive royalty statements at quarterly or even monthly intervals, rather than six-monthly.
 Sub-clause (b). The retention of sub-licence income, after the advance has been earned, until the next royalty statement is sent out has rankled with authors for years. It is good to see more and more publishers agreeing to a clause

such as this.

Sub-clause (c). Publishers have always been reluctant to divulge information about print runs and have often failed to pass on any details from sub-licences. Moreover, in many cases their royalty statements have been very difficult to understand, and therefore frequently impossible to check for accuracy. The use of a form such as the Model Royalty Statement (see p.248) will solve some of these problems, but may not protect you from inaccurate accounts, which, as the Society of Authors recently discovered, may, as a result of human error, emanate from the most respectable of publishing houses. If you have serious doubts about the accuracy of your royalty statements, most contracts have a clause similar to sub-clause (d) which you can invoke. But do make sure that you have real grounds for suspicion – the simple belief that your publisher should have sold more copies of your book than he says he has is not really enough (even if it is just as good as any of those titles on the bestseller lists).

Clause 22 Revised Editions
Not all publishers will offer a new advance when asking an author to produce a revised edition of his book. Perhaps they should, but the author who is not given extra money for the job can console himself with the hope that the book will earn far more royalties in its new form than it would have done if left to become totally outdated.

Clause 23 Assignment
Some publishers include in the preamble to their agreements some such wording as "Rows & Crowne Ltd. (hereinafter called 'the Publishers' which expression shall where the context admits include the Publishers' executors, administrators and assigns or successors in business as the case may be)". Clause 23 is much to be preferred from the author's point of view, since it will prevent the publisher from assigning his rights in the author's work to a third party to whom the author might have reasonable objections.

Clause 24 Termination
A well drawn termination clause is very necessary in all agreements between an author and a publisher. It should be specific regarding the reversion of rights to the author, but

so many different circumstances can attach to a book that it is advisable, if termination takes place, to insist that the publisher should state in writing exactly what the situation is (for example, which rights have reverted to the author, which sub-licences are still in existence and how moneys accruing from them will be dealt with, and so on).

Clause 25 Advertisements

In the years before the Second World War it was not unusual for publishers to sell space in their books to advertisers, and it would never surprise me if they were driven to do so again in order to subsidize their publications. It is to be hoped that any such advertisements would be in good taste and not such as to upset the readers of the book or to damage the author's reputation, in which case the author would surely not withhold his consent unreasonably.

Clause 26 First Refusal

The majority of publishers' contracts carry an option clause. If it specifies in detail the terms on which the publisher will be able to buy the author's next book or uses a phrase like "on the same terms and conditions as the present agreement", it is legally binding, and few, if any, authors should accept such a clause, which could be very damaging to their interests. The option "on terms to be agreed" is far less dangerous, since it probably commits the author only to the submission of his next work for the publisher's consideration and leaves him free to refuse the publisher's offer if he wishes to do so. Even better is wording such as is used in Clause 26. In practice, publishers should *earn* the right to see the author's next book. If they have behaved well towards him, and especially if they have made a success of his book, the author will probably wish to continue to be published by the same firm, and in such a case the publisher is indeed entitled to expect loyalty from his author. Some authors change publishers with alarming regularity, and one may wonder whether the reasons for their dissatisfaction lie more with themselves than with their publishers. If you are unhappy with your publisher and seek a change, you could easily jump out of the frying pan into the fire, so do be sure first that your complaints against your present publisher are justified and not likely to arise again when you go to another house. No publisher is perfect, and authors should realize that. No author is perfect, either.

Clause 27 Moral Rights
This has become an essential clause in any contract since the passage of the Copyright, Designs and Patents Act of 1988. See p.206.

The clauses in the MTA on which I have not commented are those which seem to me to be both self-explanatory and largely uncontroversial. There are, however, two further points which I should mention.

The first is the lower royalties offered for children's books. This may appear to be a cheese-paring exercise on the publisher's part, but remember that children's books are normally priced very much more cheaply than adult books, and since they are usually illustrated, the publisher also has to find room in his costings for a payment to the artist.

The second point is that phrase which occurs quite frequently, "such consent not to be unreasonably withheld". When your publisher allows you to comment on the proposed jacket design for your book, or asks you to agree to change the title of your book, try to remember that he has a certain expertise which you should respect. If you are really unhappy, let him know the strength of your feelings, but don't have a row about something quite trivial. In fact, don't have a row about anything – more will be achieved by not being unreasonable.

I now turn to more general comments.

Let me remind you that the publishers who have signed MTAs have done so only after negotiating acceptable changes with the Society and the Guild. If you are a member of either the Society or the Guild and are offered a contract by a publisher who is a signatory, it may therefore not conform exactly to the version printed in this book. In any case, every book is different, and every publishing agreement is equally likely to be different in some respects.

Do remember that this is a *Minimum* Terms Agreement. It may be possible to improve on it in some instances. The other side of the coin is that, in certain circumstances the publisher may wish, despite being a signatory, to offer you slightly less good terms (though of course he will have to present convincing arguments before he can expect you to accept.) Any agreement must to some extent be a matter of give and take, but before either side can give and take there must be full understanding of what any changes may entail and why they are necessary. This is one of the reasons why it is so important to establish a personal relationship with your publisher, and if possible a friendship, and just as the publisher should try to understand the author's problems and something of his circumstances, so the author should try to understand something about the publisher's work and the difficulties he encounters. It is worth remembering that although your publishing house is a business, it is staffed by human beings, and human behaviour can often be extremely mysterious. The more you understand of what makes your publisher tick, the easier it will be to reach agreement with him. If each side understands the other, there can be no argument, but only a discussion, and it is much easier to settle a discussion than an argument.

Although the contract between an author and a publisher is a legal document, meaning, if it is well drawn, exactly what it says, and is usually intended to last the length of the licence it covers without amendment, it is not sacrosanct, either at the time it is drawn up or later. The fact that a publisher has sent you a contract does not mean that its details cannot be altered before you sign; even if you and your publisher do not see eye to eye over some specific point, it may be possible to make an arrangement whereby the matter can be reviewed in, say, three years' time, and this is a course of action which is particularly advisable in such cases as when the publisher is asking to change from paying royalties on the published price to paying a percentage of his net receipts – you might decide to see how it works before committing yourself to it for ever. Equally, all kinds of problems or changing circumstances may occur during the writing or during the publication process or long after the book has come out which demand an alteration to the agreement, and there is no reason why you cannot negotiate changes. You can't just tear the contract up, unless you have real cause, but you may be able to amend some of its terms.

You might think, by the way, that if you have an agent you have no need to worry about the MTA, because your agent will see that you get the most beneficial agreement possible. Well, yes – a good agent will certainly do a good job and take care of all sorts of little things which you yourself might overlook. Moreover, he will usually use his own tried and tested form of contract. But it's rather interesting that a well-known agent is on record to the effect that the MTA is a better agreement than those drawn up by many agents.

In general the effect of the MTA is both to protect authors' rights and to increase their rewards. Even the most curmudgeonly of publishers might admit, if his arm were twisted, that it was about time that authors were given a little more say in the publication of their books, and he would probably also agree that, except in the case of major bestsellers, few authors are at present well paid. So why haven't more publishers signed the MTA? I suspect that many of them feel that authors, once given the right of consultation, will pester them constantly and make their lives hell (recognizing, perhaps, that the authors might be paying them back in their own coin). More importantly, and I think this is probably the main sticking point, many publishers genuinely believe that they cannot afford the additional financial benefits which the MTA gives to authors. Pleading poverty, they will point out that the only place where the extra money can be found is from the pockets of the book-buying public. Warming to the subject, they will say that publishing is a gambling business and that even the giants in the industry make comparatively small profits; in fact, they will tell you, most publishers could make a larger profit by closing down their businesses and simply investing the capital in stocks and shares or with a bank. So the extra money will have to come in the end from the people who buy books, and higher prices will mean fewer sales. And that in turn will mean fewer new books published, and not-yet-established authors will find it even more difficult to get into print.

We have heard all that before, and it has ceased to impress. The books published by those firms which have signed the MTA are not noticeably higher in price than those from non-signatory houses, and the signatories (with one possible exception, and there are other reasons for its problems) are flourishing.

Supposing that your publisher does not accept the MTA, and puts to you a contract which seems, to say the least, to be ungenerous, is there anything you can do? Unless you are a well-established author you have very little clout, but you can try a bit of gentle haggling. You will have to make your own judgement about how far the haggling can go, for if you press too hard the publisher may simply withdraw his offer and go to an author who will accept his terms without argument. But if he has gone as far as the preparation of a contract he is likely to be fairly deeply committed to your book, and he may have a little latitude on the terms. The publisher's position is often like that of someone attending an auction – he will have worked out in advance how much he can spend (or what terms he can offer on your book), but he will not necessarily bid the full amount at first. If the article being auctioned can be obtained (or your book signed up) for less than his planned maximum expenditure, he will have done well, but if he has to pay the full amount, he won't necessarily be very unhappy about it.

Your problem with an agreement may not be concerned with terms so much as simply to understand what it means. Often the legal jargon is less than clear to the lay mind, and if, as sometimes happens, the publisher's form of agreement has been poorly drafted, it may not even make sense, or you may find that it contains two totally contradictory clauses. If you have no agent and are not a member of the Society of Authors or the Writers' Guild, what can you do? The first option open to you is simply to ask the publisher to explain everything that you do not understand. If you are still in doubt, another possible answer is to consult other authors, and if you do not know any, then you might consider joining your nearest Writers' Circle, which will almost certainly include among its members some published authors with experience of publisher's contracts. Or you can consult a solicitor, but with the greatest respect to the worthy firm which deals with the sale of your house, and the making of your Will, and other such everyday affairs, it is worth going to a firm which specializes in literary matters, for your family solicitor may well be as baffled as you by some of the technicalities of the business, and may cause irritation on all sides by quibbling over matters which truly are standard and acceptable practice in the book trade and missing the points that really should be queried. Of course, you may be lucky and have a family solicitor who already knows something about publisher's contracts, or who is clever enough to work it all out accurately for himself or diligent enough to find out from others what he does not know. The point is, of course, that you should only pay for advice if you are sure that it is going to be good and informed advice, and the cheapest way of making certain might be to join the Society of Authors or the Writers' Guild.

One last important point needs to be made. Much needed through a Minimum Terms Agreement has been, and just though its provisions are, there are many cases where an author should not feel guilty at accepting lesser terms. It is a matter for your personal judgement according to circumstances; your publisher may be particularly generous in certain respects and mean in others, and you may decide that the good more than makes up for the bad; or you may be aware that the market for your writing is so competitive that you are lucky to be published at all; or you may take the view that your publisher is so active on your behalf that it is better to receive a smaller royalty or share of subsidiary moneys from him than it would be to get better terms from another publisher who would sell far fewer copies or rights; or you might be content with a lower advance, knowing that it means that royalties are payable all the sooner. Those who have struggled to get the Minimum Terms Agreement accepted would undoubtedly say that every time you accept any terms which are worse than those laid down, you are letting down every other author and allowing the continued exploitation of authors. That is true. Authors should stick together, because it is the only way of improving their lot safely and permanently. Nevertheless, it is impossible to legislate for the circumstances surrounding the publication of every book and the relationship between every author and his publisher. You have to make your own reasonable judgement.

7

Author/Publisher Relationships

Relationships between authors and publishers are often difficult, and have been so over a long period of time. The "Literature" section of *The Frank Muir Book* is full of anecdotes to illustrate this, and the list of authors who have written nastily about their publishers is lengthy and distinguished. Why there should be so much acrimony is hard to explain – not all publishers are ruthless exploiters of their authors – but I think it stems partly from the fact that very few authors understand much about publishing (which is why this book has been written), and even more from the other fact that, as a group, authors are trusting, not to say gullible.

It really is rather extraordinary. An author who would take the greatest care in the selection of any other person who is to perform some service for him, will happily place all his trust in a publisher of whom he knows nothing, and will expect him to behave with perfect efficiency, despite the fact that nothing else in this modern world, alas, can be relied upon to do so. We are all used to the trains that run late or are suddenly cancelled, to the garages which fail to cure the faults in our cars, to the builders who take longer than promised to complete their work and then charge more than their estimates. We grumble and pretend to be surprised when it happens, but we have been expecting the worst all along. Most authors, however, seem rarely to be prepared for any kind of inefficiency on the part of their publishers, and when inevitably it happens, they are not only shocked and angry, but usually very ready to believe that the publisher has done whatever it is deliberately, in a kind of personal attack. No wonder that the breaking point in the relationship can easily be reached.

The faults are certainly not all on one side. Publishers as a whole – even those editors who work closely with their authors – tend to have very little idea of what goes on in a writer's head. Even members of the general public are aware that the author's life is a lonely one – they have frequently been told so – and some of them are even prepared to believe the nonsense, put about mostly by the more pretentious authors, that it is "agony" to write; editors, on the other hand, are often willing to accept, as the general public certainly does not, that writing, though not "agony", is hard and intensive work, and they are aware of the loneliness. But that is often as far as their understanding goes. They recognize that almost all authors are totally incapable of judging their own work, but do they see just how *personal* to an author his book is, and therefore how hurtful even the most well-deserved criticism can be? Do they understand that almost all authors feel wretchedly insecure, terrified of rejection or of not maintaining the standard both in writing and in sales of their previous work? And finally publishers would probably be shocked to learn that an astonishingly large number of authors see them (not, perhaps, as individuals, but certainly as a group) as The Enemy.

The reasons why authors feel this enmity are not hard to find. Authors have believed for years that publishers exploit them – they see their editor living in his luxury house, driving his company car, lunching daily at the company's expense in exclusive restaurants, and they contrast all this with their own starving-in-a-garret-type lives. It may be an unfair view, but it has been compounded for years by the condescending attitude which many publishers have adopted, or appeared to adopt, towards their authors – an attitude which seems to be saying, "think yourself jolly lucky that I have graciously decided to publish your book", "yes, do come and talk about it, but don't expect me to give you my full attention, because I'm a Very Busy Man", "don't expect me to explain what is going on, because publishing is a Mystery, the secrets of which are revealed only to the privileged people who work in it" and "for heaven's sake don't bother me with your trivial little problems, especially if they are totally unfounded complaints about the way my firm operates". A very unfair and exaggerated view, perhaps, but it is widespread, and one which even the most rational of authors will have held at times. It is undoubtedly partly responsible for the campaign which produced the MTA. In case any publisher is still in doubt, let me say what the MTA is about: it is not just about authors getting a slightly bigger slice of the financial cake, it is not just about authors being consulted about the publication of their books, it is not even just about the recognition that authors are essentially partners with their publishers – it is all those things, but it is also about authors not being patronized, not being condescended to, being treated as human beings, with respect.

Even if a publisher is not condescending and accepts the spirit of the MTA, whether he has signed it or not, there will still probably be problems in his relationships with his authors, and the problems will almost certainly be exacerbated by a failure to communicate – strange in a business so concerned with words. It is usually the publisher's fault. In all the years that I dealt with authors I found them to be almost always understanding and co-operative when I took the time and trouble to explain what was happening. At one stage of my publishing career, when I joined a large company as Editorial Director, I promised myself that I would write regularly to all my authors to give them the latest news on their books – where we had got to in production, what luck we were having with subsidiary sales and so on. It never got done, alas, because there was just too much pressure of other work. And that reminds me to say, by the way, that you should not try to interpret the silence of your publisher as being significant or meaningful. No news is good news doesn't necessarily apply – nor does the reverse. It may be just that he's jolly busy.

Despite failures in communication, there is no reason why publishers and authors should not be friends, especially since they are both basically devoted to the same cause, providing that, as in most human relationships, there is a certain amount of give and take on both sides. The most difficult thing for an author to understand is that his publisher is also concerned with other books and other authors, and that his own book may be one among, say, three hundred that the publisher is working on during the year – it is one three-hundredth part of his year; the most difficult thing for the publisher to remember is that the book represents many months or years of work by the author, and that it is at the moment almost his entire world.

If your publisher is not as friendly towards you as you would like, you may be justified in feeling that he is, at the least, discourteous. But do remember that friendship is two-sided, and make sure that you yourself are not the cause of his attitude. If he likes your work, then he should be interested in you as a person, and in your plans and your problems, but you should equally be prepared to try to understand him and his difficulties, and to enter your relationship with him in neither too aggressive nor too defensive an attitude. If he seems to brush aside some of the things that worry you, be aware that in his eyes almost all authors have the same kind of problems: they are almost always all discontented with their sales, disappointed that their books have not been widely advertised, feel that their publishers are not making sufficient effort for them; they all get afflicted from time to time with writer's block (when the new book has got stuck, and the author despairs of making progress with it); they are all short of money (who isn't? But authors seem to live from hand to mouth, and that applies to bestselling writers too, many of whom are up to their eyes in debt to the Inland Revenue and have ex-wives to support and an expensive life-style which they refuse to abandon); and they all believe the grass is greener on the other side of the fence. The publisher has heard the same stories before and will hear them many times again; if he is a good friend, he will try not to let that show, but if he does, do try to understand, and realize too that it may not only be other authors and books which make him seem preoccupied, but also the problems of finance and administration and all the other troubles of business life which may be on his mind.

There may be more than a slight lack of friendliness in the relationship, and you may, for instance, suspect that your publisher is deliberately avoiding you if every time you phone him you are told, "I'm sorry, he's in a meeting." Of course, it may be true. Publishing used to be an autocratic business with decisions taken by the head of the house or by those individuals to whom he had delegated authority; nowadays, it is more often a question of management by committee. Your publisher may indeed be in a meeting, to discuss editorial matters, or jackets, or publicity and promotion, or sales plans, or budgets and five-year plans, or staff salaries – not to mention the possibility that he may be talking to another author on his list.

On the other hand he may indeed be trying to avoid speaking to you. Why? Possibly because he has not yet come to a decision about your book, or is having difficulty in persuading others in the firm to share his enthusiasm for it, and is reluctant to tell you yet again that you have to be patient. Or perhaps he has decided to reject your book, and being a coward, prefers to tell you so by letter rather than on the phone. Or perhaps he has forgotten until your name is mentioned that he promised to look into some matter, and not having done so, is unwilling to expose his failing. All very unsatisfactory from your point of view, but also very human, and perhaps if you try very hard you can find enough of the divine in yourself to forgive.

However, if you are constantly told that he is in a meeting, and if additionally he never rings back as promised, and fails to answer your letters, and in general takes considerable pains to avoid any contact with you, then either he is a rotten publisher (and probably has a rotten secretary into the bargain), or perhaps you are a Difficult Author. Difficult Authors are those who, among other unpleasant habits, phone daily (usually to say that their book is unavailable in such-and-such a bookshop), expect to be received immediately if they call unannounced at the publisher's offices, ask their publishers to undertake any of their research which they find too difficult, believe that it is their publisher's responsibility to make their hotel and theatre bookings, instruct the publisher to obtain books for them from other publishers at trade discount, rewrite their books at proof stage, demand that the part of the advance due on publication should be paid now, although the book is not even half way to completion, and, above all, argue over everything from a changed comma to the date chosen for publication, and who constantly complain. If you are that sort of author (and, believe me, there are plenty of them around), be prepared for your publisher not only to be permanently in a meeting, but also to reject your next book, since he may well have decided that life is too short to make it worth putting up with you.

"I recognize myself as a Difficult Author," you may bravely say, "at least in part. But the reason that I argue and complain constantly is simply that he is both rude and extremely inefficient." Well, maybe you're right. I just hope that you tried being reasonable first. In all walks of life, some people find it easy to be aggrieved, and if you are one of them, then however justified your complaints may be, your attitude may only succeed in antagonizing the one person who might be able to put right whatever is wrong, and increasing harassment on your part may simply lead to greater inefficiency on his.

On the other hand, there are of course times when authors should complain, and forcefully too. Publishers are undoubtedly often incompetent, and when they make stupid mistakes or fall down on promises, you are entitled to be angry. Why should publishers so often be inefficient? There are, I think, several factors to be considered. First of all, there is the fact that every book is different, with its own peculiarities and problems, and there is no universal formula which can be applied to the solution of its individual difficulties; this clearly multiplies the opportunities for human error. Secondly, publishing is a comparatively complex business, involving in all its processes not only a large number of people and many skills, but also quite a few sub-contractors, who are not totally subject to the publisher's control; this again makes publishing particularly vulnerable to Sod's Law ("if anything can go wrong, it will"). Thirdly, the expansion of the trade has led to additional inefficiency – and this point needs more detailed explanation.

For many reasons, publishers' output has increased dramatically compared with the numbers of books published, for example, between the two World Wars. It is partly due to the "explosion" in reading which took place during the Second World War, the higher educational standards now existing, which means that more of the population can read, and the techniques of production and marketing which have made books not only readily available but, in the case of paperbacks, much more acceptable to the general public than they were (many people still find a bookshop a somewhat forbidding place and would not think of going into one, whereas there is nothing frightening about the paperbacks in the newsagent's racks). But economic factors have also played a major role in increasing the numbers of books published. Many years ago, sweated labour in the printing and binding trade and low-paid but dedicated workers in publishers' offices made it possible to make a profit with small numbers of even comparatively unsuccessful books, and a large profit on bestsellers, especially at a time when Britannia not only ruled the waves, which was important in terms of overseas markets, but also sat firmly on inflation. Moreover, it was economically viable to print only a small quantity of sheets of a book, and to bind only part of that print run (further small quantities could be bound quickly and still cheaply), and if a small reprint were needed, it could be obtained almost overnight; if the print quantity failed to sell out, the publisher had a "safety net" in his ability to produce a "cheap edition" (which was usually the original edition with a new reduced price) and to go on reducing the price until he had sold out, but still making a profit. Nowadays, however, workers in most industries are reasonably paid, inflation goes on galloping upwards, and book prices (despite public belief that they are unreasonably high) have never rocketed sufficiently to keep pace with the financial pressure imposed on the business by the outside world. For hardcover publishers, although it is still possible to make big profits on a bestseller, the safety nets for less successful books have disappeared, part production (binding only some of the printed sheets) being economically impossible and the market for cheap editions having been taken over by paperbacks. The readiest answer to this problem has been to publish more. (And this is when, incidentally, books turn into product, which inevitably means a diminution of the human relations which should count for so much in the publication of a book.) You may make less profit on each title, but hope that greater volume will maintain your firm's overall results. This often leads in turn to the rule of the accountants (not, as I have already indicated, the most efficient way to run the business), and it will also mean an increase in staff.

Now, at the risk of labelling myself an old grouch (which I probably am), who believes the country is going to the dogs (which it probably is), I will fearlessly express the view that, despite better education for all, the general standard of work produced by junior staff in offices these days is often very much lower than it used to be before the Second World War. Many people seem more concerned about job definitions and whether or not they get luncheon vouchers, than with the quality of their work. They don't *care*. And those who do care, especially in the higher ranks, are frequently so overburdened that to their despair they cannot give the attention to detail that they would like. This is where the inefficiency comes from, this is why computers are fed with inaccurate information, this is where muddle is swept under the carpet – and this is where the sack may bring a charge of wrongful dismissal. And of course it is all a situation which lends itself admirably to the application of the Peter Principle of eventual promotion beyond the level of the employee's capability.

Whatever the cause of a publisher's incompetence, if you do encounter it you should certainly complain. But do make sure that it really is incompetence and that it really is the publisher's fault – the absence of your book from bookshops, for instance, to take a very common cause of complaint, may not be due to the publisher's failure, whatever the booksellers says (see p.187). It is worth listening to both sides of the story, so try to present your grievances in a reasoned and reasonable manner, and listen to what your publisher has to say in his defence, and be prepared to apologize if you are wrong. You are fully entitled to a hearing and courtesy from him, and he is entitled to the same from you. Incidentally, if you receive no satisfaction from your contact in the publisher's office, there is nothing to stop you going over his head (assuming that he has a superior), but again make sure that your complaint is justified.

In his biography of the founder of Penguin Books, *Allen Lane: King Penguin*, Jack Morpurgo wrote:

> Publishers are convinced that most authors are ignorant of the techniques of the publishing craft and suspect, often with justification, that many sustain this ignorance by a lofty conviction that comprehending the technical and commercial practicalities of publishing is somehow beneath their dignity and an unnecessary distraction from their prime duty, to set words, ideas or narrative to paper. Understanding the means whereby their handsomely embellished paper is to be reproduced, promoted, distributed and made profitable – to both publisher and author – is a process to which they need only give such thought as is, in their opinion, unavoidable.

Pretty harsh, you may think, but the point is that our world has increasingly become one for professionals, and even if you are no more than a part-time writer, you need to be professional in your approach, which means, among other things, learning about writing and learning something about publishing.

You also need to be professional in your approach if you become involved in a serious dispute with your publisher. Seek expert advice at an early stage and give your adviser as fair an account of what has happened as you can manage, trying not to conceal from him anything which may be to your disadvantage – he will give better advice if he knows the whole story. When you have taken advice, or even if you have not, try to write to the publisher in moderate terms – nothing is every achieved by abuse. If you have correspondence with an adviser, do not show it to the publisher. Think before taking any too hasty action.

So far in this chapter, I have referred to the author/publisher relationship, but in most cases it is more likely to be specifically an editor with whom the author has contact. A publisher's editor is not merely someone who purchases books from authors and then passes them on to be turned into printed and bound books. He is in most cases truly an editor, in the sense that he becomes involved with the actual writing of the book, perhaps as a critic who asks the author to make changes, perhaps even altering the book himself. Not many authors manage to produce a perfect book, and a good partnership between author and editor will often result in a worthwhile improvement.

Few authors are capable of viewing their own books dispassionately, and even wives or husbands, whom so many writers credit in their acknowledgements as being their most severe critics, are often themselves too close to the work in question to see it plainly. A good editor is distant enough to see the book clearly and will tell the author what, if anything, he thinks is wrong with it, but at the same time is sufficiently in tune with the author's intentions to do so sympathetically. During the whole of my publishing career, I followed the principle that in such matters the author's decision would be final – it was his book, not mine, and if he disagreed with me, then, unless my criticisms were so fundamental that I felt I could not publish the book unless he made the changes I wanted, I would give way to him. But this bargain on my part was contingent on the author's willingness to listen most carefully to my comments, to discuss them with me, and to be prepared to admit that I might possibly occasionally be right. I tried always to make it clear to the author that I was not interested in making alterations simply to justify my own existence or to boost my ego so that I could boast afterwards that the book was partly my work, but simply to make it a better book.

Of course, some editors adopt a much more dictatorial approach, and many authors complain of their arrogance. It is very difficult to deal with this kind of high-handedness, especially when it comes from someone covering up his own uncertainties with an aggressive insistence on being right. Unless you can swallow this, your only course is to go over the editor's head to his director, in the hope of getting a more sympathetic hearing. If that fails, or is impossible because the arrogant editor is himself the highest authority in the firm, then you have to choose between withdrawing your book and repaying any moneys you have received on account of it, or of letting it go through in a form which you dislike, and to do that will probably sour your whole relationship with the company and make you dissatisfied with every aspect of the publication. There is not a great deal to be gained in having an ongoing angry relationship with your publisher, and it is much better to make a clean break. But of course it is easy to say that, and not necessarily easy to find another home for the book. And that thought brings me back to the plea that you should listen carefully to the publisher's comments, and discuss them without heat, and accept his wishes if you can bring yourself to do so. Even arrogant editors are right sometimes.

If you stay with your publisher despite the disagreements, it may be possible to save yourself some of the trouble on your next book by discussing the project in much greater detail with your editor before you begin to write.

American editors tend to be far more insistent on working on an author's typescript than most of their British counterparts, and some authors find their editing very disturbing. It is difficult to know what to advise without going into specific cases, but in general the usual rules apply: plead your case as strongly as you can, having first considered seriously whether the editor might possibly be right, and if you get nowhere, then decide whether you want to stand on your dignity and cancel the contract, or whether you will cry about the alterations all the way to the bank.

It is worth repeating that an editor's intentions are always to improve the book, but that he does have more than one duty. An author once asked me whose interests came first with me – his, or my own and those of my firm. It's a difficult question to answer in black and white terms. Publishers understand very well that they are middlemen, dependent for their livelihood on authors, and in general they try to be sympathetic to writers and their work and problems. But if there is a conflict between their duty to an individual author and to themselves and their firm, they will naturally opt for the latter, and it would be foolish to pretend otherwise. We are all selfish to some degree or other.

Of course, no alterations of any kind should be made to a book without the author's consent. Should you find at proof stage that your book has been altered, and that is the first you know of it, you are entitled to object most strongly. Even if the book is the better for the alterations, you can accept the changes with gratitude, but still protest firmly that you should have been consulted. There is a vital principle here – that the author's work must not be altered without his permission – and all publishing agreements should carry a provision similar to that contained in Clause 6(c) of the Minimum Terms Agreement (see p.120). Most good publishers respect that principle, though they may feel it should not be necessary to check with the author such minor changes as the correction of typing errors, spelling and punctuation, or alterations made to bring the typescript into line with the publisher's house style (which is usually concerned with questions like the use of capital letters, whether quotation marks should be double or single, consistency in layout and the numbering of sub-paragraphs, and so on). They may also correct obvious mistakes which appear to be unintentional on the author's part and which are probably due simply to a lapse of memory. But any of the minor alterations mentioned can infuriate the author rather than please him, and it is my belief that the publisher should discuss the matter with the author before he begins any copy-editing work on the typescript, and should come to some agreement about the extent to which the author feels he should be consulted about changes. If your publisher does not raise the matter with you, ask him about it.

A question that arises frequently is the stage at which an author and an editor should work together on a book. If you have sent in a completed typescript, there is obviously no problem, but if you are an established author on the list or are lucky enough to have been commissioned, it is a very good idea to discuss the book as fully as possible with the editor before you begin to write, and perhaps to show him the early pages as you produce them. Some authors hate to talk about their books in advance, and cannot bear to let anyone read a word of the book until it is finished, but if you can let your editor see the first few chapters, it may save a lot of grief at a later stage, because he may be able to point out where, if at all, you are going wrong, or how you might improve the book. He may also of course tell you things which irritate because you are already aware of them and intend to do something about them at a later stage in the writing, but you will simply have to put up with that. One thing to try to avoid is sending your book in chapter by chapter for criticism; since your editor will have read dozens of books between your sending in one chapter and the next, he will probably have to refresh his memory by re-reading the first chapter when the second comes in, and so on, which he may well find extremely time-consuming and boring. If you are going to show your work in parts, send a good chunk at a time.

If you want him to be, your editor will probably be willing to be adviser, sounding-board, critic, comforter, shoulder-to-weep-on, inspirer and friend, despite the fact that the most kind-hearted, considerate, undemanding human beings do sometimes undergo a transformation when they become authors – not necessarily in their everyday lives, but in anything which concerns their book – turning into egotistical, thoughtless, ruthless monsters – often pleasant monsters, for most of the time, but monsters nevertheless. (Perhaps you think this sounds unduly critical of authors. "What about publishers?" you may ask. "Aren't they sometimes monsters, too?" Yes, of course, they are – indeed, many authors would say that to find a publisher who is not a monster is to find an exception to the rule.)

If you become friendly with your editor, beware – and the closer the relationship, the more need there is to take care – that you do not become the kind of monster who imposes on him. He does have a life of his own to lead, and when he is out of the office may be very glad to get away from books (even yours) for a while. So phone him at the office rather than in his home if you want to talk business. And he will appreciate a word of thanks now and then.

It always seems to me a pity when authors who live a long way away from their publishers never get to meet their editors. A face-to-face encounter is so much more helpful in establishing a relationship than any amount of telephone calls and letters. The cost of travel is such that it may be prohibitive for some authors to visit their publisher even once (though of course the expense can be claimed against tax), but if you have any opportunity to visit the city or town where your publisher works, do make a point of calling to see him, writing first to make an appointment.

How do certain editors get involved with this or that book and its author? The process is often somewhat haphazard for new authors. If the book is clearly of considerable importance, the editor who works on it will almost certainly be one of some seniority and experience. In a general publishing house most editors have certain special interests, so if your book falls into a specialist category, it will go to the editor responsible for that part of the list. Other books or authors may have been "discovered" by an editor, who will probably continue to deal with the books concerned.

Many books may be allocated to an editor much more arbitrarily: "This looks like an easy one – you'd better take it, Miss Junior"; "Who wants to read this book on Prostitution in Edwardian London? It looks as though it's very popular in approach, so we won't send it out for an expert reading until we've looked at it in house. Who wants it? No one? Then you'd better glance at it, Mr Senior – you've got less of a load this week than the rest of us." Naturally, this kind of process results sometimes in books being handled by rather unsuitable editors, but the editorial director of the firm will usually keep an eye on things and give the book to someone else if it is obvious that the original editor cannot cope.

Can an editor judge a book which is not to his personal taste or on a subject in which he is not expert? The answer is that good editors can at least recognize the merits or failings of such a book. They cannot always eliminate their personal feelings, but they try to be representative of the average reader and to judge by the standards of the genre. So you may well find someone whose literary idols are of the calibre of, say, Proust working happily and successfully as an editor of pulp fiction (well, perhaps that is an exaggeration, though the principle holds good). As for expertise, as I have said elsewhere, most publishers use expert outside readers to check the accuracy and validity of specialist books, but the experienced editor will at least be able to judge something of the quality of the book and its likely appeal to the public. He may also, in the course of working on a number of such books, have become, if not an expert, at least very knowledgeable on the subject himself.

Should you stay with the same publisher all the time? It may be of course that you are proflic and/or versatile, in which case you may need more than one publisher. Too many new books by one author appearing on the same publisher's list can, unless you are particularly well known, sometimes hamper each other's sales. Such authors sometimes use pseudonyms and often have a number of publishers. In the same way, if you write on a variety of subjects, you may need to be published by different houses specializing in your different kinds of book. It will be as well to keep your first publisher ("Publisher A") informed of your other plans, and indeed you may wish to make it clear that he will continue to have first offer of all your books in the genre with which he first began to publish you, whereas your books of a different kind will be offered to Publisher B, and a third variety to Publisher C. If A, B and C all know where they stand in relation to you and your work, there should be no cause for dissension.

For the average author, however, unless you are very dissatisfied with your publisher, and if he wants to go on publishing your books and you continue to write the kind of thing which is suited to his list, then undoubtedly you should stay with him. Publishers sometimes feel that some authors show far too little loyalty. The publisher may have brought out the first few books by an author, including perhaps work which was not of his finest, gradually building up his reputation, and then the writer produces an important book which finally establishes his success and goes off to another publisher who reaps the benefit of the first publisher's work and faith. Usually, the author is wooed and flattered by the second publisher, who offers him not only a larger advance than he has been used to getting, but promises him more promotion and publicity, full consultation, etc, etc. Beware of such offers. Many an author has moved to a different firm only to find that he is really no better off than he was before. On the other hand, if for some reason you are unhappy with your present publisher and you get an offer from elsewhere, of course it is right to move, but I think it is fair first to discuss the matter with your present publisher, presenting him frankly with your reasons for discontent and offering him the opportunity of putting right whatever it is that is wrong. If he cannot do so, then he will probably not resist your parting too strongly, for no good publisher can work to the best advantage with an author who is unhappy on his list. But again, you may find that you have exactly the same problems with your new publisher – or that they have become even worse.

Of course it is much more shattering when it happens the other way round, as it were. Here you are, having had half a dozen books published by the same house, and suddenly they turn round and say that they do not want to go ahead with your new book, which they may even admit is just as good as its predecessors. The only explanation you will probably get is that the market for your kind of book has declined to a point where it is no longer economical to publish your work. Sorry, and all that. The eminent literary agent, George Greenfield, revealed something which your publisher may be reluctant to tell you (partly because it may reflect on his abilities, and partly because it is not very flattering to you) when he suggested in his memoirs, *Scribblers for Bread*, that an author who had published six novels without steadily increasing his sales was unlikely to achieve better results with subsequent books, and that his publisher would probably therefore not wish to continue bringing out his books. Of course it does not always apply, but if it fits your case, then your only hope is to find another publisher who has perhaps a more vigorous sales approach, or lower overheads, or some other quality or set of circumstances which will allow him to take you on in the belief that he will do better for you than your previous publisher did. But it is going to be quite difficult to find such a publisher, because his optimism and enthusiasm for your work will wither away once he discovers the details of your past publishing history. Not a very hopeful outlook. Your other alternative is to write a better book – a suggestion which may not be a lot of help, I'm afraid. Another idea, which might be more rewarding, is to change to a different genre, and perhaps adopt a pseudonym into the bargain. It would mean beginning your career as an author all over again, as it were, but it might make success attainable for you.

Do study the market. It could be that the reason why your

publisher has declined your new book is simply that it is of a kind which has gone out of fashion. You may feel, with some justificiation, that your publisher should tell you if this is so, and indeed should suggest something else that you might write which would be more acceptable. Yes, perhaps he should. Nevertheless, it's something that you can and should find out for yourself. All writers should read voraciously, partly to study how other writers achieve their effects and to learn from them, but partly, including new books in their diet, to see what the latest trends are. I would also like to suggest that you read *widely*. Naturally, you will choose principally the kind of writing which interests you most, and is probably the kind that you write yourself – incidentally, I find it astonishing that some authors will boast that they never read the work of other writers in their own field, which seems a remarkably ostrich-like attitude – but if you read nothing but biography, or poetry, or fiction, or travel, or whatever it may be, you are missing a great deal.

In speaking of author/publisher relationships, I have emphasized the role of the editor. He is likely to be the person in your publishing house with whom you deal most of the time, but it is as well to meet others who will be working on your book if you can – among them I would single out the sales director, whoever is in charge of publicity and promotion, the production manager, the person who prepares the royalty statements, and the subsidiary rights manager. It does no harm either to make contact with the managing director. Indeed, the more people in your publishing house that you know, the better, and you should feel free to contact any of them direct if you have a query or complaint which falls within their sphere. Since, however, your editor is your prime colleague, it is worth making a point of keeping him informed about any dealings you may have with other members of the staff. It saves the wires from getting crossed.

All of us who write dream from time to time if not of great financial rewards from our writing, then at least of gaining the kind of recognition and respect for our work which will mean that we never again have trouble in finding a publisher and that the firm concerned will give us first-class attention at all times. (If we were in that position, we should probably have the great financial rewards too!) Well, we can dream. But being realistic, admitting that we are not in the great bestseller class or recognized as one of the twentieth century's greater geniuses, we should plant our feet firmly on the earth. No sensible author turns to writing full time unless he is assured of being able to support himself and his family, probably with an income from another source. No sensible author builds his hopes too high, nor expects everything he writes to reach the same level of success. No sensible author forgets that it is not only the quality of his work which determines how well his book does, but remembers that there are other factors, such as fashion, booms and recessions, and luck. No sensible author neglects to understand that his relationship with his publisher, however friendly it may be, is basically a business one, liable to change, or that his publisher and the rest of the staff are human and liable to make mistakes. No sensible author believes that everyone is perfect – even himself.

8
Reasons for Complaint

The publisher has lost my material

Given the fact that several hundred typescripts flow in and out of most publishers' offices every year, it is surprising perhaps that they do not get lost more often, especially since publishing tends to be a rather untidy business. If your publisher has lost your typescript, not too much harm will have been done, though it may be very inconvenient, provided you still have a copy; if he has any sense of responsibility he will pay for the typescript to be replaced or at least contribute part of the cost, despite the fact that his form letter or card acknowledging receipt of your book in his offices probably states somewhere that he will accept no liability for the loss or damage of your material while it is in his possession. If you have a word processor, it is to be hoped that your work is still on disc and it will be an easy matter to run off another copy (though I still think the publisher should pay both for the paper and something for the inconvenience caused). The loss or damage of other materials, such as illustrations, transparencies, or perhaps goods of some value which are to be photographed in order to illustrate the book, is a much more serious matter, since they may be extremely costly or impossible to replace. The only solution is to take out an insurance against loss or damage. Your publisher may be prepared to pay the premium himself, but it is more likely that at best he will agree to share it. The rights and wrongs of the matter are hard to define, depending on circumstances in each case, but broadly speaking, if you are sending the material to the publisher unsolicited, the responsibility for insuring valuables is yours, but if he has asked for them, he should, in my view, be prepared at least to share in the cost. It is important that he should understand what sum could be considered reasonable compensation for loss or damage, and you should leave him in no doubt about that.

My publisher has kept me waiting for three months for a verdict on my latest book. It is not as though I am a beginner – I am an established author on his list

I think you are right to complain, and I don't think you should hesitate to let your editor know that you think the delay unreasonable. If you don't get a satisfactory answer, then you ought to take the complaint to the top person in the firm. Incidentally, although you are probably right to believe that as an established author you are entitled to faster treatment than a beginner, no one should have to wait three months for a decision – at least, not without a reasonable explanation being given.

My book has been rejected for political reasons

If you write a book which takes a political position, or attacks or defends certain views, the book may be rejected solely because of the contents rather than because of any lack of quality. Some naïve authors believe that publishers have no right to turn down such a book and that it is their duty to publish any book which is adequately written and saleable. Not true. Publishers still, fortunately, have freedom of personal choice. If you receive such a rejection it suggests that you have not done your market research. Choose another publisher whose existing list demonstrates that he will be sympathetic to your views.

I put up an idea to a publisher who rejected it and then immediately commissioned another author to write a book on the very same subject

This is very unfortunate, especially since ideas are not protected by copyright, and in any case it would be difficult to prove that the publisher has in fact pinched the one you suggested to him. The use of someone's idea without his permission is certainly unethical and most reputable publishers would try to avoid doing anything of the kind, but

editors cannot always control their subconscious minds and
may use your idea without any intention of stealing it,
believing that it is original to themselves. "A likely story,"
you may say, but I can only repeat that good publishers do not
do naughty things deliberately. Active editors conceive a
large number of books, and get their inspiration from hundreds of different sources. Very occasionally, recognizing
that a concept stems from a book they have rejected, they
may even suggest that you should have some payment for the
idea though they want someone else to write the book. You
may not like that either, but it is difficult to know what to do
about it.

**My hardcover publisher also controls a paperback company
and other concerns which utilize other subsidiary rights. He
wants me to give him all those rights, though I would prefer to
let the competition have an opportunity to bid for them**

Many authors would think you lucky to have this automatic
interest in the subsidiary rights of your book. If you are
really unhappy about it, you should take your book
elsewhere – there are still several publishers who do not
have any direct link with the users of subsidiary rights. In
today's difficult conditions, however, you should probably
accept the offer with gratitude, especially since your
publisher will probably be willing for you to receive the full
royalty on the paperback edition, whereas if you go to an
independent hardcover house you may be expected to share
the sums which come from the paperback publisher. One of
the reasons, incidentally, that the integrated publisher can
afford to give you a full paperback royalty is that he will
probably set the book in type only once, using the same type
for both editions of the book, and may make other similar
savings, by using the same jacket, for instance, co-ordinating
the publicity plans, and so on.

   If your main worry is that you might expect a much larger
advance to be paid if the book were sent out to all the
paperback houses for them to make their bids, you might try
asking the publisher whether he would accept a "topping
right" arrangement, which would mean that he had to
submit the subsidiary rights to other concerns but would
have the right to buy them himself by topping, or improving
on, the best bids he received.

My contract bears no resemblance to the Minimum Terms Agreement

Unless your book is one of the categories specifically excluded (see p.129), the contract should not be all that different from the MTA, even if the publisher is one of the diehards who has refused to accept its terms. If you have not yet signed the agreement, don't despair – there is time to alter it, and you should be able to get some improvements made. Your best course is to join the Society of Authors or the Writers' Guild, either of which organizations will tell you which changes are those for which you should fight hard, and give you good advice about how to put your arguments to the publisher. See also p.143.

My publisher has put an unrealistic delivery date in my contract

Alter it, then – telling the publisher that you are doing so, and why. Most publishers will be reasonable about such matters. The exception is a book which will be published to coincide with some event – an anniversary, for example – in which case you may have to meet the required delivery date, or give up the whole idea of writing the book if it is impossible for you to finish it in time. Whatever the problem, discuss it with the publisher, and together you may find a way round it.

My publisher wants to break my contract

The fundamental points in a publishing contract are that the author has written or agrees to write a book and the publisher undertakes to publish it. There are many side issues which may give rise to breach of contract by either party, but they are insignificant in comparison with a decision by the publisher not to proceed with the publication of the author's book.

The publisher may have many possible reasons for such a decision. Sometimes it results from recognizable failings on the part of the author: perhaps the completed work differs substantially from the synopsis on which it was commissioned, or is much shorter or longer than the extent specified in the contract, or the author has been so tardy in delivering it that the market for it no longer exists, or the book is clearly libellous. All is not necessarily lost in such situations, since the author may be able to avert disaster by doing extra work on the book. If he refuses to do so, or is incapable of making the necessary alterations, he cannot be too indignant when the publisher wants to cancel the contract.

The agreement may be rather more arbitrarily rescinded on the basis of failings on the author's part, either real or imaginary, if there is an "acceptance" clause in the contract (see p.129), and it is often very difficult to argue in such cases since the publisher's personal taste and views are involved.

Contracts are sometimes broken because the editor who bought the book has left the firm, and there is no longer anyone working there to care about the book. Everyone in a publishing firm should care about the book. Everyone in a publishing firm should care about all the books on the list, of course, but in practice many books get published because a single person in the publishing concern is enthusiastic about them, and if that person leaves, those who take over his work may be indifferent or even hostile to those books. "I always thought we were crazy to buy that," the new editor may say. "We only took it on because So-and-so was so enthusiastic about it." To find not only that your friendly editor has left the firm, but that as a result your publishing contract is about to be cancelled, will be a terrible blow, but a book published without any enthusiasm will do little good for anyone concerned. Of course, this kind of thing does not happen with all the books on the list of an editor who leaves his firm, many of which will have wide support from the rest of the staff, and it tends to occur with books which would be borderline prospects in any publishing house. In the United States editors seem to move regularly from one publishing concern to another, but they frequently take their authors with them, so this question does not arise to the same extent.

Publishing is a business which requires a considerable amount of capital investment; consequently it always tends to have cash-flow problems and to suffer when interest rates are high. A recession during the 1980s had a major effect upon British publishers: a number went out of business, and almost all those who survived did so by reducing, as far as they could, their output of books which they considered to be doubtful propositions in terms of profitability. There was nothing wrong with the typescripts, except that perhaps they were expensive to produce and therefore showed a small profit margin, or simply that they represented too much of a gamble. The cancellation of contracts became commonplace, even for authors who had been published for many years with apparent success. Those publishing houses which came through this period of crisis did so in most cases in a leaner, tougher condition, and are (or so one hopes) in a better state to withstand any future difficulties of this kind. However, even in the slightly calmer waters through which they hope to sail in the 1990s, publishing firms do collapse. There is usually a large publishing house, or a conglomerate, which is eager to gobble up such failed businesses, but not all such giants are beneficent; they may not be willing to take over all the small firm's contracts, or there may be redundancies in the editorial department with the result that you may lose your book's champion. So contract cancellation is always a possibility – and not a particularly remote one, either.

What is the author's course of action when it happens? The first thing is to ask whether anything can be done to alter the publisher's decisions, such as cutting the book to make it more economic, or making changes designed to widen its appeal. The publisher's reply is likely to be a firm rejection of all recipes for salvaging the book, since he has probably already considered all such possibilities and decided that nothing will solve his basic problem, which is that he just won't sell sufficient copies.

You are now left with two alternatives. The first is to insist, possibly with the threat of legal action, that the publisher comply with the terms of the contract and that he publish the book despite his wish not to do so. In general, this is not a course to be recommended. It may be extremely difficult if not impossible to force him to publish, and even if you succeed in so doing, he will almost certainly print a minimum quantity of the book and make only sufficient effort at selling it to recoup his costs. Your relationship with him is bound to be a bitter one, and few authors who force their publishers to bring out a book can really rejoice in the results.

The second alternative is to be compensated by the publisher. Some publishers will try to persuade you that their liability should be limited to any part of the advance already paid, but this is hardly fair, and you should ask for at least the balance of the advance and preferably a total sum (including any advance already paid) equal to the amount that the book might have been expected to earn for you. It helps if your contract specified the number of copies which the publisher intended to print, since that will give a good indication of what the sales might have been. Each case is different, and it is impossible to lay down any hard and fast rules about the amount of compensatory payments which is fair, but if you have no agent, you should seek professional advice, either from the Society of Authors or the Writers' Guild, if you are a member, or from a good solicitor.

In any case, as well as compensation, or even if the fault lies with you and you are not entitled to any money, you should obtain from the defaulting publisher an official letter confirming that all rights in the book in question have reverted to you and that the publisher has no further claim on you whatsoever. You should also ensure that all material supplied by you to the publisher is returned. You are then free to place the book with another house if you can. Some publishers, when paying compensation, ask that the sums paid shall be returned by the author if he places the book elsewhere, arguing that he should not be paid twice for the same work. Circumstances vary, of course, and there may be some cases where it would be reasonable to agree to return part of the compensation money if you sell the book to another publisher, but in general you should never return the whole amount – at the very least, the rejection will have lost you time and caused you considerable anguish, for both of which you deserve compensation. The publisher may argue that he has already lost money on the book and that you should be prepared to share in the loss. "You have had part of the advance, and you have got all the rights back – surely that should be sufficient." It is a time to be tough. You are more likely to suffer from the non-publication than he is, and in any case he is quite likely to have already calculated the cancellation in terms of paying you a full compensation, and is now simply trying to save his firm a little money. You can't blame him for that, but you don't have to accept the terms he first offers without trying to better the deal from your point of view.

In extreme cases – if, for instance, the firm is already bankrupt – you may not get any compensation, though you should still make a claim, and also be sure that you get your rights back. However sympathetic you feel towards the publisher in his dire straits and the members of his staff who are now without jobs, you have to put your own interests first.

At the same time, I put in my usual plea for a little consideration on your part. It costs nothing for you to start off with a conciliatory attitude. Remember that the person giving you the bad news is unlikely to be enjoying the situation, which has not been devised simply to annoy you; the easier you make it for him, the easier in the end it may be for you to negotiate a settlement to your satisfaction. Litigation is to be avoided if possible.

One other circumstance might be mentioned: the occasion when your publisher declines to publish your book on the grounds that it "will do your reputation no good", but, on the assumption that it will be up to your usual standard, wishes to publish your next book. To put the book on one side may mean that you have lost the work of a year or more, and you have the choice of listening to what he says and allowing yourself to be convinced, or of parting company with him and taking the book to another publisher. Before you choose the latter course, you will have to decide whether or not your relationship with your present publisher is worth preserving, despite the disappointment he has just handed you, and that may depend not only on the way he has treated you in the past, but also on whether you believe he could possibly be right about this book. It would be in order to ask to see the reports on it, and, if you are not fully convinced, perhaps to ask that the book should be sent to another reader, without comment from the publisher and perhaps without your name on the typescript, in order to get one more independent judgement, though of course such a report would have to be very favourable to outweigh the previous adverse comments. If you already have a contract for the book, and it is decided that the publisher will not go ahead, you are back in the situation described above when some sort of compensation is in order. Just be sure that your own assessment of the work is right, and his wrong, before you finally burn your boats.

My publisher wants to reduce my royalties

As an alternative to cancelling the contract, some publishers ask authors to take a lower royalty or a smaller share of subsidiary rights than those specified in the contract. The author in this situation is facing a nasty dilemma: if he refused to accept the lower rates, the publisher may cancel the contract altogether; if he accepts them, he is not only going to make less money than he should, but may also be setting an unhappy precedent, not only for himself, but for other authors too. Publishers are often quite adept at using the ploy, "Mr Scribble and Mr Copperplate have already agreed to similar terms," to make you feel that you are being unreasonable if you demur.

I should make it clear that I am not referring to the clause in many agreements which says that the royalty payable on "small reprints shall be at the minimum rate". In that case, the publisher is only asking to revert to the royalty rate payable on the first sales of the book, even though sales have reached the level when higher rates come into force. No, I am talking here of what amounts to a re-negotiation of all the financial terms of the contract, so that, for instance, the basic starting royalty rate of 10% is to be reduced to 7½%.

The only answer is to find out all you can about the circumstances, including if possible details of the publisher's costing and expected profit, and then to make a judgement. If you insist on a full royalty, will he really either cancel the book or lose sales because its retail price will be too high? And supposing you agree to reduce your earnings, can you be sure that he is also suffering to some extent? Are you in a buyer's or a seller's market? When you have considered all the factors, you can make your mind up. If you decide to accept lower rates, at least make sure that you have it in writing that your agreement is not to be taken as a precedent.

Why are royalties so low? I have been told that, if the retail price is 100%, manufacturing costs amount to about 20%, the bookseller gets an average of 40%, and the publisher expects to take a gross profit of 30%. Why should the author be satisfied with a mere 10%?

I understand your point of view (the figures you give, incidentally, are pretty rough and ready, but let us accept them for the sake of argument). Now, if the author's royalty is to be increased (and I assume you are talking of at least doubling it), where is the extra money coming from? The bookseller will not take less than that average 40% discount, which he already says is insufficient for his survival, let alone prosperity. Out of his 30% the publisher has to pay for his overheads, which term covers the salaries of his staff (a major proportion), publicity and promotion, rent, rates, heating, lighting, telephone, postage, and so on, not to mention the fact that the Treasury will be taking its share in the form of taxes; the publisher also expects to make a net profit (and why not? – if a member of the general public can get a high rate of interest, tax-free, from investing money with a building society, why shouldn't a publisher expect a return on his investment, especially since he is in such a high-risk business?). So, I repeat, where is the extra money to come from? Let me ask another question: who pays the author his royalties? Answer: the publisher. Wrong. The publisher merely passes on a share of the money paid by the member of the public who buys the author's book. And it is that member of the public who will have to find the money to pay higher royalties. What is more, if the royalty is to be increased from 10% to, say, 20%, but leaving the publisher's gross profit at the same cash figure, that doesn't mean an increase in the retail price of the book of only 10%, but (because the bookseller's cut is based on the retail price) an increase of 25%, which is something that the bookbuyer might not be willing to stand.

Some authors do, of course, get more than 10%. They are usually the big names, whose books can be guaranteed to sell in very large quantities. The manufacturing price of such long-run books is lower as a percentage of the retail price, and the publisher will also take a smaller percentage (because his actual return in terms of cash will be satisfactorily large), so the higher royalty can be paid without passing the cost on to the book-buying public. Even if you are not in the bestseller class, if your book is reasonably successful you will probably move from the basic 10% to a higher royalty rate when your sales have reached a level specified in your agreement, and the rate will probably jump again when you have passed a second target figure.

One cost which I did not include in the publisher's overheads is that of unearned advances. You might be surprised to learn how many books do not earn anything near as much as the publisher paid out in the form of an advance. One publisher reports that this occurs so frequently that, if you include those unearned sums, he is paying authors what amounts to an average 17½% royalty. You may think that this simply indicates that he is not very good at working out what the advances should be, but it isn't as simple as that. So why does he so often pay a larger advance than he should? Because he is under pressure from agents and authors, because he always has competitors who may be even rasher than he is in calculating the size of an advance, because he is in an occupation for gamblers. I do not know of any publisher who never pays too large an advance to one of his authors, and many publishers would say that unearned advances are the rule rather than the exception. It's a pretty crazy business.

My editor has left and I don't know anyone at my publisher's now

Even if, supposing that your editor leaves your publisher, there is no question of cancelling your contract, you may be faced with the lesser but nevertheless worrying problem of not knowing who will be dealing with your book in future. When an editor, or any other member of the staff, leaves, his work is naturally passed over to a successor, or sometimes shared out between a number of people. Whoever has taken over responsibility for you and your book should write and introduce himself, and perhaps suggest a meeting so that you can get to know each other. Sometimes, however, it is not done – perhaps because, with the best of intentions, your new contact finds himself so overburdened with his new responsibilities that he just doesn't get around to writing to you, or perhaps because publishers are human and, as with any other group of men and women, include some who are lazy or inefficient or discourteous, or all three.

If after a while you have heard nothing except that your former editor has departed, write to the head of the department, if there is one, or to a director of the company, and ask to be put in touch with your new editor. You shouldn't have to do this, but it is better than just sitting at home waiting for a word which may never come. Then, when you have written or spoken on the phone, if your new editor makes no suggestions of a meeting, propose it yourself.

It may happen that when you meet your new editor, you do not get on with him – and we all meet people from time to time to whom we are not sympathetic. In this case I suggest that you write a tactful letter to his superior in the publishing house, asking if there is anyone else that you could deal with. If you make it clear that you accept that there may be faults on both sides, no one's feelings will be badly hurt, and a change may be possible. Of course, your new contact may now be the only editor in the firm, or perhaps is the Managing Director himself. Your only solution then is either to grin and bear it or to find another publisher.

My publisher has made editorial changes to my book

I hope you are referring to what might be termed fairly minor alterations – punctuation, spelling, the occasional change in phrasing. Publishers regularly make such changes in authors' typescripts before they are sent to the printer. Since extraordinarily large numbers of authors cannot spell, know little about punctuation, are frequently inconsistent and often inaccurate, the service that publishers provide in these respects is something to be grateful for. If you happen to be meticulous in such matters and indeed feel strongly about your commas and full stops, or if you are deliberately using a particularly kind of spelling for effect, or indeed are departing from the normal rules in any way, it is as well to discuss the matter at an early stage with your editor, and to put a note at the front of the typescript, addressed to both copy editor and printer, asking them to respect your intentions and not to alter your work.

In any case, unless the publisher's alterations are of the most minor kind and you have already given blanket permission for them to be made, you should be given the opportunity of seeing and approving the changes before the typescript goes to the printer.

If the editorial changes under discussion go beyond the scope of normal copy editing – in other words, if major alterations have been made to your work – or if you strongly disapprove of the changes, however minor they may be, particularly if the basic structure, or emphasis or spirit of the writing has been seriously tampered with, you should protest in the strongest possible terms, and you will be within your rights to insist on the reinstatement of your original version, even at proof stage. Nothing should be done to your typescript without your consent. But at the same time do be reasonable, listen to the copy editor's justification of what has been done, and if the changes improve the book, be ready to acknowledge the fact and to thank the person who carried them out.

I get no editorial help

It has long been said that British editors are over-reluctant to help their authors to improve their books (or perhaps incapable of doing so), whereas American editors go to the other extreme and often virtually rewrite books which had no need of such treatment. If your editor does not help you, it may be simply that he doesn't see anything wrong with the book (in which case it is either perfect as it stands, or more likely he is a less than perfect editor), or that he knows that something is wrong, but cannot really put his finger on what it is, or cannot clarify the problem sufficiently for you to understand it too; or it may be that he expects you, as the author, to have a more dispassionate view of your work than in fact you have, so that if he says, for instance, that it needs a bit of cutting, or that such and such a part needs strengthening, you will understand. If that is the problem, you can try asking him to explain in much greater detail. If he cannot do so, then once again you are faced with a less than perfect editor, and your only course is probably to change publishers if you can.

Of course, one other possible reason why you do not get editorial help is that you have demonstrated in the past that you really don't want it. With some of their authors, editors have to tread extremely delicately, knowing that the least hint of criticism will be greeted with anger, abuse, hysterics, the sulks, argument, or at very least will be totally ignored, despite the fact that the author begged for comments and advice. Criticism hurts, but it should always be listened to.

My editor, who doesn't seem to understand my book, has asked me to make major changes to it, of which I strongly disapprove

Oh, dear. This sounds as though it may easily develop into a pretty unhappy situation, because there's going to be an argument, and arguments have a habit of making the "love factor" (see p.65) disappear like magic. You obviously need to have a cards-on-the-table talk with your editor. When you do so, remember that he is entitled to his opinion, and that his aim is to enhance the book's chances of success. Listen carefully to what he has to say, and be ready to concede if he has valid points to make. At the same time, he must remember that it is, after all, *your* book and as its creator you are entitled to feel very strongly about how it should or should not appear. You must present your own point of view as firmly and clearly as you can, and do your best to convince him that you are right – but keep it friendly. If, at the end of the conversation, he still doesn't appear to understand the book and is still asking for these radical changes, you have two courses of action open to you: you can refuse to make the changes, or you can carry them out. If you choose the latter course, the argument is over. If you refuse to make the changes you may find that he collapses and accepts the book the way you want it to be; you must also be prepared, however, for him to stick to his guns and to say that he will not publish the book as it stands. So you then either start peddling it to other publishers, or you decide to be the one to collapse and make the changes.

The title of my book has been changed without my approval

Everyone agrees that a good title is extremely important, and the only problem is to decide what constitutes a good one. We can all recognize them after the event, but not always beforehand. The story has often been told of that great publisher Stanley Unwin consulting booksellers about a book which he was going to publish and which had already earned itself some reputation. Many advised him to change the title, saying that "expedition" was an old-fashioned word to use for a true adventure story, and that no one would be able to remember or pronounce the second word of the title. He refused to change it. The book was of course *The Kon-Tiki Expedition*.

As a general principle, it should go without saying that a title should not be changed without the author's approval, but in this business the old adage that two heads are better than one is often true, and if a publisher wants to change a book's title, and is prepared to explain sensibly his reasons for doing so, the author should be prepared to be convinced. If he is not, he may be able to force his publisher to use his original title, but no one is going to be very happy about it.

My proof corrections have not been followed

When your publisher sends you proofs to correct and you mark them up, using all the standard signs, making sure that all your corrections are totally unambiguous, it is very disappointing to find sometimes that in the finished book the corrections have not been made, or that new errors have occurred. By all means protest to your publisher if this happens, but unless the errors are of a very serious nature, it is unlikely that he will be able to do anything about it, at least until he reprints the book (if he does). Why are corrections ignored, and why do new errors appear? In both cases, usually as a result of carelessness on the part of the printers; the marked correction may not have been noticed (perhaps two pages of the proof were turned at once); as for the new errors, sometimes to correct a mistake a whole line or even a paragraph has to be re-keyed, and in this process it is possible that the original mistake will be corrected but that a new error will be made. This kind of error is likely to be less frequent with the use of computers. If you do suffer in this way, however, there is little you can do, except to hope that your publisher will use one of the better printers next time, and that the printer's staff will be among those who still take a pride in the quality of their work.

In times gone by, most printers demanded a very high standard from their compositors, and literal errors were rare; moreover, printers employed expert and often very erudite readers who would mark corrections and queries on the proofs before they were sent out to the author. Nowadays, alas, standards are much lower, and often the proofs are not read by the printer at all.

Another cause of complaint is when printing errors are not corrected in a reprint, despite the fact that the author has given the publisher a list of them. Why not? Inefficiency. What can you do about it? Little, except perhaps to find out beforehand if you can when your publisher is going to reprint the book again, and send the production manager a repeat list of the corrections in good time and ask him to ensure that they are carried out.

My publishers have deducted an enormous sum from my royalties, which they say is the cost of my proof corrections, although I didn't make all that many changes.

Publishing contracts usually contain a clause saying that the author must bear the costs of proof corrections, apart from printer's errors, by the amount by which those costs exceed 10% (or in the MTA 15%) of the cost of composition of the whole book. That *sounds* very generous. It *sounds* as though you could alter 10% of the book without incurring any charge. In fact, however, the cost of carrying out proof corrections is extremely high, and comparatively few changes can soon mount up to 10%, or even 15%, of the original composition cost. Moral: get your typescript to as near a perfect state as you can and don't start improving it at proof stage, unless it is absolutely essential to do so.

I must say that I think your publishers should have warned you, when they saw your corrected proofs, that you were likely to incur this "enormous" deduction. You might then have decided not to make all the changes you had originally marked. As it is, I doubt if you can do much about it except to be more circumspect when you read the proofs of your next book.

It is a terrible hassle to get the illustrations for my book, and permission to use them, to say nothing of being extremely expensive. Surely this should be the publisher's responsibility?

It seems to me that in most cases the obtaining of illustrations and of permission to use them should be the author's responsibility rather than the publisher's (and the same applies to quotations from other authors' writings, to an index, to any extraneous material which is not your own work). The question of who should pay for the necessary permissions is less clear-cut. The basic MTA suggests that the publisher should be responsible for the cost of permissions, or should contribute up to £250 towards them, but you may find that your publisher is less generous. However, when you discuss the point (preferably before the contract is signed) don't let yourself be bullied into taking responsibility for all these payments, and resist as firmly as possible if the publisher suggests increasing the advance to cover the extra costs. Whatever arrangements are agreed between you and the publisher, the whole matter should be decided before the contract is signed, and the details then incorporated in the agreement or in attached correspondence.

It is important, incidentally, to make sure if you are obtaining permission to reproduce material, whether it is illustrative or textual, that you get permission for the appropriate territories. Your publisher should make clear to you whether he requires clearance for world use or only for the British exclusive market and the Open market, and he will need to be specific about the territories concerned. These details can make a great difference to the fees.

I have masses of good illustrations available for my book, but my publisher refuses to use more than a few

There are three factors which may have come into play in this case. Firstly, it may have been a question of simple economics – adding more illustrations means adding to the production costs of the book, which would perhaps have resulted in a higher retail price than the publisher believed the book could stand. Secondly, some of the illustrations may not be suitable for reproduction – a faded old photograph may be all the more interesting because of its condition when you hold it in your hand, but when it is reproduced in a book its faint or blurred state makes it look of very poor quality. Thirdly, it may have been an editorial decision not to include certain illustrations – the editor may have felt that they were far less interesting than you believe them to be, especially, perhaps, if they are family photographs, which will probably mean much more to you than to the general public.

My publisher insists on using a professional indexer, for whose services I have to pay half the fee (a lot of money), although I am quite capable of preparing the index for my book myself

The preparation of an index is a skilled business, and the Society of Indexers insist on the highest standards from their members. If the book is a long and complex one, it is probably best to use a professional. It depends, however, on what potential readers of the book will want from the index, and if their requirements will be fairly simple, you may indeed be capable of preparing it yourself. Discuss it with your publisher. If you do provide it yourself, you may find that a professional indexer will make scathing remarks about the quality of the index in a review of the book. That happened to me once. Ah, well, you can't win 'em all, as they say.

I was asked to write a blurb for my book, but instead of using it my publisher has written one which gives the whole plot away

That's silly of him, and you have good reason for being upset. It's probably too late to do anything now, but you should complain, and if you have another book published by the same house you should insist on a clause in the contract giving you the right to be consulted about the blurb (and other matters, such as the jacket), and you should make it plain that the clause must be honoured.

The jacket design is a travesty of my book

Increasingly, contracts with publishers, even if they are not signatories of the MTA, include a clause giving the author the right of consultation over the jacket design. Why do publishers resist this? For two reasons, the first being that they believe (sometimes with justice) that they know more about how to sell their books (and the jacket is an important factor in that process) than the author, and secondly because if the author has to be consulted the publisher may be subjected to long arguments and additional delays.

If you are consulted, you should try to restrict your criticism to matters of fact, such as discrepancies between the illustration and the descriptions in your book, and only if you feel very strongly indeed about the design as a whole should you attempt to veto it. You may have the right of consultation, but the publisher has control. If he has any sense, he will listen to you, provided that you are reasonable.

Of course, the most frequent cause of complaint concerns fiction and is that the artist has not followed your descriptions of the characters or the scene which he has portrayed. Really good jacket artists understand that they should reflect the contents of the book, but there are many who feel that they have licence to adapt in order to make what they consider a better picture, and this is why, for instance, your blue-eyed blonde heroine may turn up on the jacket looking like a Spanish señorita. Why doesn't the publisher make the artist change his painting? Usually because to do so would seriously delay publication of the book – but that, it seems to many, is a poor excuse. Other problems arise from a practice of some publishers of buying stacks of artwork with no particular book in mind; when a jacket has to be prepared, the art director looks through his available artwork and chooses something which is often no more than vaguely appropriate. It's a poor way of working, and the author is entitled to make a strong protest.

My book has been very badly produced, on poor paper and in small print

Publishers insist that the manner in which they produce books is their responsibility alone. Sometimes, in their efforts to economize and keep the retail price of the book down, they go too far, and the result is a very unattractive volume. Whether, unless the book is quite ludicrously unpleasing or is physically difficult to read, this will affect the sales, it is hard to say. Books can be very beautiful objects, and some people collect them as such, but the majority are bought to be read, and ugly though some of them may be, are in fact read, if they have something worthwhile to say.

I have to wait a ridiculously long time between delivery of the typescript and publication

Most authors quickly accustom themselves to the fact that there is normally a long delay between the acceptance of their typescript and publication. The reasons why publishing seems to be such a slow process are explained in Chapter 5. What is more worrying is the postponement of scheduled publication. The most frequent cause of this is that there has been some unforeseen delay in the manufacturing process – perhaps the printer has not kept to his schedule, or the paper for the book has been discovered to be faulty, or there has been a strike, or editorial work on the book has taken much longer than anticipated. If the publisher can give you a reasonable explanation of what has caused the delay, then you can only accept it with as good a grace as you can manage. If he cannot explain it to your satisfaction, you have few courses of action open. You can decide to leave him, you can sue him for breaking his contract, or you can, after protesting, go away to lick your wounds.

By and large, publishers do not want to delay publication of their books, however difficult that may sometimes be to believe, since the sooner the book is published the sooner they can begin to recoup the very considerable sums of money they have already spent on it.

It is also worth remembering that sometimes books are delayed because the publisher believes that a later publication date will actually be beneficial to the sales. In such a case, he should be willing to explain his reasoning.

My biography of X has been delayed so long by my publisher that another author's biography of the same person has come out first and taken all the attention and sales

A very difficult problem. Delays happen for all sorts of reasons, and some books seem to be jinxed in this respect, while others sometimes go through all the publishing processes remarkably quickly. Perhaps the other publisher knew of your book and speeded his own in order to pre-empt you. If you become aware of a rival book early enough before publication, you should warn your publisher (who is often surprisingly ignorant about what his competitors are doing, publishing often being a very inward-looking business) in the hope that he may be able to get things moving more quickly. Occasionally publishers of rival books will agree to publish at the same time so as to be fair to both, but not everyone agrees that this is a good idea, and most houses will attempt to steal a march if they can. There is not much you can do about it, except to accept the fact that this is a business in which luck or ill-luck plays a tremendous part.

My book has been wrongly categorized by my publisher

In an attempt to group sections of their lists together, publishers will sometimes gather together some rather odd bedfellows. It might, for example, upset an author to find his book listed under "Hobbies" when it is aimed very firmly at a professional market, or his work on astronomy nestling next to a sensational book about ghosts. Such categorization is, however, unlikely to have an deleterious effect on sales, and the main damage will be to the author's *amour-propre*.

No one will buy copies of my book at the ridiculously high price the publisher has put on it

Well, I hope you're wrong. The public at large does believe that books are expensive (all authors should constantly preach the gospel that they are, on the contrary, cheap) and may indeed be put off if the price of a particular book seems to be out of line with others. But, believe me, publishers don't fix their retail prices arbitrarily, and they take into account not only their costs, but also the size of the market and what they believe the market will bear. A really good book, which is authoritative, and especially if it is on a subject which is comparatively unusual, will often be given what seems to be an exceptionally high price. The publisher does this in the belief, usually justified, that those people who are interested in the subject will not care about the cost because so good a book will be essential in their eyes.

My publisher made a great to-do of consulting me about publicity and promotion, but did not follow it up

The probable reason for failing to follow up the author's suggestions is lack of money. The publicity department's budget is frequently altered by intervention from higher authority in the firm, which sees a cut in publicity spending as the first and easiest of economies in times of difficulty, or by outside influences such as inflation, or by such circumstances as the addition to the list at the last moment of a book on which a great deal of attention and money is to be spent. Or it may be that the suggestions were not followed up because the notes were misfiled or forgotten, or for some equally irritating example of inefficiency.

Without a written undertaking from the publisher, there is nothing much you can do in these circumstances, unless you have the money and the facility to provide your own publicity. If you do decide to do anything like that, tell your publisher first, just to make sure that you do not duplicate efforts.

There is one other point to be made here, and it is an important one since it can apply to a great many aspects of the author's relationship with his publisher's staff. When an editor, or a publicity manager, or a royalties clerk, or the managing director, or the postboy talks to an author, there is usually a desire to be friendly and to please the writer, and it is therefore very much easier at the time, especially for the inexperienced, to promise the author everything rather than possibly have a row by saying "no". Without wanting to add anything to the mistrust which so often unfortunately exists between authors and publishers, I would caution you to take a grain of salt with what your publisher tells you, especially if the person concerned is clearly inexperienced. If you have doubts, ask for a commitment in writing. Whatever it is may still not be carried out, but you would then have legitimate grounds for complaint and for asking that the situation should be remedied.

My book is not advertised, and of course, since it has not been advertised in them, none of the national papers has reviewed it

Few publishers will concede that advertising, especially in the National Press, which is very expensive, actually sells books. The literary editors of national newspapers would strongly deny that the space devoted to a particular publisher's books is directly related to the amount of money he spends in advertising his wares in that paper. See also p.98.

My book has received no reviews

Only a tiny number of books receive reviews in large numbers. Space for reviews in newspapers and other media is strictly limited and since many literary editors believe that the most important part of their function is to see that "important" books (i.e. literary works and books by authors with well-known names) are reviewed, the chances of notices for less important books, especially popular fiction, are poor. However, this is true mainly of the National Press. Provincial and local papers are often more ready to put in notices of books which are not necessarily either literary or by famous writers. Why not have a word with the editor of your local rag? Your publisher should have done so, but you, as a local resident, may be more persuasive. See also p.101.

All my reviews have been unfavourable

Don't expect your publisher to do anything about this. A protest to the literary editors of the papers concerned will do nothing. If the reviews are inaccurate, you may wish to write to the paper pointing out the reviewer's errors, but this frequently results only in a reply from him in which you suffer still more. Obviously you cannot let a gross distortion of the facts about your book go by, but on the whole it is probably wisest to put up with bad reviews, if you get them, consoling yourself with the thought that any publicity is better than none (which isn't necessarily true, of course). You might also stop to wonder whether all the unfavourable notices are in fact justified.

My publisher doesn't send me copies of the reviews of my book

He is not usually contractually obliged to do so. Most publishers subscribe to a cutting service (which authors can also do if they are wealthy enough to feel it worthwhile), and can often be persuaded to make a photocopy of reviews or to send the author duplicates if they have them. Some publishers send the author all the reviews a certain time after the publication of the book in question, keeping a record only of the quotable words, and clearing their files by this method. If your publisher does not send you reviews, then all you can really do is to ask him to do so.

My book is not available in bookshops

Every publisher is constantly bombarded by letters and phone calls from authors complaining that their books cannot be found in bookstores, particularly the author's local bookshop, or that their friends have not been able to buy copies. Sometimes this is the publisher's fault, but not always. There is nothing that compels any bookseller to stock any given book, not even the fact that the author lives in the same town. All the publisher and his representatives can do is to try to persuade the bookseller to order copies. If he refuses, then you and your friends are going to be disappointed.

Of course, publishers are sometimes to blame – they lose orders, they supply the wrong books, they sometimes take an unbelievably long time to invoice and despatch books, they make all kinds of human errors – but by and large they do not refuse to send books to booksellers without good reason. Books lying in warehouses do no good for publishers, but only cost money. Believe it or not, publishers do actually want to sell books, because it is the only way that they can recoup their outlay in publishing books and gather in the money which will pay the author's royalties, and their wages and overhead expenses and perhaps make them a profit which will enable them to stay in business. "What about their income from subsidiary rights?" you may ask. Well, that certainly helps, but it is almost invariably of much less importance than income from sales of copies of their own edition of the book, unless it happens to be one of those books where the hardcover sales are small, but the paperback is a major bestseller. The reason for this is that on copies of their own edition they are likely to get from the bookseller something between 50% and 65% of the retail price, whereas from subsidiary rights they get no more than a share of the royalties. "By their fruits shall ye know them" certainly applies to publishing; successful publishers attract new books and new authors, and the one recipe for success is to sell books in large quantities.

Don't, therefore, immediately blame your publisher if your book is apparently not available in the bookshop. He may be tearing his hair over the situation just as much as you are. The distribution of books, the full penetration of the potential market, is the greatest problem any publisher has to face, not excluding such perennial favourites as cash flow and Difficult Authors. What is the potential market for a book, and how do you reach it? Let us take a typical example. You have written a book on Pig-Sticking, and you tell your publisher of the huge demand there will be for it. "There are five thousand members of the Pig-sticking Society for whom it will be required reading," you say. "Then there are some ten thousand occasional pig-stickers in Britain and the overseas markets, who are less committed, but still interested – let's say that half of them will buy the book. At least a thousand copies will go to people in the Anti-Pig-Sticking League, who will want to read it so that they know what our latest thinking is. Add in your own standard market, through bookshops and libraries, and it seems to me that you will end up with a printing quantity of at least 15,000 copies." The publisher tries to disillusion you, explaining that the vast majority of your totally committed pig-sticking enthusiasts will not in fact buy the book, but will borrow it, either from each other, or more likely from the public library, which is also where the members of the Anti-Pig-Sticking League will undoubtedly go, if they bother at all. Pressed by you, he may agree that there is in fact a realistic specialist market potential of some 2,000 copies. But how does he reach them? Even if he sends each of the sixteen thousand people from whom these two thousand buyers will come an order form to pass to their local bookseller, there is little likelihood that they will take any action (the average response to a mailing shot is not much more than 1%), and if they are persuaded to go to a bookshop, the bookseller may well have declined to order the book in the first place, and the customer may be so put off by not finding the book readily available that he may give up all idea of buying it. Or it may be that the bookseller to whom that customer goes is one that the publisher has decided that he will no longer supply, perhaps because the bookseller neglects to pay his bills, or regularly breaks the net book agreement, or indulges in early selling (i.e. having a book on sale before its publication date), or for some other valid reason.

But why should the bookseller be so reluctant to order the book? Well, for example, the last time that something similar came along, he was persuaded to take a dozen copies, because the author lived nearby and swore that he had twelve friends who had promised to buy the book. One of them bought the book from that bookseller and two others borrowed that copy, one bought it from a different shop, three got it out of the library, two bought the bookclub edition, two decided to wait until a paperback came out, and one didn't ever intend to read the book anyway. The bookseller was left with eleven unsold copies. That was all right, you might think, since he had bought the books on sale or return and could send back the unsold copies for credit. "Yes," the bookseller would reply, "but while the books were in my shop they were taking up space that I could have devoted to other books that would have sold. Sale or return arrangements help me, but they are the lesser of two evils – especially since returning the unsold books to the publisher is a time-consuming chore. I do my best to order only those books that I am sure of selling."

A fact which does not make the life of the publisher's sales manager any easier is that authors seem always to believe everything that booksellers tell them. Good booksellers do not lie, but others, more prone to human weaknesses, may decide that it is simpler to deal with a dissatisfied customer, especially if he is an author who does not actually want to buy copies of his book, but only to see that they are on display, by putting the blame on the publisher, saying that his order hasn't been filled or even that he has been told that the book is out of print. And we have all met the incompetent bookseller's assistant who seems to have no knowledge of the wares in the shop or any desire to serve customers, and who will say anything which will get an awkward inquirer out of the shop and leave him in peace. If you have a complaint about your book not being available, be prepared to ask your publisher whether what you have been told is true, before you go off the deep end. And it will help if you can name the bookshop concerned, and report accurately what has been said.

I do not want, on the other hand, to put all the blame on booksellers, large numbers of whom do a very good job. Imagine being faced with tens of thousands of new books every year, plus the necessity of keeping stocks of backlist books and standard works such as Bibles and dictionaries. Small wonder that they do not stock all books. Naturally, the larger the bookshop the better chance there is of finding your book in it, and if it is not there, the large bookseller may find it easier to order copies than his smaller *confrère*, because he can do so directly from the publisher, whereas the small shop will probably get books from a wholesaler – but this latter method can, if you are lucky, provide a fast and efficient service.

It is particularly galling, of course, when your book is not available in the shops for some special occasion, especially as such events do often help to sell books and are ephemeral in nature, so that the sales won't be achieved when the books eventually arrive, as they frequently do, two or three days after the whole thing is over. There is nothing you can do, except to complain loudly and hope that your publisher won't be so inefficient in future.

"But why," you may ask in justifiable exasperation, "is it apparently so difficult to get books speedily from the publisher to the bookshop, sometimes taking five or six weeks?" First of all, it may be that the bookseller has not sent your order off immediately, not because he is inefficient (though that could also be a reason for delay), but because it makes considerable economic sense for everyone concerned, even including the customer, who may avoid having to pay a surcharge on a single copy order, if the bookseller lumps together the orders he receives for books which have to be ordered from one particular source. Next there is the question of delays in the post, which we all suffer from time to time, especially with second-class mail. When the order arrives in the publisher's office, it may not be entirely clear and may have to be referred back to the bookseller, but even without that complication it may have to take its place in a queue of orders waiting to be processed, and similarly when the invoice and packing instructions reach the warehouse, it may not be possible to deal with the order immediately. At any one of these stages additional time may be lost if weekends happen to be awkwardly placed in relation to the progress of the order, and holidays and illnesses can also cause delay. Nevertheless, some publishers manage to be far more efficient than others in processing orders. Why? Well, it may be that the efficiency is produced by employing many more staff and by always using first-class post, and by other such practices which can speed the processing of orders, but which will perhaps prevent the publisher in the end from carrying out that first duty to the author, already quoted earlier in the book, of remaining solvent. Efficiency has to be measured in cost-effectiveness as well as in excellence of service. The truly efficient publishers have better management and staff – it's as simple as that.

The solution to all these problems is to write an enormous bestseller. It will also remove most of the other causes for complaint dealt with in this chapter. But since for most authors that is just a dream, some more practical advice may be in order. Do let your publisher know if your book is not available in the bookshops, but try to do so in a friendly rather than a complaining way, and don't keep on and on about it. He is probably well aware of whatever is wrong, and is doing what he can to put it right.

If all else fails, some publishers will allow their authors to buy copies of their books for re-sale to their friends. There is a standard clause in most authors' contracts which allows the author to buy copies of the book at trade terms, *but not for re-sale*. If you buy your books from the publisher at trade terms you must therefore have his permission before selling them to your friends. Such sales will presumably be at full retail price and you will make a profit: remember that you will have to declare such earnings to the Inland Revenue. You should also, if your publisher agrees to the arrangement, use it with care, making sure that you do not take sales away from a bookseller by so doing, and if your local bookseller steadfastly refuses to stock your book, it might be as well to tell him that you propose to sell copies yourself.

I have the feeling that my publisher is only interested in selling to libraries

You may be quite right. Some books, particularly in the field of popular fiction – romances, westerns, and so on – are published virtually exclusively for the library market, and the publisher makes little or no effort to sell the titles to bookshops. He doesn't do so because he knows full well that the bookshops won't order the book. Bookshops in this country, especially outside London, sell very little fiction, and that applies to so-called "literary" novels as well as to "entertainment" fiction. Apart from the work of a limited number of bestselling authors, fictions sells in hardcover in Britain almost exclusively to libraries. You need to be realistic. If your publisher sees your book as one for the library market and makes no effort in other directions, he is almost certainly right. He is also possibly a specialist in that kind of publishing, so before you rush off to another house, which does try to sell to outlets other than libraries, make sure that you're really going to be better off.

My publisher's firm is so small that his books are not distributed by the major chains such as W.H. Smith

A problem indeed, for the publisher as well as the author, and one to which I can offer no solution. If your book is of a very specialist nature, it may not matter a great deal that it is not available in the major chains, provided that your publisher knows how to sell it in its own market, but if it is a general book, its chances may well be damaged. The really small firm may be able to attract splendid authors, may have a marvellous editor, may publish beautifully produced books, but almost always will have selling and distribution problems (any author who tries self publishing will soon find himself up against similar difficulties – the real killer is getting his books where the buying public will see them). There is always the hope that the small firm will get bigger (as many in fact have done in the past) or will produce such stunning books that the chains have to take its output.

It is only fair to say that the W.H.Smith organization does make some effort to support small publishers, but the amount of time and energy which a chain can devote to such concerns is clearly minimal. Nevertheless, it might be worth your publisher's while to try to talk to the top people at W.H.S.

My previous books have always sold more copies

This does not mean necessarily that your publisher is making any less effort – indeed, he may be trying harder than ever in the past. The plain fact is that over the last twenty years or more the market for hardcover books has declined and continues to decline.

My publisher refuses to reprint my book

Publishing is a chancy business. No one can predict for certain how a new book will perform – whether it will sell as expected or in excess of or below its target. Fixing print quantities for books is a gamble. Many factors are considered: the publisher's experience with books of a similar nature, the editor's enthusiasm, the reaction of subsidiary rights buyers prior to publication, the jacket, advance orders from bookshops, and of course some kind of estimate of the book's potential, and so on. It is very difficult to get the answer right, and failure to set print quantities at the exact level to obtain all possible sales without being left with an overstock is the reason why publishers, as a whole, are not wealthy men, and why their businesses are particularly vulnerable in adverse trade conditions. More often than not the publisher is over-optimistic and prints too many copies, and has to remainder or pulp the surplus, almost always losing money on such copies. Many years ago, conditions were much easier; it was the habit to bind small quantities of the printed sheets of a book, binding more as and when the demand came along, thus minimizing the amount of capital tied up in finished stock; moreover, it was not uneconomic to keep quantities of a book available over a long period of time, even though sales were very slow. Nowadays, the whole of an edition is normally printed and bound at one time, and the storage of books is an extremely expensive business. Books which do not sell quickly cannot be allowed to take up valuable warehouse space, and in an effort to avoid overstocks, the publisher will sometimes print too few copies. The book sells out on publication or shortly thereafter, and the author is then dismayed when the publisher refuses to reprint. Why does he do so? Usually because the information that he gathers from his sales representatives and from bookshops leads him to believe that the unsatisfied demand is not large enough to warrant reprinting, which cannot be done economically for anything but a large quantity, often virtually as big as the original print run. Although the charges for setting the book in type have been met, and the initiation of artwork and illustrations has been paid for, the cost of putting the plates back on the printing machine and of doing all the other things necessary to manufacture the reprint is so high that a large printing is needed if the unit cost per book is to be kept to a level which will be profitable. This is one of the reasons why authors whose sales have brought them to a higher scale of royalties are asked to revert to a minimal royalty on "small" reprints of 1,500 or sometimes 2,000 copies or less. The more elaborate the book, especially if colour illustrations are involved, the most costly the origination of the reprint will be.

Sometimes the sales reports will suggest that there is sufficient demand to justify a reprint, but that it will take many years before the entire quantity is sold, and the publisher may regretfully have to decide that he cannot tie up the required capital for that length of time.

Knowing all this does not console the author who sees lost sales (and the publisher will not be happy about it either), but at least he can feel sure that the publisher is more likely to be receptive to his next book than if he had over-printed the first one.

I have been asked to revise and update my book, but the publisher has not offered me a new advance

The MTA suggests that advances should be paid for revisions, but most publishers' contracts simply say that you agree to update the book if it is necessary, and make no mention of paying you to do the work. But an updated, revised edition should generate a whole lot more sales for a book which might otherwise have died of old age, so you will get payment for your work in the form of continuing royalties. Lucky you.

My book is to be remaindered

When the sale of a book has stopped or has petered down to almost nothing, the publisher is often left with a stock of unsaleable books. The growth of the paperback market has largely taken away from the hardcover publisher his ability to produce cheap editions (which in the distant past were often simply the original edition made available at a lower price), and his usual practice is to "remainder" the book, that is to say, to sell off the remainder of his stock at a low price, which is usually below his manufacturing cost. The merchant who buys this "remainder" stock then markets it to the public at bargain prices. Apart from the problem of whether or not the author receives any royalty on remainder sales (see p.136), the author is often angered because his book has been remaindered within too short a period of original publication. The MTA gives the publisher the right to remainder a book twelve months after publication, but it seems to me that the justice in this matter depends to some extent on the kind of book involved. If one is talking of a serious work of non-fiction which is not essentially topical and ephemeral, it is entirely reasonable for the author to ask that it should not be remaindered until a minimum of two years after its first publication. However, if the publisher can demonstrate that the book has stopped selling completely, for whatever reason, even in such cases the author might agree to remaindering, trusting that his publisher would not advocate such a course if he believed that he could make more money by keeping the book alive on his list – which he will surely do if the sales income is going to bring him even a small profit as opposed to the almost certain loss of remaindering. But the author's consent should be sought.

If, however, we are considering fiction, it is an unfortunate truth that the majority of novels are virtually moribund six months after publication. If the publisher wishes to remainder your novel within a comparatively short period, though you might well ask him to keep it going for a few months longer, or perhaps to remainder only a part of his stock so that he still has copies available through normal trade channels, it seems to me reasonable for you to consider his request favourably. You may say that he should make a renewed sales effort to dispose of the overstocks, but this just does not work, unless there is some outside influence to affect matters, such as the release of a film of the book. Booksellers, faced with scores of new books appearing every month, will not look kindly on the attempt to sell them a novel which they first considered six months or more ago, and which cannot be said to have exactly leapt off the shelves.

Authors are also incensed, and rightly so, when their books are remaindered without their knowledge. If the book is to be remaindered, the author should always have the opportunity of buying copies at the remainder price, and it is outrageous that some books are sold off in this way without the author being told. Unfortunately, by the time he discovers what has happened, it is usually too late to do anything about it, but a vigorous protest to the publisher has sometimes resulted in the latter at least buying back from the remainder merchant the number of copies that the author wants.

Of course, if your book is remaindered, there is nothing to stop you buying copies at the remainder price and then selling them at the full retail price shown on the jacket or cover, or at least at a price which will give you a good profit on the deal. If you give talks, or go to writers' gatherings such as the Summer School at Swanwick, you will certainly be able to dispose of copies. You should, of course, report the profit you make to the Inland Revenue as part of your income. However, do be careful about how many you buy, making sure that there's a chance of getting rid of them within a reasonable length of time.

When your book is remaindered, you should check whether it is a full or a partial remainder, and whether any sub-licences for the book are still active. If there are none of the latter and if the publisher has no remaining stock, then you are entitled under most publishing contracts to have all rights in the book returned from the publisher to you. You should seek confirmation of such reversion of rights.

I was not told of the bookclub sale until the royalty statement arrived

You are right to feel annoyed. It's bad-mannered and stupid of your publisher not to have told you something like that, especially as it was good news. How did it happen? Well, the subsidiary rights manager probably thought the editor was writing to you, and the editor thought the sub-rights person was writing ... and in the end no one wrote. Protest, and ask that nothing similar should happen in future.

Incidentally, although I said in the previous paragraph that the bookclub deal was good news, it has to be admitted that there are some authors who are very much opposed to bookclubs, usually because they believe that bookclub sales work against bookshops (though they may be motivated by the fact that bookclub royalties are very low). Most booksellers would agree that their livelihood is seriously damaged by bookclubs, but the bookclubs argue that their members are not normally bookbuyers, and indeed normally never darken a bookshop's doors. It is fairly noticeable that most of the authors who refuse to let their books appear in club editions are those who regularly produce bestsellers. While admiring them for defending bookshops, one cannot help thinking that it is always easier to stand on one's principles when one does not have to count the pennies.

My publisher has sold his own edition of my book in the United States rather than selling the rights to an American publisher

This situation normally applies only to highly illustrated books, especially those which have a number of pages in full colour. The only way in which the book can be made economic is for the British and American publishers to work together so that a double-sized print quantity can be ordered. Books of British origin are manufactured in such cases by the British publisher, who usually sells the sheets to the American publisher at a fairly low price which is inclusive of royalty, and the same thing works in reverse with books of American origin. Sometimes foreign language editions are also involved. The reward to the author on these deals is minimal, but it is often true that if no such arrangement could be worked out, the book would not be published on either side of the Atlantic, and this is why in many cases the British (or American) publisher will not sign a firm contract with the author until he has sold an edition of the book to an American (or British) publisher.

If there is no such cost problem and it is a perfectly ordinary book, it is surprising that the British publisher should try to sell his own edition in the States, and he is unlikely to have much success. However, if he has tried unsuccessfully to sell the American rights, a few extra sales of his own edition are better than nothing.

No effort has been made to sell subsidiary rights in my book

Are you sure? If your publisher has really made no effort to sell subsidiary rights, he is either a fool or incompetent, and you should leave him if you can find someone else to take you on, and providing your contract allows you to do so. But do try to find out first whether it is simply that, despite considerable industry on his part, all the subsidiary rights buyers to whom he has submitted your book have rejected it. Paperback publishers, bookclub editors, serial editors for magazines and newspapers are all faced with an embarrassment of riches, and reject far more books than they accept. Some years ago Sir Robert Lusty suggested that only one hardcover book in twenty also achieved bookclub or paperback sales; with the proliferation of bookclubs since then the chances may have improved a little, but would probably not be better than one in fifteen.

If your book has not sold any subsidiary rights, you may have been unlucky, or it may be that your book is just not good enough, but it doesn't necessarily mean that your publisher hasn't tried. If you ask him, he may be able to tell you to whom he has submitted the book and possibly whether they have given any reasons for rejection, and this may be useful information to bear in mind when writing your next book. He may also tell you why he has *not* submitted the book to this or that paperback publisher. If, for instance, the editor of a paperback house has repeatedly told your publisher that he does not want any historical fiction, your publisher would be foolish to send him your historical novel – unless it is of such outstanding quality that he can say to the paperback editor, "I know you don't want historical fiction, but this one is so brilliant that you must read it." If the paperback editor knows that your publisher would not say that unless the book really were extraordinarily good, then he might make an exception and consider it. But if the book is as splendid as that, your publisher will have had no difficulty in selling it to one of the other paperback houses anyway.

My publisher turned down a subsidiary rights offer as not good enough; it has now been withdrawn, and no other offer has come in

Bad luck. I keep telling you it's a gambling business.

I am an internationally known, bestselling author. My hardcover publisher has been taken over by a conglomerate which is fully integrated, having its own mass-market paperback concern. They are going to revert all the paperback rights in my books from the house which has successfully published them for years, and with whom I have excellent relationships, so that they can publish them under their own imprint. And they are doing this without consulting me.

I am not surprised that you are angry. Unfortunately, for many years in the past it was standard practice to give hardcover publishers full control of paperback rights, without any need to consult the author about their sale or reversion. Legally, you probably have no recourse; morally, however, you are entitled to make as big a fuss as you can, and if you shout loud enough you may be able to shame the conglomerate into behaving properly. At the very least, of course, you will change your hardcover publisher for your future books, and make sure that every contract you sign gives you the power to veto any deal concerning subsidiary rights.

It is unfair that I have to wait so long for my share of subsidiary rights income

Publishers who sell subsidiary rights receive moneys from those to whom they sell, and then divide them according to the proportions set out in the contract between themselves and the author. Now, it has been standard practice for many years that the advance originally paid by the publisher to the author is against all sums due under the contract, which means that the author receives no extra payment until the advance has been earned, whether by royalties on the original edition or from the author's share of subsidiary rights, or a combination of the two. Let us suppose that the publisher has paid an advance of £1,000, and has sold subsidiary rights for a sum of which the author's share is £600. £600 of the original advance has now been earned, but that money will not be paid to the author, nor will any further sums be payable until the remaining £400 of the advance has been earned. This is not necessarily unfair, especially since publishers frequently take into account their expectations of receipts from subsidiary rights when calculating how much the original advance should be.

What is less fair is the practice of some publishers of retaining the author's share of subsidiary rights moneys *after* the original advance has been fully earned until they next send a royalty statement to the author. This could mean that for a considerable period of time moneys due to the author are kept and used by the publisher. Supposing that after the advance has been earned your publisher sells certain subsidiary rights in your book for a sum of which your share is £500. If his royalty accounting periods end at 30th June and 31st December, and if it so happened that these subsidiary rights moneys came into him on 1st July, he could retain the £500 until the following 31st March, when he would normally be rendering to you the royalty statement for the six months ending 31st December. Many authors, agents and especially organizations such as the Society of Authors and the Writers' Guild believe this practice is not merely unfair, but pretty near to being criminal. It is not criminal, of course, in the legal sense, if your contract allows the publisher to retain these moneys, and publishers can certainly claim that it was "the practice of the trade" until comparatively recently. But if the advance has been earned, any publisher who still refuses to pass on the author's share of subsidiary rights income immediately on receipt (or within, say, a maximum of thirty days) ought to be ashamed of himself. But note that the MTA makes provision for such moneys to be passed to the author only when they amount to £100 or more. If your advance has been earned and your publisher is holding back a large amount of subsidiary income due to you, even if the publisher is justified in what he is doing by the terms of your contract, it is still worth protesting. Some publishers do have a conscience.

I have just discovered that a large company has made several dozen photocopies of my book and distributed them among its staff. Can they do this?

No, they can't – at least, not without permission. Check that your publisher has not made any arrangement with the firm concerned (though if he has, he should have told you about it). Unless such an arrangement exists, your publisher should then give all the details to the Copyright Licensing Agency (see p.228), which will be happy to take the matter up, and, if necessary, take proceedings.

The hardcover edition of my book is out of print, and the publisher refuses to reprint, but he is still taking his cut of the paperback royalties

Most publishing contracts include a clause which allows the publisher to retain rights provided that any sub-licensed edition of the book is in print, even if his own edition is not. A reprint may be impossible to contemplate, for even though the book may still be selling in the sub-licensed edition, the market for the original edition may now be non-existent or too small to justify the reprint. In these circumstances some publishers will occasionally agree to increase the author's share of the subsidiary income, but very few will release all rights to the author, arguing that the fact that they took the initial risk with the book, and that if they had not done so the subsidiary rights in question would not have been sold at all, and it was they who conducted the negotiations for the sale, is a valid justification for them taking their share, and will remain so throughout the life of the sub-licence in question. Legally, unless your contract does not have the kind of clause referred to above, you have no cause for redress. Morally, it depends somewhat on the kind of sums involved. If the publisher has already received a very substantial sum in the form of his share of subsidiary rights income, then perhaps he has less justification for still taking his full percentage than if the moneys involved are small. But that's a difficult one to argue.

My royalty statements are late and/or inaccurate

As I have already explained earlier in this book, publishers maintain that the complexity of their royalty accounts means that they cannot possibly produce them in less than three months after the end of the relevant royalty period. Computerization should certainly make it possible to produce the statements more speedily, and there is no excuse at all for lateness.

As for those publishers who want to move against the tide and provide one annual statement only, authors should resist such suggestions as strongly as possible.

Of course, royalty statements should never be inaccurate, but the occasional mistake is probably inevitable, simply because human beings are concerned with the preparation of the accounts, and human beings are fallible. All authors should check their royalty statements carefully, and bring any errors to the notice of their publishers. Some royalty statements are very difficult to understand, and if you have that kind of problem, you should ask your publisher to explain his form in detail. If you believe your royalty statements to be seriously inaccurate you may need to invoke your right, given under most contracts, to examine the relevant parts of the publisher's account books.

My royalty statement has a percentage of sales deducted for returns

For an explanation of this practice, see pp.135–6.

I have just read about an author who has signed a deal with a publisher giving him a million pounds for his next two books. I'm green with envy.

So am I. Enormous advance payments to certain authors have been with us for some time now, and seem to be a phenomenon which has come about largely because of the need that the big publishing conglomerates feel to attract major authors and simultaneously to show off their wealth and power. "Cheque-book publishing", as those publishers who can't afford it are wont to describe it, seems to me to be unfortunate, in that it inevitably reduces the amount of money available for other authors and their projects. However, the publishers who spend all these astronomical sums have usually taken out insurance by selling various subsidiary rights for equally huge amounts, so that their risks are diminished. I'm not sure that I really do envy the author you mention – just think of the responsibility that sums like that place on him. On second thoughts, yes, I still do envy him.

I am sure that a small advance means no promotion and no effort or, indeed, interest

There is some truth in this, but it isn't the entire story. When a publisher pays a really large sum of money as the advance on a book, it is indeed likely that he will also spend quite a lot on promoting it and he will print a large number of copies, and devote a lot of his time and that of his staff to it. But there are comparatively few such books on any publisher's list, and it does not mean that the rest are neglected. They may not get star treatment (it is not an equal world), but they are nevertheless important to the publisher, who does not live on bestsellers alone. If your publisher doesn't pay an advance of thousands of pounds for your book, then in terms of his effort and interest it really won't matter a great deal whether the advance he pays is £50 or £750 or nothing at all. He is committed to spending a substantial sum on the manufacture of any book on his list, and his desire to recoup his outlay guarantees you at least a modicum of effort and interest. Occasionally a genuine ugly duckling comes along – a book which no one expected to be a big seller, but which suddenly takes off into the realms of success. The amount the publisher paid as an advance doesn't affect his effort and interest in that book, and since the advance was small, the author's first royalty cheque is all the nicer.

My book was published six months ago, but already my publisher has lost interest in it

In most cases, a very high proportion of the sales of a book has been achieved before and within six months of publication, and thereafter sales may virtually have ceased. Additional promotion and effort by the publisher will not stimulate additional sales, unless there is some justification for it, such as the release of a film based on the book. Even then, the new publicity may result only in the sale of those copies of the book already in the bookshops, without much re-ordering. Books which survive for a longer period usually continue to sell on their own momentum, and again additional attention does not often produce much effect.

Your publisher's lack of interest in your book is largely due to the fact that he is concerned with the new books on his list. He has to keep on producing new books and his attention is bound to be focused on them.

My book, which was a failure, was remaindered and is now out of print, dead and forgotten. Nevertheless, I've been advised to ask the publisher for the rights back. Why should I bother?

You sound depressed about your book, and that's not surprising, but you should never give up hope. Get the rights back, and then see if you can sell them yourself. You may not be able to get a hardcover publisher to take the book on, but perhaps you could sell paperback rights, or large-print rights; or perhaps, without you doing anything about it, a film producer will come across a copy of the book and decide that it would make a really smashing film. Stranger things have happened. If any subsidiary rights in your book are sold, now or in the future, you will have to share the proceeds with the publisher if the rights have not reverted to you, but if you've got them back, all the money will be yours. Anyway, it's not a difficult thing to arrange – just write to the publisher and ask him to confirm that, since the book is out of print, all rights have reverted to you.

Whenever I complain to my publisher, he just fobs me off with some unconvincing explanation

This sounds like a rather unhappy situation. Either the publisher is incompetent and does not know the answers to your queries, and hasn't the courage to tell you that he doesn't know, or more likely he is ashamed of his firm's inefficiency and is trying to cover up. Loyalty to his firm and to his colleagues may be preventing him from confessing how right you are and how justified your complaints. Not only that, but to tell you the truth might mean that you would lose any remaining faith in the firm that you might have. I think he's wrong, and that honesty is always the best policy for a publisher dealing with his authors.

Of course, the trouble might be that you are a Difficult Author ...

My publisher is greedy

Very probably. If you think so, tell him. He may be able to explain to you why he appears that way; he may even respond by being more generous towards you. But do remember that one of his functions is to help make his firm profitable, and that may mean saving as much money as is consistent with not losing good publishing opportunities as a result of apparent parsimony. Don't blame him for trying to strike a good bargain. Try a little haggling.

9

Legal Matters

Publishers' Contracts

The contract that you sign with a publisher is, of course, a legal document, and so is the correspondence with him which deals with any commitment on either side which is not covered by the agreement. These papers should be kept carefully in a safe place, and you should stick rigidly to all the terms and conditions in them – your signature on the contract is a statement of your acceptance of all the terms. If later you find that your contract is irksome in some respect or commits you to something which you cannot fulfil – the delivery date for the completed typescript of your book, for instance – talk to your publisher and persuade him, if you can, to alter the contract accordingly. Get it in writing, so that there can't be any argument later.

The contract and any relevant correspondence will be needed if you ever reach the unhappy position of being involved in a law suit with your publisher. You will certainly need professional advice in such a case. If you are already a member of the Society of Authors or the Writers' Guild such advice will be readily available to you from whichever of those bodies you belong to, but neither organization will provide assistance for a member in a legal dispute which was already in existence before that member joined.

Copyright

Copyright is granted by law to the creator of a work, giving him the exclusive right to reproduce and publish it in whole or in part. The law of copyright is enormously complicated and the Copyright, Designs and Patents Act of 1988, while clarifying some matters has left others in a confusing state of obfuscation, especially when the author writes something for and at the behest of his employer, in which case the copyright usually belongs to the employer, though the concept of "moral rights" (see below) may complicate the issue.

However, the average author, fortunately, needs to know only certain basic facts about copyright, which will be set out below, and if he should require more detailed advice he will find it readily available from the Society of Authors or the Writers' Guild.

Your book (or, indeed, anything that you write) is protected by copyright as soon as it is committed to paper. Some authors feel it is useful to establish the date of the work's completion, which can be done, for instance, by depositing a copy of it with your bank and obtaining a dated receipt. The authors who do this are usually afraid that if they don't protect themselves and their work in this way it may be copied or stolen by an unscrupulous publisher. I must say I know of no professional author who bothers with such a performance. Most publishers give full respect to the copyright of any material submitted to them.

On publication, the printing in the book of the symbol ©, the name of the copyright owner and the date of the first publication secures protection in all countries which are signatories to the Universal Copyright Convention, numbering over sixty nations throughout the world. Before the Universal Copyright Convention (which the United Kingdom ratified in 1957) came into existence, many countries adhered to an earlier international recognition of copyright, the Berne Convention, which was first drawn up in 1886, has been frequently amended since, and is still in force.

Unfortunately, many countries of the world, especially in the Far East, have little regard for copyright. In Taiwan, Singapore, Korea and the Indian sub-continent, for example, pirate publishers flourish, publishing books by European and American authors without authorization and without payment of royalties. If you learn of the pirating of one of your books, inform your agent and/or your publisher or, if you are a member of the Society of Authors or the Writers' Guild, tell them, and do so immediately. Often they will be powerless to do anything, because in some cases the pirates are actually encouraged in their illegal work by their governments, but at least you should keep them informed. The same advice applies, incidentally, if you discover that your work has been plagiarized or that your copyright has been infringed in any other way. Don't suffer in silence. However, before rushing too precipitately into action, you should bear in mind that while a direct quotation of your words may be a clear-cut case of plagiarism, it is rather more difficult to prove that similarities of plot have been pinched by one writer from another.

Copyright in a work published during the author's lifetime extends for fifty years after the author's death, and this applies in most countries of the world, though in some the term is shorter and in others longer. When you die your copyrights become part of your estate, and unless you leave them in your will to a specific person, will pass to your residual legatee. As assets, they may be liable to tax, and your publisher or agent will be asked to place a value on them so that the Capital Taxes Office can make the necessary assessment.

Unless there are very special reasons for doing so, you should never surrender the copyright in your work, but instead should grant your publisher a licence for a limited period and with clauses which will ensure that all rights revert to you in due course or if he fails to carry out the commitments of the agreement. There are some circumstances in which a publisher may wish to buy the copyright in your work, usually offering an outright fee. Since the fee is frequently a sum larger than the author might expect to receive simply as an advance against royalties, he may be tempted to accept it. But he should think carefully before doing so. Once he has parted with the copyright, the publisher will be able to go on producing the work, possibly in very large quantities, without paying the author any additional money, and the outright sum he received may end up looking very small against the royalties that the work's sale would have brought in, even if those royalties had been on a low scale. And if the publisher has bought the copyright in your book he is free to edit it, change it, abridge it, and indeed do anything he likes with it, without consulting you or paying you any more money, no matter how much it may earn for him. Parting with your copyright is not only foolish, but normally pretty irreversible – even if the firm to which you sold it goes out of existence you are unlikely to get your copyright back. However, a sensible course of action if you are asked to give up your copyright, is to take professional advice (from the Society of Authors, for instance), since there are some rare circumstances in which it may be an acceptable option.

Do remember, by the way, that just as laws of copyright protect you, so they protect other authors, and you must not infringe their rights any more than they must play around with yours. See the section on Permissions below.

The copyright in letters, incidentally, belongs to the person who writes them, not to the recipient. As for photographs, the copyright usually belongs to the person who takes the photograph, but if the photographer is asked to take a given photograph and is paid for doing so, the copyright will probably be owned by the person who commissioned it.

There is no copyright in ideas. Many authors worry about this, fearing that their bright ideas will be stolen by unscrupulous publishers. There may be some justification for their worries, but, as explained on p.164, the majority of publishers will not knowingly pinch ideas.

There is no copyright in titles either, nor in author's names. You are entitled to call your book *A Brief History of Time* or *The Day of the Jackal* if you want to without infringing anyone's copyright. However, even if it appeared under your own name as author rather than that of Stephen Hawking or Frederick Forsyth, you could in either of those cases be sued for "passing off", which is to say for attempting to con the public into buying your book in the belief that it was the famous one (even if that was not your intention). And I wouldn't advise you to call yourself Jeffrey Archer or Catherine Cookson, for the same reason. If your name really is Jeffrey Archer or Catherine Cookson, however unhappy you may feel about it, it will probably make sense for you, when you write, to use a pseudonym or at the least to add an initial or a middle name and to call yourself, for instance, something like Jeffrey C. Archer or Catherine Jane Cookson.

As a final point, there is no copyright in generally accepted facts. See the section on Plagiarism below.

Moral Rights

Moral rights are basically those of "paternity" and

"integrity". The former guarantees that the author will be identified in any use which is made of his work, whether in whole or in part; the latter protects him against the distortion or mutilation of his work in any adaptation or other treatments of it. Moral rights have been enshrined in law for the first time in the recent Copyright, Designs and Patents Act of 1988, but the protection that the law gives does not become effective in respect of the "paternity" of the work unless the author "asserts" his rights, which he does by printing a notice to that effect in his book or at the end of his article. The following wording is suitable.

The right of (Author's name) to be identified as the author of this work has been asserted by him/her in accordance with the Copyright, Designs and Patents Act 1988

Most book publishers appear to be willing to conform to the law as far as Moral rights are concerned, but authors who work in other fields, like films and television, may not always find a similar willingness on the part of those who commission their work. Point out to such people that Moral rights are actually part of the law of the realm, and they will simply take their commission to an author who either does not know that he should insist on retaining the rights, or does not care. Authors must stand firm, and shoulder to shoulder, on this issue.

Libel

The laws of libel are pretty complex, and it is not the province of this book to give a complete survey of them. However, some helpful points may be made.

First of all, the essence of libel is that it is damaging to the victim, so you are in no danger if you write about real-life people provided that you do not say anything unpleasant about them. You do not even need to be all that bland in your comments, as long as what you write does not damage the person's reputation or expose him to hatred, ridicule or contempt. Of course, you have to be careful, because something which you may consider to be the mildest of criticisms may be thought by the subject of your remarks to be offensive in the extreme.

The next point to remember is that you cannot libel the

dead. Even with this freedom, however, there is a danger, because a remark about a dead person could be considered by his living descendants to be libellous of them if in some respect it damages their reputations. For instance, if you were to write, "Lord Blank came from a family noted throughout history for lechery, duplicity and total incompetence in high office", you might be referring in your mind only to Lord Blank himself, but his descendants might not be at all pleased.

There are several possible defences which an author can make to a charge of libel, the first and best of which is that the matter complained of is true. If you say in your book that Mr X is a liar, a thief, a taker of bribes, a lecher, a coward and anything else uncomplimentary you can think of, you can answer the libel suit that he brings against you simply by proving that all those things are true. The trouble is that little word "simply" – it is rarely a simple matter to prove the truth, and it may not only be difficult, but extremely expensive too, to do so in a court of law.

The next possible defence is one of "fair comment". This is what protects journalists from actions against them when they say rude things about public figures such as politicians. You may still have to show that your "fair comment" is a matter of opinion, rather than fact, and that you wrote in good faith and without malice.

A somewhat similar protection exists primarily for reports of judicial or parliamentary proceedings, and is known as "privilege".

And lastly, there is the defence of "innocence", if you can prove that you had no intention of libelling the person concerned and did so by accident. This defence would work best if you could show that you did not even know of the plaintiff's existence, and, even better, if you could demonstrate that you had taken some steps to find out whether there was anyone of that name and had failed to trace it. To explain that, let us suppose that you have written about a fictional criminal medical practitioner for whom you have invented the name "Doctor Y". You are horrified when a real-life Doctor Y turns up and sues you for libel. If you can prove not only that you had no personal knowledge of the existence of Doctor Y, but also that you had checked in the BMA register and had found no mention of him (because he had qualified since the printing of the register which you saw), you have quite a strong defence. You would still, however, have to issue an apology, and the whole thing would probably cost you a great deal of money.

You may have yet another answer. "Z won't sue," you may say, "because it's not worth his while. He hasn't got the time for a court case, and if he did sue, he knows I haven't got the money, so even if he wins he won't get anything out of me." Or you might suggest, "Z wouldn't dare sue me. He knows that if he did, far worse things than I have written would come out in the trial." Well, yes, but honestly I don't think any publisher could be blamed for being very wary indeed about such an approach.

The best answer is to avoid libel like the plague. If you write non-fiction, it is quite easy to recognize potentially libellous matter. It is more difficult with fictional characters. Some authors of novels, short stories, plays and other imaginative work believe that if they model one of their characters on a real-life person, all they have to do, if the portrait they have drawn is a libellous one, is to change the name. This is not so. If the person libelled recognizes himself (and he probably will, despite the myth that people never see themselves in fictional characters directly based on them), and especially if his friends and acquaintances can also recognize him, he will have a case against the author, whatever the character in the story may be called. It is not even enough, necessarily, to change the person's physical appearance, although this may help, for it depends on how impenetrable the disguise you have given the character is – if he and his buddies can still recognize him, then you are still in trouble. The moral is to change everything – name, physical appearance, age, occupation, and even sex. Yet another danger lurks in the fictional presentation of certain public figures; if, for instance, you were to write a novel in which you showed a fictional Chairman of the Coal Board in a very unpleasant light, the real-life holder of that office might have a case against you even though you had changed his name, appearance and other characteristics. One thing which can sometimes help is to introduce the original of your libellous character in a more recognizable form as one of your "goodies", in the hope that he and his friends will see himself in that characterization rather than in the unpleasant one. An even better moral than the one given a few lines above is to make sure that all the characters about whom you write libellous material are wholly imaginary, and, if they happen to be in one of the professions, to check that there is no doctor or clergyman or lawyer or whatever it may be with that particular name.

The notice that appears in the front of many novels, indicating that the characters in it are imaginary and bear no resemblance to any person, living or dead, is of little use. I doubt if it would even scare off someone who is thinking somewhat frivolously of suing (if anybody ever does such a thing), and it certainly won't save you if anyone really believes that you have libelled him.

If there is anything in your book which you consider to be of a potentially libellous nature, you should bring it to the attention of your publisher. Additionally, if you are worried and your publisher does not do this, you can submit the book to a solicitor for his opinion, though it is as well to choose one who is a specialist in the field. Your publisher will know the names of suitable firms.

Permissions

You are permitted to quote short passages from copyright material for purposes of criticism or review, or to illustrate a point that you are making, but you must always acknowledge the source of any such quotation. Although such short extracts can usually be used without payment of fees, it is always a good idea to check with the publishers that there is no objection to their use (they will also tell you what form your acknowledgement should take). Long quotations will almost always attract a fee. If you are preparing an anthology, you will be expected to pay for all the copyright material you include, even if the extract is a short one. The fees often vary considerably, so it is a good idea to find out what they are before you make up your mind to use the pieces in question, and you should always check with your publisher to find out exactly what permission you need to get – whether, for instance, you need World English Language rights, or perhaps only British and Commonwealth rights. Whatever the length of the extract, it has always been expected that the author should be identified, but now, with the inclusion of Moral rights (see above) in copyright law, it has become essential.

Works written by authors who have been dead for more

than fifty years are usually out of copyright, but there are occasional exceptions to this rule, and it is always as well to check.

Plagiarism

If you deliberately copy someone else's work, without permission or acknowledgement, pretending that it is your own, you are guilty of plagiarism, a crime for which you can be sued. If your book has been published and is deemed to contain plagiarized material, it will probably have to be withdrawn and fairly substantial damages will be payable to the author whose work you have stolen. "Then how much of my research," you may ask, "may I use?" That depends on what you are talking about. If you are referring to facts, which are generally accepted, there is usually no problem – if you have checked the date of, let us say, the assassination of President Kennedy, and intend to use that information in your novel, there is no question of plagiarism. However, if you go on to describe the assassination, using the actual words in the book you consulted, you may be infringing the author's copyright and be guilty of plagiarism. In fact, there's no "may" about it – you *will* be guilty of plagiarism. If you insist on making use of someone else's material, you will have to paraphrase – that is to say, you will have to put everything in your own words. And is that enough? No, almost certainly it is not. You can't get away with changing the words if you still use the same sentence structure, and the same kind of paragraphing, and all the same facts. In particular, you must avoid what might be called the idiosyncrasies of the author whose work you are using – if, for instance, you were rewriting the section above on Libel, you would be foolish to copy too closely my device of saying, "the moral is ..." and then later, "an even better moral is ...".

Plagiarism is, of course, not only a matter of copying another author's words and the way in which they are presented or of following too closely the method he has used to organize his material. You will be guilty of the same crime if you use the plot of someone else's novel. That, you may think, presents a real problem, since it is well known that there is only a handful of basic plots on which all fictional material must be based. And you wonder how on earth the writers of romantic fiction can avoid plagiarism, since all their plots are almost bound to have many similarities. Yes, but they aren't all told in exactly the same way, they don't all have the same characters, the subplots vary considerably, and the main theme of the story will twist and turn in different ways. It is still possible to be original in your treatment. But if you follow the pattern of another author's story too exactly, then you are a plagiarist.

It is really a matter of common sense. Don't pinch other writers' ideas or work. Don't even "borrow" from them. "Borrow" in this context is simply a euphemism for "steal". But if you do use existing material, at least rework it so that it has truly become your own – and so that it is not recognizable to the original author.

Supposing you plagiarize another author by accident? This is more likely to happen with a plot than with the actual words. It is certainly possible that two novelists could come up with the same basic story and could choose to tell it in exactly the same way. It is also possible for an author to have read someone else's book some time ago, to forget all about it, and then to dig it out of his subconscious in the belief that it is an entirely original idea. In the former case, if you can prove that you had never read the other author's book, you may get away with it – but that's a pretty difficult thing to prove. In the latter case, you're probably firmly guilty of plagiarism, even if it was not, as it were, premeditated.

Obscenity, Blasphemous Libel, Sedition and other Offensive Material

It seems unlikely that obscenity, blasphemous libel and sedition will cause an author much trouble nowadays, when anything goes and freedom of speech is sacrosanct. However, even in a liberal society, laws do exist to protect people from the publication of offensive material (or what those who legislate may consider to be offensive).

It is still, for instance, possible to be prosecuted for publishing pornography, the police periodically raid bookshops, and court orders are given for the destruction of obscene material (and of course there is an outcry when some perfectly respectable books get caught up, as inevitably they do from time to time, in such a prosecution).

Equally, there are laws which prohibit the promulgation

of blasphemous material; at the time of writing, this protection is given only to the Christian religion, but there are moves afoot to change the regulations, either totally abolishing the anti-blasphemy laws or extending them to cover other religions.

The idea of sedition dates back to a time when all power was in the hands of the king who needed to protect himself against any attempt by his enemies to topple him from the throne; in today's climate, arguments for the overthrow of the government, for the establishment of a Communist régime or of a Fascist dictatorship, or indeed for the dissolution of the monarchy can be put forward in books with impunity, but there are still restrictions, which come under this heading, against the publication of material which the government of the day wishes to remain secret.

Finally, everyone must be aware of the laws which are designed to protect the ethnic minorities against abuse, and most of us also understand that there are other somewhat similar "-isms" to be avoided, even if they are not prohibited by legal statutes, such as sexism, ageism and classism.

This awareness of what is offensive should prevent you from getting into trouble – or at least it should mean that if you have written questionable material you have done so with your eyes open, as it were, knowing the dangers that you are courting. Your publisher, and the printer of the book, will be in the same boat, of course. One of the troubles is that, in this context, what you have written needs to offend one person only to bring down the whole force of the law on the heads of all three of you.

Wills

Everyone should make a will, simply because it will save all kinds of hassle after one's death. But are there any special words of advice for authors? Your literary properties may go on earning money after your death, and, for tax purposes, your executors will have to have some assessment made (possibly by the publishers concerned or by your agent, if you have one) of the value of these assets. If you do not mention them specifically in your will, they will form part of your general estate and be inherited by your principal heirs; on the other hand, you may wish to leave special directions as to the disposal of such moneys. You could, for instance, direct that all income from a specific book should go to your favourite nephew, or to one of the charities for authors, such as the Authors' Foundation or the Royal Literary Fund, or perhaps to an organization such as the Society of Authors, or the Writers' Guild, or International PEN, or Book Trust. Equally, you could simply direct that a sum of money from your general funds should go to one of these bodies. If you are wealthy, you might even consider setting aside enough money to fund a prize (possibly to be administered by the Society of Authors or Book Trust). Whatever you decide to do, your solicitor should be able to draw up an appropriate clause in the will, but it is probably worthwhile to consult any organization concerned who will be able to give specific advice on the wording.

10

The Rewards of Writing

Every now and then considerable publicity is given to the success story of certain bestselling authors. We learn of the astronomic sums paid in the United States for the paperback rights to their books, we are told of colossal sales of the film rights, we hear they themselves have had to become tax exiles. No wonder many people think that writing is an easy way of making money. Most of them never get beyond thinking about it, but if they do try to write they are likely to discover that it is much harder work and demands far more skill than they thought. And of course, it is not just a matter of putting all those thousands of words on paper – there is also the business of planning and construction (which is what we are doing, as all we authors know, when we are discovered apparently asleep at our desks). Oh, yes, it is very hard, and the skills are not easily acquired.

But there is another shock waiting for our friend who thinks that writing is an easy way of making money, for if he manages to complete a book and get it accepted for publication, he will discover that the average author's earnings are pitifully small. Very few can make writing a full-time career unless they have means of some other kind.

Perhaps our friend will have some little success with his first book, and will then believe that his future as an author is assured. But he will find that earning his living from writing is a totally uncertain business. His next book may be a failure and he may never be published again. He may write a number of books and eventually have the right to consider himself as "established", but his income from his writing may still vary from book to book and from year to year quite unpredictably. Even if he becomes a household name, he will probably need a whole string of bestsellers before he can feel certain that anything else he writes will automatically bring him in a large and steady income. But he's more likely anyway to be one of the thousands to whom their books bring no more than pin money.

So what are the rewards of writing? First of all, and despite the fact that I can hear some of my readers giving a hollow laugh, there is the reward of writing for its own sake. Some authors like to talk about the agony of writing, but though it is certainly very hard and requires considerable stamina and application, I have yet to find an author who really and truly finds his work an agony. On the contrary, most will admit, if pressed, to the pleasure it gives them. There is a sense of achievement in putting words to paper, a joy in the creativity involved, and there can sometimes be great happiness in reading something that you have written and finding satisfaction in it, feeling that you have managed to express exactly what you were intending to say, and in the best possible manner.

When, earlier in this book, I replied cynically to the statement that everyone has a book in him by saying that it should usually stay there, I was really making a commercial judgement; "everyone" more often than not has neither an interesting enough story nor the skill with which to tell it to make the book a likely candidate for publication. But my cynicism ignores that simple pleasure which "everyone" may get just from writing his story, so if you have never written before, but believe there is a book inside you, then go ahead and bring it out.

Few authors, except perhaps for ardent diarists, and even they may have half an eye on the main chance, write only for themselves. Again there can be rewards, even if your writing remains unpublished, for it may give great pleasure to your family and friends. I think particularly of those autobiographies with which every publisher is familiar, which do not get published because their authors are unknown and their lives neither unusual enough nor distinguished enough to be of wide, and saleable, interest. Those stories will probably be of great value to the family. Don't we all regret how little we know of our grandparents and the generations before them?

So if this is the kind of book you think of writing, do go ahead – write it for your own enjoyment and that of your family. Don't expect to be published commercially, though of course there is no harm in trying to interest a publisher, and if you succeed in that, you will have earned yourself a nice bonus. Or if you write poetry or science fiction or treatises on unpronounceable chemical compounds or a manual of Pig Sticking, or even an account of your package holiday in Playa El Populario, Majorca, or the hilarious story of your house-moving – whatever you write, don't let anyone stop you or discourage you, and above all don't be too disappointed if you do not achieve publication. Remember that there are other rewards in writing.

However, you are probably still interested in the financial question. Let us suppose that you have something to say, are equipped to say it, and that it is of book length. (By "something to say", I do not mean necessarily that you have to have some sort of message for the world, but that you have a story to tell, or information to impart; by "equipped to say it", I mean that you have a modicum of writing ability, can express your thoughts on paper, perhaps have some understanding of the shape and form that a book requires, and the stamina to complete it; and by "book length", I mean that, unless it falls into a category such as children's books or poetry where much shorter lengths are acceptable, the typescript when completed would be at least thirty to thirty-five thousand words in length – and preferably nearer to sixty thousand words, unless it is intended for a series in which the books are normally of shorter length than that. So you write your book, and then have the good fortune to find a publisher who agrees to publish it. What can you expect to earn from it?

I cannot tell you. You could make a fortune, or you might barely cover your expenses, or end up out of pocket. You are likely to receive an advance from your publisher which might be as little as £100, or a more reasonable £1,000 or £1,500. The advance could equally be in a much higher bracket if the publisher can envisage a really large sale, or if he is reasonably sure of making sales of subsidiary rights for substantial sums.

If the advance is low, you will have some chance of earning royalties which exceed it, but remember that for a book priced at £15, one thousand copies have to be sold at a royalty of 10% to earn you £1,500, and many books nowadays fail to reach that sales figure. If the paperback rights are sold, the paperback publisher will probably pay an advance of upwards of £750, but you will have to share those moneys with your hardcover publisher in proportions determined in your contract. Translations may bring in extra sums, and if the US rights in your book are sold, the increase in your earnings could vary from modest to substantial. But it is all extremely chancy, and if you end up making £3,000 out of your book you have been far from unlucky. When you consider the fact that you have spent a great deal of time and effort in writing the book, and that the income does not usually arrive in one nice cheque, but may be spread over a long period – even several years – it is plain that you are not going to be rich. Even if you multiply those earnings by ten, meaning that you have had a fairly substantial success, it will probably take at least four years from the time you began to write until you have received the whole of the £30,000, so it scarcely adds up to a princely annual income.

Most of your income from books will come to you under the terms of the contracts you sign with your publishers or any other persons or organizations which you license to use your work in some way, and this applies whether you sign it up directly or use an agent. There are, however, two important sources of moneys which may come to you without the intervention of either publisher or agent. These are Public Lending Right and fees collected by the Authors Licensing and Collecting Society (see pp.225–8).

Another possibility is that you will receive a grant. The Regional Arts Associations sometimes award bursaries, usually when an author is working on a book and needs extra funds for research purposes, and moneys are also available for similar purposes from various sources, such as the Authors' Foundation, which is administered by the Society of Authors. If you think you have a good case, make an initial inquiry to your local Arts Association or to the Society of Authors.

Then the many prizes which are on offer must not be forgotten. The *Writers' and Artists' Yearbook* takes no less than twenty-four pages to list all the prizes available, and just about every conceivable kind of writing seems to be eligible for one or other of them. Many are for published work, and in such cases it is usually up to the publisher to enter them, but there are also several which can be awarded to unpublished work, which obviously has to be submitted by the author. The most prestigious prize of all, and by far the largest, is the Nobel Prize for Literature, which of course is given only to the most eminent of authors when they have established an international reputation and one which is expected to survive (though it must be admitted that many of the past winners are now almost totally forgotten). In Britain the most important of the major prizes is generally considered to be the Booker, awarded to the novel which the panel of judges consider to be the best published in the year under consideration, and its nearest challengers in terms of value and public interest are the Whitbread Literary Awards (which include the Whitbread Book of the Year), the *Sunday Express* Book of the Year Award, and the Betty Trask Awards.

It cannot be repeated too often that bestsellerdom is not always solely a question of your ability as a writer, important though that is, but also depends to a frightening extent on luck – the luck of choosing the right title, finding the right publisher, being published at the right time, receiving the right kind of publicity, finding the public in the right mood to respond to your work. Many potential bestsellers are published every year, of which a few make it to the top, and the others sink without trace – and it is a matter of luck. Certainly some publishers are more vigorous than others in forcing their books on to the bestseller lists, and some authors feel that it is a great advantage to be published by one of the big concerns because of the extra weight they can bring to bear and their flexibility and strength of resources; others believe that you get far more personal attention, and therefore perhaps a better chance of becoming a bestseller with a small publishing house. Whichever kind of publisher you have and however hard he may try to make you into a bestseller, he will have to have a little bit of luck – no, a fairly large bit of luck – to succeed.

The element of fortune is something that, if you are wise, you should accept. Some authors are for ever bemoaning their failure to hit the jackpot, frequently blaming their publishers for their lack of success, whereas others content themselves with making a nice little addition to their income by writing and publishing new books regularly, but without hankering too continuously for rewards that they are never likely to earn. They keep their envy of luckier (or perhaps more skilful) authors in check, and allow their dissatisfaction to focus on the quality of their own work – and of course, no good writer is ever satisfied entirely with what he writes. This is not to say that you should have no confidence in yourself and your writing. I think every writer should say to himself every day, "My new book is the best I have ever written – but it won't make me a fortune." The first part of that may help to keep up your morale, while the second half may help to ensure that your bank manager loses no sleep over you.

Of course, there are many, many prudent authors who manage their affairs without ever falling into debt, and who take a realistic view of the potential earning capacity of their work. Even when their publishers greet their new book with excited little cries and begin to talk hysterically of enormous sales and US and foreign language and subsidiary rights buyers queuing up for the chance to bid for the book, these sober, sensible authors, instead of cracking a bottle of champagne to celebrate, will take a large pinch of salt with all that is said, and wait to see what happens. If the publisher is right, the champagne will keep for the few months before he is proved so; if he is wrong, a good cup of tea or coffee will be much cheaper and almost as cheering. It goes without saying that I am just such a sensible author, and I am sure that you, who are reading this now, are another.

Remember that any income you receive from writing has to be reported to the Inland Revenue, and you will be taxed on it. If you are a professional author, it is almost essential to get a good accountant, and preferably one who understands something of the author's position *vis-à-vis* the tax authorities. There are many expenses that authors can legitimately claim, such as the cost of writing and typing materials and other stationery, research expenses including the purchase of books for that purpose, postage and telephone including telephone rental, travel and motoring costs, secretarial charges (which can include some remuneration for your spouse who takes messages, checks proofs, helps with research) and so on. Of course, all these costs must be incurred solely for the purpose of your writing, and in the case, for instance, of telephone rental, unless you have a separate business line which you use solely as an author, only a proportion of the charges will be allowable. You should keep all bills and receipts in connection with your writing for your accountant's use. Your accountant will also in certain circumstances be able to arrange for the "spreading" of your writing income, which to some extent allows you to even out the good and the bad years. Advice on these matters is often available from agents, and the Society of Authors or the Writers' Guild may be able to help, but there is really no substitute for a capable accountant. Few publishers are qualified to give reliable tax advice.

I referred at the beginning of the last paragraph to "professional" authors. If you are writing in your spare time from another job, which provides your main livelihood, can you really consider yourself a professional author? It depends on your attitude. If your whole approach to writing is professional, the fact that it is a spare-time job is irrelevant. Being professional means dedication and perseverance, and a determination never to fall below the highest standards that you can attain.

My favourite quotation about the writing business comes from the American author of humorous, witty novels and verse, Peter de Vries. He says, "I write only when I'm inspired, and I see to it that I'm inspired at nine o'clock every morning." It may sound like a joke, but that attitude is symptomatic of real professionalism. It is an attitude which, if true of his approach to all aspects of his work, guarantees to any writer with sufficient talent that he will indeed reap a reward from his efforts.

That positive and uplifting pronouncement should have been the end of this chapter, but realism insists on forcing its way in. It is possible that, however professional your approach may be, you will fall upon hard times. If this should happen, there are, alas, unlikely to be any long-term solutions to the problem, but some possible sources of temporary help do exist. For instance, the Society of Authors has a Contingency Fund, from which grants may be made in the event of sudden financial hardship, and equally the Royal Literary Fund is available for authors who find themselves in difficulties.

11
Organizations For Authors

Being an author is often a very lonely business. It is not just that one tends to write in a private world, shut off by the act of creation even from one's family and friends; it is also frequently very difficult to know where to go for unbiased advice regarding one's dealings with publishers, and for the companionship of others whose problems and pleasures may be somewhat similar.

In the matter of advice, it is hoped that this book will be of some help, but it clearly cannot cover every problem that may arise. You may feel that you can rely on your agent for sound advice, but supposing that you want to find out whether he himself is behaving towards you as he should? And if you have no agent anyway, where can you go?

The Society of Authors

The Society of Authors, founded in 1884, exists primarily to further the interests of authors and to defend their rights. It therefore acts as an advisory body to its individual members, but also represents authors' interests in negotiations with Government departments (over such matters as VAT and PLR) and with publishers, either individually or through the Publishers Association, and with any other bodies which may be concerned with authors and their work. It also administers various prizes and funds, and acts for the estates of some deceased authors.

After a referendum of its members, the Society became, in 1978, an independent trade union. It is not affiliated to the TUC, and is completely non-political. Only those members with extremely strong principles against becoming union members found it necessary to resign when the Society took this step.

The Society offers free legal advice and, in some cases, representation to its members, but does make the rule that it cannot be involved in a legal dispute which is already in existence at the time you join the Society – in other words, if you are in the middle of a legal argument with your publisher, for instance, it is no use rushing off to join the Society of Authors and expecting it immediately to take on your case with all the attendant expenses. If you are already a member and were before the dispute began, that is a different matter.

The Society also offers free business advice to its members, and this includes two services in particular which members find of great help: the provision of information about publishers and agents, and the clause-by-clause vetting of publishing agreements.

Medical insurance and pension schemes are also available to members, plus fringe benefits such as books and stationery for purchase at specially reduced rates.

The Society includes a number of specialist sub-organizations: Broadcasting, Children's Writers, Educational Writers, Medical and Technical Groups, and a Translators Association. It publishes a quarterly magazine, *The Author*, and it has available a most useful set of "Quick Guides" to such subjects as Copyright, The Protection of Titles, Income Tax, Libel, Value Added Tax, Publishing Contracts and Authors' Agents, and "Bulletins" on such subjects as Translators as Authors and Teachers as Authors. These leaflets are free to members, and available to others at a modest fee.

The Society of Authors is principally concerned with advisory and representational activities, but it also organizes seminars and other events which combine the useful and the merely social. Full membership is open only to those who have been published, but associate membership is available if you have had a manuscript accepted for publication, or if you have an established reputation in another medium, or if you have contributed occasional scripts to the media. The annual subscription is a set sum (currently £50 in most cases). It includes free and automatic membership of the Authors' Licensing and Collecting Society (see below). Full details may be obtained from: The Membership Secretary, The Society of Authors, 84 Drayton Gardens, London SW10 9SB. Telephone: 071-373 6642.

If you are a published author (or have had a book accepted for publication) but are not a member of the Society of Authors, I would earnestly ask you to consider joining, and for three reasons: firstly, the wider and stronger the membership the more power that the Society (and the Writers' Guild) can wield in negotiations with the Government (over such matters as PLR and VAT) and with publishers (over the MTA, for instance); secondly, the reasonable deal that most authors receive nowadays from publishers is due in no small measure to the efforts of the Society over the past century, and I think that joining can be regarded as a necessary expression of gratitude for that work, and of hope for future improvements; thirdly, the services which the Society offers are in themselves of considerable value, including of course the fact that if you are a member and have a book accepted by a publisher who is a signatory of the Minimum Terms Agreement you will be entitled to have all the benefits of that arrangement incorporated into your agreement.

The Writers' Guild of Great Britain

Originally called the Television and Screenwriters' Guild, this organization has in recent years widened its scope to include representation for all kinds of authors, and it has a special Books section. Nevertheless, it is still primarily orientated towards the film, television, radio and theatre writer.

The Guild's principal aims are twofold. Firstly, to give individual advice and help to members on the whole range of issues involving their business life as writers, including legal advice, taxation and contracts; and secondly, to negotiate minimum terms agreements in each of the five industries using a writer's work. The Guild currently has agreements providing for protection to its members in film, television, radio, theatre and books. It publishes a monthly Newsletter.

Membership of the Writers' Guild of Great Britain is open to anyone who has had work published, broadcast or performed (using a somewhat complex points system for minor works), and to any writer who has had a contract offered, even if it has not yet been signed. The current annual subscription (which includes free and automatic membership of the Authors' Licensing and Collecting

Society – see below) is £50 plus 1% of the author's income from writing during the previous year. Full details are available from the Membership Secretary, The Writers' Guild of Great Britain, 430 Edgware Road, London W2 1EH. Telephone: 071-723 8074.

The Writers' Guild of Great Britain and the Society of Authors work amicably and closely together on such issues as PLR, the MTA and reprography (reproduction by photographic means – primarily by photocopiers). Many of the members' benefits offered by the Guild parallel those offered by the Society, and indeed there is a considerable area of overlap as far as the operation of the two organizations is concerned. Amalgamation has been proposed, but while this would make sense in many ways, the two groups are sharply divided on some issues. One of these is that, although the Guild makes it clear that it is non-political, has no involvement with any political party and pays no political levy, it is nevertheless affiliated to the TUC and to other individual unions in the Entertainments industry. The Society is not so affiliated.

Public Lending Right

As long ago as 1951, John Brophy (at that time a popular novelist, but now, alas, largely forgotten), convinced of the unfairness of a system which gave the author no reward for the thousands of borrowings of his or her books from Public Libraries, proposed "the Brophy Penny". The suggestion was that an author should be paid one penny every time one of his or her books was borrowed from a Public Library.

The issue was taken up by the Society of Authors, which persuaded A.P. Herbert to spearhead the campaign to bring in the necessary law. Various schemes were drawn up, which various Ministers for the Arts considered and altered or rejected, and the matter dragged on unsatisfactorily for year after year. In 1972, the formation of the Writers' Action Group, led by Brigid Brophy (John's daughter) and Maureen Duffy, brought a new vigour to the battle. All authors owe an enormous debt of gratitude to Ms Brophy and Ms Duffy – without their determined leadership, Public Lending Right would certainly not have become law as soon as it did and in a form which was acceptable to most authors. They did not achieve success entirely alone – they were supported by the Society of Authors and the Writers' Guild, by individuals, by agents and other interested parties – but let no one take away the credit due to them. It was not easy – indeed, it took seven years of intense lobbying from the time that the Writers' Action Group was formed until an act was finally passed in 1979 and Public Lending Right was brought into being – or almost into being (for administrative reasons it was not implemented until 1983/84). Authors would register their books with a central authority; all books borrowed from a number of libraries in various parts of the country would be recorded for a period of twelve months; from these sample figures would be extrapolated the supposed borrowings for the country as a whole; the government would provide an annual sum of £2 million, which, after the deduction of administration costs, would be divided among the authors concerned in proportion to the number of times their books had been borrowed. Various conditions were subsequently built in, such as restricting the most popular authors to a maximum payment of £5,000, and limiting the scheme to authors who were still alive.

When PLR finally came into operation, in the year 1983/84, the sum which the government made available remained at £2 million, the figure allocated in 1979, despite the fact that substantial inflation had taken place in the intervening years. Since that time various adjustments have been made to the scheme, mostly to widen the scope of those who may benefit from it, and the money has been increased (though the increases have never caught up with inflation). In that first year, 7,562 authors had registered for the scheme, the rate of payment was 1.02p per loan, forty-six authors received the maximum payment of £5,000, 5,327 received £99 or less, and 1,449 registered authors got nothing (each book had to earn a minimum of £1 before any payment for that book was made). By 1990 the number of authors in the scheme had risen to 17,594, the rate of payment was 1.39p per loan, sixty-three authors received the maximum payment, by now increased to £6,000, 13,266 received £99 or less, and 3,394 registered authors got nothing (at this point an author had to earn a minimum total of £1 from all his registered books before any payment was made to him). A sum of 1.39p per borrowing is not a large amount of money, and although all authors will agree that even the most niggardly payment is better than nothing, many will remember that the Brophy Penny was a penny in the old money and in purchasing power its present-day equivalent would be at least 5p, and probably something nearer to 10p.

One of the provisions of the Act, and this has not been changed by any subsequent amendments, is that PLR payments belong exclusively to the author. Publishers do not receive any part of them, and neither, since the moneys are paid direct to the author, do authors' agents. Any attempts by publishers or agents to take a percentage of PLR earnings should be firmly resisted.

The responsibility for registering for PLR remains with authors. It is not undertaken by your publisher or your agent – you, the author, are the one who has to send details of your book or books to the PLR Office. It is easy to do, and will cost you no more initially than a couple of postage stamps (one to get a form, and one to send it back when completed). Thereafter you can easily add any new books to your list. For full details write to: Public Lending Right Office, Bayheath House, Prince Regent Street, Stockton-on-Tees, Cleveland TS18 1DF.

The Authors' Licensing and Collecting Society

Set up by writers in 1977, this organization collects sums of money which are due to authors for certain subsidiary rights in their works (rights which are not licensed to publishers), but which for special reasons cannot be paid to the authors directly. The Authors' Licensing and Collecting Society (ALCS) then distributes the moneys to the authors concerned. Among such payments are fees for cable transmission of television programmes, and educational off-air recording fees, but the bulk of the money paid to the authors of books comes from two sources – public lending right in foreign countries, and photocopying fees.

Britain is not the only country to have PLR. It exists also in Germany, for instance. German PLR due to British authors cannot by German law be distributed directly to the authors; it is therefore transmitted to ALCS and passed by them to the authors concerned. As the principle of PLR becomes accepted throughout the world, more and more countries are likely to be making payments through ALCS to British authors.

ALCS is the joint owner, together with the Publishers Licensing Society (PLS), of the Copyright Licensing Agency (CLA), which exists to license and collect fees, in respect of the photocopying of copyright material, from organizations such as schools, universities, industry, government offices and various professional organizations and societies. The moneys it collects are split between authors, represented by ALCS, and publishers, and at the time of writing the authors' share, since the organization was founded in 1982, has amounted to some £2 million. That sum is likely to increase substantially as, with the law behind it, CLA expands its licensing to cover the ever-widening use of photocopying machines. CLA is also watching with extreme care the developments in the fields of electronics which could involve the storage and use of copyright material, and will be vigilant in its protection of the interests of both publishers and authors, and will collect and distribute any fees due.

To join ALCS, write to The Membership Secretary, ALCS, 33/34 Alfred Place, London WC1E 7DP. The annual subscription is currently £5.75, but members of the Society of Authors and the Writers' Guild are entitled to free membership of ALCS, and are automatically entered on their books.

PEN – The World Association of Writers

This international organization was founded in 1921 to promote friendship and understanding between writers and to defend freedom of expression within and between all nations. The initials P.E.N. stand for Poets, Playwrights, Editors, Essayists, Novelists, but membership is open to any writer or translator (or indeed anyone who works in virtually any capacity in the book business), provided that he is of good standing and subscribes to these fundamental principles. PEN Centres are spread throughout the world; each is autonomous and organizes various seminars and other events for its members, and many of the centres issue regular journals. An International Congress takes place every year. One of PEN's most important concerns (and indeed a good reason for joining) is with the plight of writers who are imprisoned or otherwise persecuted for daring to express views which do not coincide with those of the régimes under which they live. PEN Centres have campaigned for the freedom of such writers, and even when their efforts have met with failure, they have sometimes been able to pass greatly appreciated messages of encouragement to the authors – clearly something which deserves the support of every writer in the free world. Full details may be obtained from: PEN International, 7 Dilke Place, London SW3 4JE. Telephone: 071-352 6303.

Book Trust

Worthy of support by all authors, Book Trust exists to promote books and reading in any and every possible way. While it receives the support of all branches of the book trade, it is in no way dependent on any of them, and for this reason and because of its charitable status it is able to speak for books to bodies who might be suspicious of a commercial purpose or vested interest. Membership is open to everyone interested in books and reading. Book Trust (formerly The National Book League) has a useful book information service giving information about books published in the UK and USA; it arranges exhibitions; it has a Children's Book Reference Library and the Mark Longman Library, a collection of books about books, publishing and bookselling. The Trust administers various Literary Awards and book ventures, such as the School Bookshop Association and the National Book Committee. There are varying rates of membership for individuals and for groups or organizations. Membership offers a quarterly magazine, *Booknews*, and use of the Trust facilities, including the Licensed Snack Bar. Full details may be obtained from: Book Trust, Book House, 45 East Hill, Wandsworth, London SW18 2QZ. Telephone: 081-870 9055.

Writers' Circles

Many authors find congenial companionship in attending Writers' Circles. The membership usually comprises both regularly published authors and those whose work has not appeared in print, and standards of ability are liable to vary greatly within the group. A programme of lectures and social activities is usually arranged, but the reading of new work by members to the assembled company, which is then free to criticize it, is always one of the main functions of the group, and can be very helpful, provided that you are not too thin-skinned. You should be able to find details of your local Circles in the public library. A directory of Writers' Circles is available from: Mrs Jill Dick, Oldacre, Horderns Park Road, Chapel-en-le-Frith, Derbyshire SK12 6SY.

Writers' Conferences

Arising out of the Writers' Circle movement and as an extension of the functions of such groups, many residential courses for writers take place up and down the country. Fees are usually modest and those who attend find the diet of lectures from experts, discussion groups, brief instructional courses and social activities very much to their taste. The people who go to these conferences include writers in every genre, from journalism to poetry, from children's books to biography, from drama to all varieties of fiction, and they range in experience from complete beginners to bestselling authors. Many writers have been attending these conferences year after year for donkey's ages, and they do so at least in part for the pleasure of talking to others who share the same interest in all aspects of the writing business.

The most popular, longest-established of these residential courses is the Writers' Summer School, which takes place at Swanwick in Derbyshire for a week every August. Full details may be obtained from: Mrs Philippa Boland, The Red House, Mardens Hill, Crowborough, East Sussex TN6 1XN. Telephone: 0892 653943.

Other popular gatherings include:

Writers' Holiday, held in Caerleon, Gwent, in late July. For details write to Mrs D.L. Anne Hobbs, 30 Pant Road, Newport, Gwent NP9 5PR.

Southern Writers Conference held at Chichester, West Sussex, in mid-June. For details write to Ms Ann Hutton, 6 Blandford Road, London W4 1DU.

Writers' Weekends, held at Scarborough, North Yorkshire, in April and November. For details write to Mrs Audrey Wilson, 7 Osgodby Close, Scarborough, North Yorkshire YO11 3JW.

SAMWAW (South and Mid-Wales Association of Writers) Weekends, held at Cardiff, South Glamorgan, in May and September. For details write to Mrs Marguerite

Prisk, 48 Baron Road, Penarth, South Glamorgan CF6 1UE.

The Arvon Foundation

This organization offers people of all ages over sixteen the chance to meet, talk and work in an informal way with practising artists. At the time of writing there are two Arvon centres, one in Yorkshire and one in Devon, but I understand that a third centre, in Scotland, will be opening shortly. The centres provide a full programme of five-day courses in various fields of writing and related art forms. Full details may be obtained from: The Arvon Foundation, Lumb Bank, Heptonstall, Hebden Bridge, West Yorkshire HX7 6DF, or from The Arvon Foundation, Totleigh Barton, Sheepwash, Beaworthy, Devon EX21 5NS. Incidentally, many of the Regional Arts Associations are willing in certain cases to subsidize would-be writers who wish to attend one of the Arvon courses, so it is worthwhile for such persons to contact the local Arts Association in this matter (for addresses see p.233).

Adult Education Creative Writing Classes

Creative writing classes are of course intended primarily for those who have not been successful in achieving publication, but many successful authors do attend them. Their value naturally depends largely on the ability of the Tutor taking the classes, which in some ways differ from the average Writers' Circle only in that the Tutor is there as a kind of superior authority when the members' work is discussed, though he may devote part of the time to formal lectures. Some people attend the classes more for the sake of a pleasant evening among fellow writers than for the instruction. Details are available from Adult Education offices and from public libraries.

Some Other Useful Organizations

The Association of British Science Writers, c/o British Association for the Advancement of Science, Fortress House, 23 Savile Row, London W1X 1AB. Telephone: 071-494 3326.

The Authors' Club, 40 Dover Street, London W1X 3RB. Telephone: 071-499 8581.

The Authors' Guild of Ireland Ltd, 282 Swords Road, Dublin 9. Telephone: 375974.

The British Copyright Council, Copyright House, 29-33 Berners Street, London W1P 4AA.

The British Fantasy Society, c/o 15 Stanley Road, Morden, Surrey SM4 5DE.

The British Guild of Travel Writers, c/o 90 Corringway, London W5 3HA. Telephone: 081-198 2223.

The British Science Fiction Association Limited, c/o 33 Thornville Road, Hartlepool, Cleveland TS26 8EW.

Broadcasting Group, The Society of Authors, 84 Drayton Gardens, London SW10 9SB. Telephone: 071-373 6642.

Catholic Writers Guild, c/o 1 Leopold Road, London W5 3PB. Telephone: 081-992 3954.

Children's Writers Group, The Society of Authors, 84 Drayton Gardens, London SW10 9SB. Telephone: 071-353 6642.

The Crime Writers' Association, c/o Thistles, Back Lane, Little Addington, Kettering, Northants NN14 4AX.

Educational Writers Group, The Society of Authors, 84 Drayton Gardens, London SW10 9SB. Telephone 071-353 6642.

The Fellowship of Christian Writers, c/o She-Dy-Vea, 151a Bedford Road, Marston Morteyne, Beds. MK43 0LD. Telephone: 0234 767470.

The Institute of Journalists, 2 Dock Offices, Surrey Quays, Lower Road, London SE16 2XL. Telephone: 071-252 1187.

Medical Writers' Group, The Society of Authors, 84 Drayton Gardens, London SW10 9SB. Telephone: 071-353 6642.

The National Union of Journalists, Acorn House, 314 Gray's Inn Road, London WC1X 8DP. Telephone: 071-278 7916.

The Poetry Society, 21 Earls Court Square, London SW5 9BY. Telephone: 071-373 7861.

The Romantic Novelists Association, c/o Half Hidden, West Lane, Bledlow, Nr Aylesbury, Bucks HP17 9PF.

The Royal Literary Fund, 144 Temple Chambers, Temple Avenue, London EC4Y 0DT. Telephone: 071-353 7150.

Scientific and Technical Authors' Group. The Society of

Authors, 84 Drayton Gardens, London SW10 9SB. Telephone: 071-353 6642.

The Society of Indexers, c/o 16 Green Road, Birchington, Kent CT7 9JZ.

The Society of Women Writers and Journalists, c/o 13 Warwick Avenue, Cuffley, Herts EN6 4RU.

Theatre Writers' Union, c/o The Actors Centre, 4 Chenies Street, London WC1E 7EP. Telephone: 071-631 3599.

The Translators Association, The Society of Authors, 84 Drayton Gardens, London SW10 9SB. Telephone: 071-353 6642.

The Regional Arts Associations

East Midlands Arts, Mountfields House, Forest Road, Loughborough, Leicestershire LE11 3HU

Eastern Arts Association, Cherry Hinton Hall, Cherry Hinton Road, Cambridge CB1 4DW.

Greater London Arts, 9 White Lion Street, London N1 9PD.

Lincolnshire and Humberside Arts, St Hugh's Newport, Lincoln LN1 3DN.

Merseyside Arts, Graphic House, Duke Street, Liverpool L1 4JR.

North Wales Arts Association, 10 Wellfield House, Bangor, Gwynedd LL57 1ER.

North West Arts, 12 Harter Street, Manchester M1 6HY.

Northern Arts, 9-10 Osborne Terrace, Newcastle-upon-Tyne NE2 1NZ.

South East Arts Association, 10 Mount Ephraim, Tunbridge Wells, Kent TN4 8AS.

South-east Wales Arts Association, Victoria Street, Cwmbran, Gwent NP44 3YT.

Southern Arts, 19 Southgate Street, Winchester, Hants SO23 9DQ.

South West Arts, Bradninch Place, Gandy Street, Exeter, Devon EX4 3LS.

West Midland Arts, 82 Granville Street, Birmingham B1 2LH.

West Wales (Association for the) Arts, Red Street, Carmarthen, Dyfed SA31 1QL.

Yorkshire Arts, Glyde House, Glydegate, Bradford, West Yorkshire BD5 0BQ.

Glossary

Advance   The moneys paid to an author in advance and on account of the earnings of his book. Normally non-returnable. Often referred to in the USA as a "guarantee".

ALCS   The Authors' Licensing and Collecting Society (see p.227)

Backlist   After a book is first published it becomes, if it continues to sell, part of its publisher's backlist. A publisher cannot exist on the sale of new books alone, but is constantly looking for books which will sell over a period of years – i.e. potential backlist titles.

Bastard title   Another term for "half title" q.v.

Biblio page   Another term for "imprint page" q.v.

Binding   Hardcover books are usually bound by being sewn and cased, i.e. the signatures are sewn together and a stiff binding is then attached by means of the end papers. Paperbacks are more often "perfect bound", i.e. the back edges of the signatures are trimmed, so that each page is separate, then glued and the stiff paper cover is then drawn on.

Bleeding   Illustrations which go off the edge of the page, so that there is no surround to the illustration, are said to "bleed".

Blues   See Ozalids.

Blurb   The advertising copy which the publisher uses on the jacket or cover of a book, in his catalogue and in various other ways. A blurb is not to be confused with a synopsis (q.v.), and should not attempt to cover in detail all the contents of a book. It usually consists of some indication of what the book is about, couched in terms which are designed to intrigue the reader, plus a number of statements, which cannot always be relied upon to be entirely truthful, intended to persuade a potential purchaser that the book is one he cannot afford to be without. The best blurbs are short and pithy, and have both a "selling" and a "teasing" quality – rather like a good trailer for a film.

Boards The stiff cardboard used in binding a hardcover book. As a descriptive term in a catalogue, "boards" means that the book has a hardcover binding (the boards often being covered with a decorative paper), but no jacket.

Brasses The title of a book, the author's name, and sometimes decorative designs are printed on to the binding of a hardcover book by means of brasses (which are nowadays more likely to be made of other metal and called "zincos").

Camera-ready copy Many printing processes involve photography, for which material has to be produced which is error-free, with everything correctly positioned as it is to appear on the page, and which can therefore be called "camera-ready copy".

Cancel page A page inserted in a printed book in place of a page which contains an error or other material which it is essential to change, even at the cost of this expensive process.

Case The binding of a hardcover book.

Case The tray in which type is stored, the upper part containing capital letters and the lower part small letters. "Upper case" has become a synonym for capitals and "lower case" for small letters.

Cast off A word count usually prepared in a publisher's production department or by a printer. Calculated with care, the object is to work out as accurately as possible the number of printed pages that the book in question will occupy, given a specified type size and type area.

CLA Copyright Licensing Agency (see p.228).

Cloth Nearly all hardcover books used to be bound in real cloth – a woven fabric. Nowadays, "cloth" is more often a special kind of very hard-wearing paper, frequently embossed with a pattern to give the impression that it is the genuine article.

Co-edition A book produced simultaneously for two or more publishers and for different areas of the world, or languages, in order to reduce printing costs.

Colophon The term is usually used in the book trade to

describe the device which publishers use as their sign or trademark. It is often to be found on the titlepage and in many cases on the spine of the jacket, while paperback publishers also place it on the front cover of their books.

Composition   The conversion of the author's copy, which has been produced on a typewriter or word processor, into the type in which it will appear in the finished book. The composition is usually done on a computer, producing a tape from which film of the composition can be made. This process involves re-keying all the copy, but use of the author's word processor discs can eliminate most, if not all, such labour.

Cover   See Jacket.

Double spread   When an illustration runs across two facing pages, without other illustrations on the same pages, it is called a "double spread". The same term may be applied to a publisher's advertisement on two facing pages of, for instance, *The Bookseller*, or to two facing pages devoted to one book in a catalogue.

Dummy   A book made of the paper to be used in the finished article, and bound in the style that will be used for the book, but without the pages being printed. The dummy is used, among other things, for the preparation of the jacket, since it shows the size of the book, including the width of the spine. Dummies are sometimes prepared with a few pages of printed material, especially in the case of highly illustrated books, to give foreign publishers and bookbuyers an impression of what the final book will look like.

Edition   An edition of a book is not the same as an impression. Each impression of the book, that is to say the first and subsequent printings, contains the same material. Each edition, on the other hand, is altered substantially from the previous edition.

Em   A unit of measurement in printing. Since it is based on the width of the letter "m", its size obviously can vary with the size of the type. However, the term is frequently taken to mean a standard 12pt "m", equalling roughly $\frac{1}{6}$ inch. See also Point.

End papers   The four pages at the beginning and end of a hardcover book by means of which the case is attached.

Extent   The length of a book in words, or in typescript pages or in printed pages.

Flap   The part of the jacket which is folded inside the cover of the book. "Front flap" and "back flap" are terms which are frequently used.

Folded and Collated   After printing, the sheets of paper are folded into signatures, and the signatures are collated or gathered into groups, so that each group contains all the signatures which make up the book.

Folio   Although this word has a number of definitions relating to sheets of paper (a single sheet, for instance, or the size of sheet obtained by folding a standard sheet once), in printing and publishing it is normally used to mean the page number.

Format   The size and shape of a book.

Gutter   The "join" where two facing pages of a book meet.

Half-title   A page of a book on which is printed the title of the book, or the title of a Part (in which case it should really be called a "part-title"), but which does not normally carry the author's name or that of the publisher.

ISBN   These initials stand for International Standard Book Number. A world-wide system of identifying books by means of a ten-digit number. The first digit identifies the book's country of origin, the next four the publisher, the next four the individual title, and the final number is a check digit.

Imposition   The arrangement of the pages for printing so that when the sheet is folded the pages will appear in their correct sequence.

Impression   A printing of a book. New impressions of a book are reprints without changes having been made to the content. See also Edition.

Imprint   The publisher's name printed at the foot of the title-page is his "imprint". The printer's imprint, consisting of his name and address, is usually printed at the foot of the biblio or imprint page.

Imprint page   The page of a book which contains the copyright notice and assertion of the author's moral rights, the printing history of the book, the ISBN, the publisher's name and address, British Library Cataloguing in Publication Data, the printer's imprint and any other similar necessary information. It is usually on the back, or verso, of the title page.

In print   Books which are "in print" are available from the publisher, as opposed to those which have sold out and will not be reprinted and are designated "out of print". The phrase "in print" is also used to indicate the number of copies printed of a book since it was first published – "There are fifty thousand copies of this book in print, made up of nine impressions", or "I have published ten of this author's books, totalling over two million copies of his works in print in paperback editions."

Jacket   Sometimes called "dust jacket" or "dust cover" or "wrapper". The loose paper cover on a hardcover book, often carrying an illustration on the front and a blurb and the retail price on the front flap. Paperbacks do not normally have jackets, and their stiff paper bindings are known as "covers".

Leading   Space between lines of type.

Letter spacing   Space between the letters of a word, often used when the word is entirely in capitals, as in a title.

Limp   Binding in which boards are not used. Paperbacks could technically be described as having a limp binding, but in practice the term is normally only used for books bound without boards in cloth or imitation cloth.

List   A publisher's list of titles – "We are glad to announce that X has joined our list", or "Our list contains general non-fiction and medical books, but does not include fiction."

Literal   The equivalent in composition of a typing error. In America the term "typo" is used.

MTA   Minimum Terms Agreement (see Chapter 6).

Net   Under the Net Book Agreement, books must not be sold to the public at less than the price fixed by the publisher, which is the "net" price. Most books published in Britain are "net", though school books are frequently "non-net". Bookclubs can offer net books at a discount because of the conditions they attach to membership.

Orphan   When the last line on a page happens to be the first line of a paragraph it is called an "orphan". It is clearly a companion term to that other great typographical sin, the "widow" q.v. "Club line" is a less picturesque synonym, in this context, for "orphan".

Ozalids   Proofs of highly illustrated books often come in the form of "Ozalids". Authors are often appalled by them, but should be reassured that they do not reflect the quality of the finished printing. Since Ozalids are blue, they are often referred to as "blues".

PA   The Publishers Association, to which some 300 publishers, including almost all the major houses, belong.

Paper   Three main kinds of paper are used for books: antique, a fairly rough-surfaced paper, used for most books without integrated tonal illustrations; calendered paper, which has been subjected to a smoothing process, used for illustrated books; art paper, coated with china clay or other material to give a glossy surface for the fine printing of illustrations.

Paper sizes   The most popular sizes of paper for books are Metric Crown, Metric Large Crown, Metric Demy and Metric Royal, of which quad sheets (i.e. sheets four times the basic sizes) measure in millimetres 768 × 1008, 816 × 1056, 888 × 1128 and 960 × 1272 respectively. The terms "quarto (4to)", "octavo (8vo)", "sixteenmo (16mo)" and so on refer to the number of times the basic sheet of paper is folded to produce a signature; quarto is folded twice, producing a Crown page size, for instance, of 252 × 192mm; octavo is folded three times, producing a Demy page size, for instance, of 222 × 141mm; and so on. Paper is used not only in quad sheets, but in larger sizes, and also in reels.

Paste-up   A paste-up is usually prepared for highly illustrated books, taking the proofs of the text and of the illustrations and pasting them into the blank pages of a dummy to show the printer the exact position required.

Perfect binding   See Binding.

Plant costs   This term normally refers to all the costs of production prior to the actual printing of the book. It includes therefore composition, preparation of film, manufacture of binding brasses, etc.

PLR   Public Lending Right (see p.225).

PLS   Publishers' Licensing Society. Joint owner with the Authors' Licensing and Collecting Society of the Copyright Licensing Agency (see p.228).

Point size   The size of type is indicated in points, this showing the height of the block on which the individual letter stands. So one refers to "10pt type" or "36pt type". A point equals approximately 1/72 inch.

Prelims   The first or preliminary pages of a book, including half-title and title pages, imprint page, contents, etc, before the text begins.

Printing processes   Virtually all books nowadays are printed by offset lithography. Letterpress – printing direct from type – which used to be the standard method for all short-run production and was basically the same process as Caxton used, is now quite outdated.

Print run   The number of copies of a book printed at any one time.

Proofs   Proofs come in various forms. Galley proofs are long strips of paper on which long columns of print, not yet split up into pages, appear. Paged galleys are also long strips of paper, but the columns of type on them have been split into pages, though these have not yet been imposed. Other proofs look like computer print-outs. Page proofs normally look much like paperbacks, the type having been split into pages and the pages imposed.

Recto   Open a book: the left-hand page is called the "verso"; the right-hand page is called the "recto".

Remainder   When a publisher finds that one of his books appears to have stopped selling, he may try to sell off his stock at a very low price to certain traders who specialize in such purchases. Books sold in this way are called "remainders" and the people who buy them are "remainder merchants". The word "remainder" is also a verb – "I shall have to remainder these books."

Running head   The headline at the top of a page. Sometimes the title of a book is repeated on all pages, but more often the book title appears on the verso and the chapter title or title of a sub-section on the recto.

Sheets   When a book is printed the sheets have to be folded and collated before the book can be bound. Sometimes, however, the publisher does not wish to bind all the copies that he has printed at that point in time, and he may keep part of his stock in the form of either flat or folded and collated sheets. Sheets may also be sold unbound – to library suppliers, for instance – and in many co-editions the originating publisher will supply the other publishers concerned with sheets rather than bound stock.

Signature   When a printed sheet has been folded into pages it is called a "signature". Signatures usually consist of sixteen or thirty-two pages (although it is possible to have signatures of four or eight pages). For this reason the extent of a book is usually a multiple of thirty-two or sixteen, although this may not always be apparent if the publisher has chosen to ignore the prelims and to start numbering the book so that page one is the first page of the main text.

Spine   The back of a book, and especially the back of the binding case, frequently rounded.

Subscription When a publisher sells his books to book-sellers and other trade outlets prior to publication he "subscribes" them. Such advance sales are "subscription" sales. The word "subscription" is also used to mean the total number of copies of a book sold before publication – "This book has had a good subscription."

Subsidiary rights Strictly speaking, all rights in a book other than those of the original publisher to produce his own editions of the book. In many contracts, however, the clause concerning subsidiary rights does not include paperback, bookclub, United States or translation rights, which are dealt with under separate headings.

Synopsis A summary of the complete contents of a book, usually prepared by an author in the hope of persuading a publisher to commission the book, or at least to agree to read it. A synopsis usually confines itself to factual details of what the book is about, rather than including comments designed to "sell" the product, which are the province of the blurb (q.v.). Synopses range in length from a mere list of chapter titles to several thousand words detailing, for instance, the characters and the twists and turns of plot of a long, complex novel.

Title Apart from the obvious meaning of the name of a book, publishers use this word as a synonym for "book" – "I am publishing twenty titles this Spring."

Trade paperback This term is usually applied to a paperback edition produced by a hardcover publisher, using the type from which the hardcover edition is printed. It is therefore often in a large format, but its paper is probably of a lesser quality and it is likely to be perfect bound rather than sewn. Since the edition is comparatively small and not intended for the mass market the price usually falls somewhere between that of the hardcover and that of an ordinary paperback. It might be regarded as a cheap edition.

Verso See Recto

Volume rights A somewhat vague term, subject to varying interpretations, but usually taken basically to mean the right offered or granted to a publisher to produce the work in book form, plus the right to issue bookclub, paperback and other reprint editions (or to license others to do so).

Widow A short line appearing as the first line of a new page. Typographers dislike "widows". They also dislike (only not quite so much) "orphans" – the first line of a paragraph appearing as the last line on a page.

Wrapper   See Jacket.

Appendix I   Proof Reader's Marks

The symbols for correcting proofs are taken from a British Standard BS 5261: PART 2 1976 *Copy preparation and proof correction – Specification of typographic requirements, marks for copy preparation and proof correction, proofing procedure.* Extracts from the new Standard are reproduced below with the permission of BSI. Complete copies can be obtained from them at Linford Wood, Milton Keynes, Bucks., MK14 6LE. All authors, printers and publishers are recommended to adopt the new correction symbols.

Instruction	Textual Mark	Marginal Mark
Delete and close up	through character or through character e.g. charaacter characcter	
Substitute character or substitute part of one or more word(s)	/ through character or through word(s)	New character or new word(s)
Wrong fount. Replace by character(s) of correct fount	Encircle character(s) to be changed	⊗
Change damaged character(s)	Encircle character(s) to be changed	✗
Set in or change to italic	____ under character(s) to be set or changed	⊔
Set in or change to capital letters	≡≡≡ under character(s) to be set or changed	≡
Set in or change to small capital letters	≡≡≡ under character(s) to be set or changed	≡
Set in or change to capital letters for initial letters and small capital letters for the rest of the words	≡ under initial letters and ≡≡≡ under rest of word(s)	≡
Set in or change to bold type	⌇⌇⌇ under character(s) to be set or changed	⌇
Change capital letters to lower case letters	Encircle character(s) to be changed	⧣
Change italic to upright type	Encircle character(s) to be changed	⊔

Instruction	Textual Mark	Marginal Mark
Invert type	Encircle character to be inverted	↻
Substitute or insert full stop or decimal point	/ through character or ⅄ where required	⊙
Substitute or insert semi-colon	/ through character or ⅄ where required	;
Substitute or insert comma	/ through character or ⅄ where required	,
Start new paragraph	⌐	⌐
Run on (no new paragraph)	⌒	⌒
Centre	[enclosing matter to be centred]	[ ]
Indent	⊏	⊐
Cancel indent	⊷⊏	⊐
Move matter specified distance to the right	enclosing matter to be moved to the right →	⊏

Instruction	Textual Mark	Marginal Mark
Take over character(s), word(s) or line to next line, column or page		
Take back character(s), word(s) or line to previous line, column or page		
Raise matter	over matter to be raised / under matter to be raised	
Lower matter	over matter to be lowered / under matter to be lowered	
Correct horizontal alignment	Single line above and below misaligned matter e.g. $mi_{sa}l^{ig}n_ed$	
Close up. Delete space between characters or words	linking characters	
Insert space between characters	between characters affected	
Insert space between words	between words affected	
Reduce space between characters	between characters affected	
Reduce space between words	between words affected	
Make space appear equal between characters or words	between characters or words affected	

Appendix II
Model Royalty Statement

The Society of Authors
84 Drayton Gardens
London SW10 9SD

19(c)/79

Telephone: Littlewick Green 3104
Telegrams: Scholarly, Maidenhead
Registered Number 522538 England

Our Ref: 123456

EDWARD ARNOLD (PUBLISHERS) LTD.
Woodlands Park Avenue,
Woodlands Park,
Maidenhead, Berkshire.

H. W. Smith,
Royalty Manager

31st March, 1979.

"MODEL" ROYALTY STATEMENT (See FRONT LINE, SPRING 1979 *AUTHOR*)

ROYALTY STATEMENT NO. 1.

Period Covered 1st July 1978 to 31st December 1978

To: **C. O. Mittee Esq.,**
19 Bedford Square,
London WC1B 3HJ.

Author:	GUILD & MITTEE
Title	Royalty Statements for Authors
SBN:	0 7131 4142X
Date Published:	9th October 1978
Printing Qty:	Previous Periods: —
	This Period : 50,000

SALES DETAIL		Published Price	Proceeds £	Royalty Rate	Royalty £	p
General Sales	10,000	£1.00	n.a.	10% of PP	1,000	00
General Sales†	2,000	£1.00	n.a.	12½% of PP	250	00
Special Sales:						
Flat sheets to USA	5,000	n.a.	2,250	12½% of Rec	281	25
Subsidiary Rights as detailed		n.a.	n.a.	n.a.	25	00
Cumulative Sales	17,000					
†Change of rate after 10,000 General Sales						
Note: n.a. = not applicable						
Total Royalties etc. Payable					1,556	25

	£	p
Royalties Payable Your Share = 50%	778	12
Less: Advances Paid	*250.00	
Unearned Balance brought forward		
Deductible Corrections and Contributions	* 18.85	
Reserve for Returns		
Authors' Goods Purchased	7.50	
	276	35
Sub-Total	501	77
Add: VAT @ 8% on * items	40	74
Balance Payable/(Unearned)	£542	51

Telephone: Littlewick Green 3104
Telegrams: Scholarly, Maidenhead
Registered Number 522538 England

EDWARD ARNOLD (PUBLISHERS) LTD.
Woodlands Park Avenue,
Woodlands Park,
Maidenhead, Berkshire.

Our Ref: 123456

H. W. Smith,
Royalty Manager
31st March, 1979.

ROYALTY STATEMENT NO. 1 — DETAILS OF SUBSIDIARY RIGHTS

Author: Guild & Mittee   Title: Royalty Statements for Authors   SBN: 07131 4142 X

Date	Details	Total £ p	Author's Share %	Author's Share £ p
29 Oct 78	AMOUNT RECEIVED FOR EXTRACT REPRINTED IN THE BOOKSELLER	50.00	50	25.00
31 Dec 78	TOTAL Carried to Attached Statement			£25.00

ROYALTY STATEMENT NOTES

1. Publisher's imprint: i.e. if different from publisher's name.

2. Date: i.e. date on which the Statement is issued. Note, however, that if the Statement should be issued on or before 31st March in any year and the date of issue is in fact later than 31st March, tax problems may arise if the Statement is not pre-dated to the 31st March or before.

3. Royalty Statement No.: i.e. "No. 1", "No. 2." etc., adopting consecutive numbering for Statements issued in respect of each publication and, in the case of Statement No. 1, stating the publication date after "Title".

4. Sales details: i.e. cumulative sales, specifying each relevant category:

   > Home
   > Export
   > Special (with appropriate detail)
   > Remainder
   > Subsidiary Rights

   and, where relevant, stating the point at which the royalty rate changes.

   A separate detailed statement may be required for subsidiary rights.

5. Royalty rate: stating the basis of calculation, e.g. 10% × PP or 12½% × Rec.

6. If the publication has gone out of print since the previous Statement it would be helpful if the tabulation were to state, above the lower horizon line, "Put out of print on...............(date)".

7. Printing numbers: if sheet or other stock has been transferred from one edition to another, confusion about the printing number may arise. It would therefore be helpful if

relevant details were set out, as briefly as possible, above the lower horizontal line.

8. Royalties: Only some of these items will be relevant. It may be easier not to pre-print this part of the Statement but to insert to typewriter or by computer printer the required items, sub-totalled and totalled.

9. VAT: i.e. VAT payable on relevant items, identified by an asterisk under "sales details".

N.B. It is unnecessary to insert stock details.

Index